BENCHMARK SERIES

Microsoft®

OUTLOOK 2002

Fanshawe College
London, Ontario

DENISE SEGUIN

Senior Developmental Editor	Sonja M. Brown
Associate Editor	Courtney Kost
Special Projects Coordinator	Joan D'Onofrio
Senior Designer	Jennifer Wreisner
Senior Design and Production Specialist	Leslie Anderson
Editorial Assistant	Susan Capecchi
Copy Editor	Sharon O'Donnell
Proofreader	Gretchen Bratvold
Indexer	Nancy Fulton

Publishing Team—George Provol, Publisher; Janice Johnson, Director of Product Development; Tony Galvin, Acquisitions Editor; Lori Landwer, Marketing Manager; Shelley Clubb, Electronic Design and Production Manager

Acknowledgments—The author and publisher wish to thank the following reviewers for their technical and academic assistance in testing exercises and assessing instruction:

• Kay M. Newton, Commonwealth Business College, LaPorte, Indiana
• Jeannie Whitty, Fanshawe College, London, Ontario

Library of Congress Cataloging-in-Publication Data
    Seguin, Denise.
        Microsoft Outlook 2002 / Denise Seguin.
            p.cm. – (Benchmark series)
        ISBN 0-7638-1608-6
                1. Microsoft Outlook. 2. Time Management—Computer Programs. 3.
        Personal Information Management—Computer Programs I. Title. II. Benchmark series
        (Saint Paul, Minn.)

Z42.5.M73 R836 2002
652.5'4369—dc21   2082045782

Care has been taken to verify the accuracy of information presented in this book. However, the author, editor, and publisher cannot accept any responsibility for Web, e-mail, newsgroup, or chat room subject matter or content, or for consequences from application of the information in this book, and make no warranty, expressed or implied, with respect to its content.

Trademarks: Some of the product names and company names included in this book have been used for identification purposes only and may be trademarks or registered trademarks of their respective manufacturers and sellers. The author, editor, and publisher disclaim any affiliation, association, or connection with, or sponsorship or endorsement by, such owners.

Text: ISBN 0-7638-1608-6
Order Number: 01576

© 2002 by Paradigm Publishing Inc.
    Published by **EMC**Paradigm
    875 Montreal Way
    St. Paul, MN 55102

    (800) 535-6865
    E-mail: educate@emcp.com
    Web site: www.emcp.com

Printed in the United States of America
10 9 8 7 6 5 4 3 2 1

CONTENTS

Chapter 5

Configuring and Customizing Outlook 169

Chapter 6

Integrating and Managing Outlook Components 225

OUTLOOK

OFFICE

Microsoft Office XP is a very popular suite of programs designed to improve productivity and efficiency in workplace, school, and home settings. The major programs included in Office are Word, a word processing program; Excel, a spreadsheet program; Access, a database management program; PowerPoint, a slide presentation program; and Outlook, a scheduling, contact management, and e-mail program.

The Office suite offers significant advantages over individual programs. The programs in the Office suite use similar toolbars, buttons, icons, and menus providing easy transfer of knowledge from one program to another, decreasing the amount of time required to learn the features of a program. The compatibility of the programs creates seamless integration of data within and between programs and lets the operator use the program that most easily and efficiently completes the required tasks.

USING OUTLOOK 2002

Microsoft Outlook 2002 is an application that provides tools to send and receive e-mail, organize schedules and events, and maintain contacts lists, to-do lists, and notes. Outlook also includes a journal that automatically logs everything you do on your computer. Information in Outlook can be integrated with other applications in the Microsoft Office suite. Using Outlook is different from using other applications such as Word or Excel. In Outlook, you open a folder related to the item you wish to create, edit, or view.

Skills taught in this text:

✔ Using Outlook for e-mail
- Create and send an e-mail message
- Reply to, print, and delete e-mail messages
- Attach files to a message

✔ Managing schedules
- Schedule appointments and events
- Schedule recurring appointments
- Change the calendar view
- Print the calendar
- Edit and move appointments
- Use Outlook to schedule meetings
- Create an appointment from the Contacts folder

✔ Managing Outlook folders and contacts
- Create folders and move messages between folders
- Create, print, edit, and delete contacts
- Change the contacts view
- Perform a mail merge using the Contacts list

✔ Organizing your work using tasks
- Create a tasks list
- Mark a task as complete
- Create a recurring task
- Print a task

✔ Customizing Outlook and using advanced features
- Create, edit, view, and print journal entries
- Use and customize Outlook Today
- Save a calendar as a Web page
- Assign a Web page as the folder home page
- Create, specify, and synchronize folders for offline use
- Import a vCard and vCalendar file into Outlook
- Send and receive instant messages and newsgroup messages

USING OUTLOOK FOR E-MAIL

P E R F O R M A N C E   O B J E C T I V E S

Upon successful completion of chapter 1, you will be able to:
- Identify Outlook components and display folder contents
- Compose, send, open, and print messages
- Reply to, forward, and delete messages
- Attach a file to a message
- Use the address book when creating messages
- Assign importance, sensitivity, and tracking options to a message
- Create a signature
- Find and flag messages
- Change the current view
- Organize messages by sorting and grouping methods
- Create and use a mail template
- Save a message as a text or HTML file
- Create a folder and move messages between folders
- Change the mail format and e-mail options for new messages
- Find information in Microsoft Help resources

Outlook Chapter 1

(Note: There are 2 student data files required for this chapter.)

Microsoft Outlook is an application that is often referred to as a *Desktop Information Management (DIM)* or a *Personal Information Manager (PIM)* program. Information management programs organize items such as e-mail messages, appointments or meetings, contacts, to-do lists, and notes. Outlook also includes a journal that can log everything that you do on your computer to track time spent and/or activities completed. In an environment where the computer you are using is connected to an internal network or the Internet, information within Outlook, such as your calendar, can be shared with other users. Data stored within Outlook can be integrated to and from the other applications within the Microsoft Office XP suite. In this chapter you will explore the basic features of Outlook and the Inbox component that is used for managing e-mail messages.

The first time that you start Outlook 2002 after Microsoft Office XP has been installed, you might be required to navigate through a series of dialog boxes that are part of the startup wizard. The startup wizard searches your computer for existing mail accounts and in most cases will allow you to import the information into Outlook. If Outlook cannot upgrade or import from an existing account, you will be prompted to enter the required information to create a new e-mail account to send and receive messages. Your e-mail provider can provide the server type and server name settings for this process.

Starting the Outlook Window

Launch
Outlook

To start Outlook using the menu, click the Start button on the Taskbar, point to Programs, and then click Microsoft Outlook. The Microsoft Outlook application window will appear as shown in figure 1.1. You can also start Outlook by clicking the Launch Microsoft Outlook button on the Quick Launch toolbar displayed on the Taskbar.

FIGURE

1.1 *Microsoft Outlook Window*

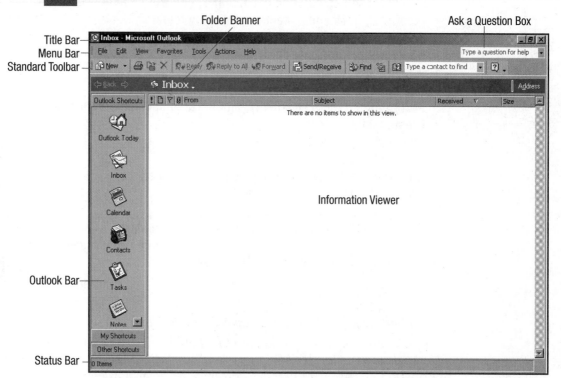

The Outlook window contains elements standard to Windows-based applications such as the Title bar, Menu bar, Standard toolbar, and Status bar that contain features similar to those found in the other programs within the Microsoft Office suite.

By default, the *Inbox* folder is active when Outlook is first started. In Outlook, information items within each component are stored within a separate folder for that component. For example, mail messages are stored within the *Inbox* folder and appointments are stored within the *Calendar* folder. Clicking an icon on the Outlook bar will display the contents of the folder within the Information Viewer. Table 1.1 identifies the items that are stored within each Outlook folder.

OUTLOOK

The Folder banner displays below the Standard toolbar and displays the name of the active folder. Clicking the current folder name on the Folder banner will display the Folder List where you can view the folders within Outlook or change to a different folder.

TABLE

1.1	*Outlook Folders*

Folder Name	Contents Stored within Folder
Inbox	E-mail messages that have been received. Other folders for e-mail are *Deleted Items*, *Sent Items*, and *Drafts*.
Calendar	Scheduled appointments, events, and meetings.
Contacts	Information such as name, address, telephone, e-mail address, and other data about the individuals with whom you regularly communicate.
Tasks	Descriptions of activities that you need to complete for which you want to keep track.
Notes	Reminders or other pieces of unstructured information for which you want to keep track.

Exploring Outlook Components

The Outlook bar icons are shortcuts to some of the commonly used folders in Outlook. Clicking an icon on the Outlook bar will change the active folder and display the folder's contents in the Information Viewer. The Folder List accessed from the Folder banner can also be used to change the active folder. The Folder List displays all of the folders within Outlook in a hierarchial arrangement similar to Windows Explorer.

exercise 1

CHANGING THE ACTIVE FOLDER AND VIEWING FOLDER CONTENTS

1. Click the Start button on the Taskbar, point to <u>P</u>rograms, and then click Microsoft Outlook, or click the *Launch Microsoft Outlook* icon on the Quick Launch toolbar.
2. If necessary, key your user name and password at the Enter Password dialog box.
3. Change the active folder using the Outlook bar by completing the following steps:

   Step 3a

   a. Click the *Calendar* icon on the Outlook bar. The current day is displayed within the Information Viewer and *Calendar* is displayed in the Folder banner.
   b. Click the *Contacts* icon on the Outlook bar and then view the layout of the Information Viewer.
   c. Click the *Tasks* icon on the Outlook bar and then view the layout of the Information Viewer.

4. Change the active folder using the Folder List by completing the following steps:
   a. Click *Tasks* on the Folder banner.
   b. Click the *Inbox* folder name in the Folder List.
   c. Click *Inbox* on the Folder banner.
   d. Click the *Notes* folder name in the Folder List and then view the layout of the Information Viewer.
5. Change the active folder back to the *Inbox* using the Outlook bar or the Folder List.

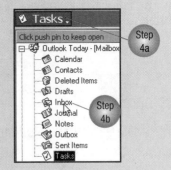

Using Menus and Toolbars

In a default installation of Microsoft Outlook 2002, the menus and toolbars are personalized as you work with the application. When you click an option on the Menu bar, such as File, the drop-down list of menu items that is shown are only the options referred to as *first-rank options*. These are the options that are considered to have the most usage. At the bottom of the menu you will see down-pointing triangles. This indicates that additional menu items (referred to as *second-rank options*) are not currently displayed. Use any of the following techniques to expand the menu and see the full list of options.

- Double-click the menu option.
- Click the down-pointing triangles at the bottom of the menu.
- Wait a few seconds and the menu will expand automatically.

If you click a second-ranked option on a menu, the next time you access the same menu, the option will have moved in precedence to a first-rank option and will be visible immediately. This feature is called *adaptive menus*. Complete the following steps if you prefer to work with Outlook with the adaptive menu feature turned off. This means you will see the full list of menu items whenever you click an option on the Menu bar.

1. Click Tools and then Customize.
2. Click the Options tab in the Customize dialog box.
3. Click the Always show full menus check box in the Personalized Menus and Toolbars section.
4. Click the Close button at the bottom of the Customize dialog box.

Toolbars in Outlook are also adaptive. When you open a message window, the Standard and Formatting toolbars occupy one row in the window. A Toolbar Options button displays at the right end of the Standard and Formatting toolbars. Click the Toolbar Options button to view additional buttons that are not visible. Once you click a button that was not previously visible, the button moves to the main toolbar. Outlook can be customized so that the toolbars are shown on two rows in the message window. Open a message window and complete steps 1 and 2 as described above. Click the Show Standard and Formatting toolbars on two rows check box in the Customize dialog box with the Options tab selected and then click Close.

Creating and Sending E-Mail Messages

Electronic mail (e-mail) is communication between individuals by means of sending and receiving messages electronically. E-mail usage continues to increase because of its ability to deliver a message within seconds anywhere around the world. Most businesses have moved to e-mail as the standard method of communication due to the speed and low cost. Routine business correspondence is now mostly conducted electronically replacing paper-based letters and memos. Individuals use e-mail regularly to communicate with relatives and friends all around the world.

To send and receive e-mail, you need to have a connection to a *mail server*. The mail server acts as the post office, routing messages sent and received to the appropriate recipients. The computer that you use to create messages and read the messages that you have received is called the *mail client*.

Multiple users will be connected to the same mail server just as one post office serves many people within a community. Each individual connected to the mail server is assigned a *user name* and *password* for unique identification and security to mail services. Messages are held in the *Inbox* until you log in to the mail server at which point the messages will be downloaded to the mail client and stored locally. It is possible to instruct Outlook to leave a copy of all messages on the mail server in case you want to have access to the Inbox from multiple locations.

The exercises and assessments in this chapter assume that you will be connected to a mail server through a local area network (LAN) at school. If you are working from home, you will need to establish a dial-up connection or have a continuous high-speed connection through a cable/digital modem to a service provider that provides the mail server prior to starting an exercise or assessment.

To create an e-mail message, click the New Mail Message button on the Standard toolbar in Outlook with the *Inbox* folder active. An Untitled - Message window opens as shown in figure 1.2.

New Message

FIGURE

1.2 *New Mail Message Window*

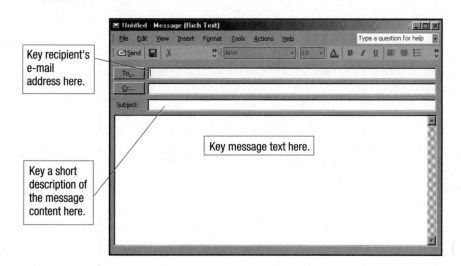

The address that you key in the To text box is either the user name of the recipient if you are sending the message to someone on the same mail server as you are, or the full Internet address of the recipient such as *username@mailserver.domain* if you are sending the message to someone outside your network. Key multiple addresses separated by a semicolon and one space. For example, *JDoe@school.net; MSmith@mail.net*.

The message window's Title bar initially displays *Untitled - Message* until you key text in the Subject text box. The subject text then appears in the Title bar of the window. The formatting toolbar in the message window is used to change the font, font size, font color, font attributes, text alignment, to key a bulleted list, and so on.

exercise 2

CREATING AND SENDING A MESSAGE

(Note: To complete most of the remaining exercises in this chapter you must be connected to a mail server. Check with your instructor for specific instructions on whom you should send the e-mail messages to. The instructor may have designated an e-mail partner to each person in the class to whom you will send messages to and receive messages from. If necessary, you can send the messages to yourself.)

1. Make sure *Inbox* is the active folder.
2. In a default installation of Microsoft Outlook 2002, the default e-mail editor is set as Microsoft Word. For purposes of learning the Outlook features in this chapter, Microsoft Outlook should be set as the e-mail editor. Complete the following steps to change the e-mail editor, if necessary, on the computer you are using:
   a. Click <u>T</u>ools and then <u>O</u>ptions.
   b. Click the Mail Format tab in the Options dialog box.
   c. If necessary, click the Use Microsoft <u>W</u>ord to edit e-mail messages check box to deselect it. *(Note: Skip this step if the check box is already deselected.)*
   d. If necessary, click the Use Microsoft Word to <u>r</u>ead Rich Text e-mail messages check box. *(Note: Skip this step if the check box is already deselected.)*
   e. Click OK to close the Options dialog box.
3. Create and send a new mail message by completing the following steps:
   a. Click the New Mail Message button on the Standard toolbar.
   b. Key the e-mail address for the recipient in the To text box. For example, *username@mailserver.net*. Check with your instructor for specific instructions on to whom you should send this message.
   c. Press Tab twice to move to the Subject text box.
   d. Key **Mail Viruses**, and then press Tab to move to the message text window.
   e. Key the following as the message text:

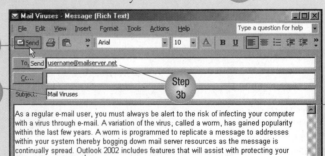

OUTLOOK

As a regular e-mail user, you must always be alert to the risk of infecting your computer with a virus through e-mail. A variation of the virus, called a worm, has gained popularity within the last few years. A worm is programmed to replicate a message to addresses within your system, thereby bogging down mail server resources as the message is continually spread. Outlook 2002 includes features that will assist with protecting your system from infection.

  f. Click the <u>S</u>end button on the message window toolbar to send the message to the recipient. The message window automatically closes once you have clicked Send.

4. Check the mail folders to see where the message has been placed by completing the following steps:

  a. Click *Inbox* on the Folder banner to view the Folder List. The message will appear in one of two folders. If the mail server is busy, the message will be queued in the *Outbox* folder. If the message has been routed through the mail server, the message will be in the *Sent Items* folder.

  b. If the message is in the Outbox, the folder name *Outbox* is in bold and the number of messages in the queue displays in blue. Click *Outbox* to view the message header in the *Outbox* folder. Proceed to step 4c if *Outbox* is not displayed in bold.

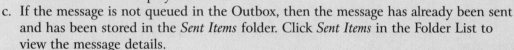

  c. If the message is not queued in the Outbox, then the message has already been sent and has been stored in the *Sent Items* folder. Click *Sent Items* in the Folder List to view the message details.

5. Redisplay the Inbox by clicking *Sent Items* or *Outbox* in the Folder banner, and then clicking *Inbox* in the Folder List.

Opening, Printing, Replying to, and Forwarding Messages

Messages appear in the Information Viewer of the Inbox in the order they were received with the most recent message at the top of the list. The message header for messages that have not yet been opened are in bold text. The sender's name, subject, date and time the message was received, and the message size are listed in the message header. An icon of an envelope will also appear in the system tray at the right edge of the Taskbar. By default, when new mail is received while you are working online, you will hear a chime and the pointer will change briefly to an icon of an envelope as the message is placed in the Inbox.

  To read a message, double-click the message header in the Information Viewer. A message window opens where you can read the contents. The Standard toolbar in the message window contains buttons to <u>R</u>eply, Reply to A<u>l</u>l, For<u>w</u>ard, or Print the message to someone else as shown in figure 1.3.

1.3 *Opened Message Window*

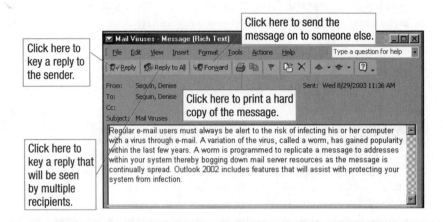

Click here to send the message on to someone else.

Click here to key a reply to the sender.

Click here to print a hard copy of the message.

Click here to key a reply that will be seen by multiple recipients.

Replying to a Message

Reply

When you click the Reply or Reply to All button on the Standard toolbar, a new message window opens layered over the original message with the sender's e-mail address already entered in the To text box, and *RE:* inserted in front of the Subject text. The original message text is copied at the bottom of the message window a few blank lines below the insertion point. The original message is included in the reply so that the reader will see the source text. This is referred to as a *thread* and is very beneficial to someone who sends or receives several messages in a day and may not immediately recall what she or he had sent to you. Reply text is displayed in blue above the original message text.

If you are replying to a message that was sent to multiple recipients and you would like all of them to read your reply to the sender, click the Reply to All button to have the sender's e-mail address and the e-mail addresses of the other recipients of the original message automatically inserted in the To text box.

Forwarding a Message

Forward

When you click the Forward button on the Standard toolbar, a new message window opens layered over the original message with the insertion point positioned in the To text box, and *FW:* inserted in front of the Subject text. The original message text is copied a few blank lines below the beginning of the message window so that the reader can read the threaded text.

Key the e-mail address of the person to whom you want to forward the message and if necessary, include a few explanatory lines of text in the message window above the original message for the benefit of the recipient. Text keyed at the top of the editing window of a forwarded message is displayed in blue.

 **exercise** 3

OPENING, PRINTING, REPLYING TO, AND FORWARDING A MESSAGE

(Note: To complete this exercise another student must have sent you the message created in exercise 2.)

1. Make sure *Inbox* is the active folder and that a new message appears in the Information Viewer.

2. Open, print, and reply to the message by completing the following steps:

    a. Double-click the message header to open the message and then read the message text.

    b. Click the Print button on the Standard toolbar in the message window. In a few seconds a hard copy of the message will print on the printer.

    c. Click the Reply button on the Standard toolbar in the message window.

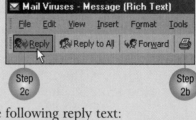

    d. With the insertion point automatically positioned at the top left of the message text window, key the following reply text:

    Thanks for the information. I have been hearing about computer viruses for some time now. We should investigate this further so that we know how to protect our computers.

    e. Click Send. The reply message window closes and you are returned to the original message window. A yellow information box appears above the sender's name with the date and time you sent the reply.

    f. Click the Close button at the right end of the message window Title bar.

3. Now that you have read and replied to the message, you decide to send both the original message and your reply to someone else by completing the following steps:

    a. Change the active folder to *Sent Items*. To do this, click *Inbox* in the Folder banner and then click *Sent Items* in the Folder List.

    b. Double-click the message header for the message you just sent in step 2 in the Information Viewer. *(Note: If the message does not appear in the* Sent Items *folder, it is in the* Outbox *folder. Click the Send/Receive button on the Standard toolbar to upload the message to the mail server. In a few seconds, the message should appear in the Information Viewer.)*

    c. Click the Forward button on the Standard toolbar in the message window toolbar.

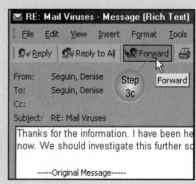

d. With the insertion point positioned in the To text box, key the e-mail address of the person for whom you want to forward the message.

e. Click at the top of the message text window and then key the following text: **I thought you might be interested in reading this information on Mail Viruses.**

f. Click Send. The forward message window closes and you are returned to the original message window. A yellow information box appears above the sender's name with the date and time you forwarded the message.

g. Click the Close button at the right end of the message window Title bar.

4. Display the contents of the *Inbox* folder. The envelope icon in the message header changes to indicate the message status as follows: opened when a message has been read; a purple left-curved arrow on the opened envelope when you have replied to the message; and a blue right-curved arrow when you have forwarded the message.

Deleting Messages

Delete

The mail messages stored in the *Inbox* and *Sent Items* folders are stored permanently. After a period of time these folders will become filled with messages that are no longer needed and should be deleted. To delete a message, click the message header to select the message and then press the Delete key on the keyboard or the Delete button on the Standard toolbar. The message will be moved to the *Deleted Items* folder. The message can be opened, replied to, or forwarded to someone else while it resides in the *Deleted Items* folder.

More than one message can be deleted at one time by following standard Windows conventions as follows:

• If the messages to be deleted are a group of adjacent messages, click the message header to select the first message in the list, hold down the Shift key, and then click the message header of the last message in the list.

• If the messages to be deleted are not adjacent, click the message header to select the first message, and then hold down the Ctrl key while clicking the remaining messages.

From time to time the *Deleted Items* folder should also be cleared out using the same techniques as the messages that were deleted from the original folder. To delete all of the messages in the *Deleted Items* folder in one step, complete the following steps:

1. Make *Deleted Items* the active folder.
2. Right-click the *Deleted Items* folder name in the Folder banner.
3. Click Empty "Deleted Items" Folder at the shortcut menu that appears.
4. Click Yes at the message box that appears asking if you are sure you want to permanently delete all of the items and subfolders in the *Deleted Items* folder.

1. With the *Inbox* folder active, change to the *Sent Items* folder.
2. Delete the first message that you sent from exercise 2 by completing the following steps:
   a. Click the message header in the Information Viewer for the message you sent in exercise 1.
   b. Click the Delete button on the Standard toolbar.
3. Delete the two messages that you sent from exercise 3 by completing the following steps:
   a. Click the message header for the first message that you sent from exercise 3 in the Information Viewer.
   b. Hold down the Shift key and then click the message header for the second message that you sent from exercise 3. Both messages are now selected.
   c. Press the Delete key on the keyboard.
4. Display the *Deleted Items* folder and then empty the folder by completing the following steps:
   a. Change the active folder to *Deleted Items*.
   b. Right-click the *Deleted Items* folder name in the Folder banner.
   c. Click Empty "Deleted Items" Folder at the shortcut menu.
   d. Click Yes at the message asking if you are sure you want to permanently delete all of the items and subfolders in the "Deleted Items" folder.
5. Change the active folder to the *Inbox*.

Attaching Files to Messages

Any file that you want to send to another individual can be attached to an e-mail message. Office documents created in Word or Excel, pictures, Web pages, and applications are routinely distributed by e-mail. To attach a file to a message, click Insert on the message window Menu bar and then click File. Browse to the location of the desired document in the Insert File dialog box and then double-click the file name for the file that you want to attach.

The recipient of the e-mail with a file attachment can choose to open the file from the mail server or save it to disk. To open a file attachment from the mail server, open the message and then double-click the icon for the file attachment in the message window. Depending on the size of the file and the purpose, saving an

Insert File

attachment to disk is often preferable. A message with a file attachment is differentiated in the Information Viewer with the icon of a paper clip next to the sender's name in the message header.

exercise 5

(Note: Make sure you have copied the student data files for chapter 1 before completing this exercise.)

1. With the *Inbox* folder active, click the New Mail Message button on the Standard toolbar.
2. With the insertion point positioned in the To text box, key the e-mail address for the person to whom you want to send the message with the file attachment.
3. Click in the Subject text box and then key **E-Mail Virus Tips**.
4. Click in the message editing window and then key the following text:
   I created this Word document with a few tips on how to protect your computer from infection as a result of an e-mail virus. Let me know if you have any additional tips I should add to the list.
5. Attach the Word document named Virus_Tips.doc to the message by completing the following steps:
   a. Press Enter twice to move down the message editing window a few lines.
   b. Click Insert on the message window Menu bar and then click File.
   c. Click the down-pointing triangle next to the Look in list box in the Insert File dialog box and then click *3½ Floppy (A:)* in the drop-down list. *(Note: Select a different location if your student data files are stored on a drive and/or folder other than the 3½ Floppy.)*
   d. Double-click the file named Virus_Tips.doc in the file list box. The file is added to the Attach row below subject.
6. Click Send.

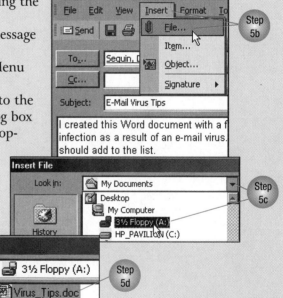

exercise 6

(Note: To complete this exercise another student must have sent you the message created in exercise 5.)

1. With the *Inbox* folder active, look at the message header for the message received with the subject E-Mail Virus Tips. Notice the paper clip icon next to the sender's name in the Attachment column of the Information Viewer.

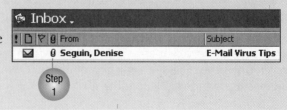

OUTLOOK

2. Double-click the message header to open the message. Attachments can be opened directly within the message window by double-clicking the icon for the file. In this exercise, however, you will learn how to save the file attachment to a disk.

3. Save the Word document to disk by completing the following steps:

a. Right-click the *Word* icon for the attached message and then click Save As at the shortcut menu.

b. With the file name Virus_Tips.doc already selected in the File name text box of the Save Attachment dilaog box, key **Ch01Ex06**.

c. Click the down-pointing triangle next to the Save in list box, click 3½ Floppy (A:) in the drop-down list, and then click the Save button.

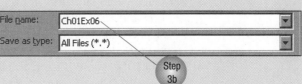

d. Click the Close button at the right end of the E-Mail Virus Tips message window Title bar.

4. Open the file attachment saved to disk by completing the following steps:

a. Click Start, point to Programs, and then click Microsoft Word.

b. Click the Open button on the Standard toolbar.

c. Change the Look in location to the 3½ Floppy (A:).

d. Double-click the file named *Ch01Ex06*.

e. Read the text in the document and then click the Print button on the Standard toolbar.

5. Exit Microsoft Word.

Maintaining Address Book Lists

Address Book

The Address Book is used to store the names and e-mail addresses of people to whom you send mail often. Addresses can be stored in Outlook in different locations. In a default installation of Outlook, the address book is dynamically linked to the *Contacts* folder. Adding an entry in the Address Book while in the *Inbox* folder, is essentially creating a record in the *Contacts* folder.

If you wish to keep track of some e-mail addresses independently from the *Contacts* folder, one personal address book can be created that is stored separately from *Contacts*. A personal address book is created using the E-mail Accounts Wizard.

If the computer you are using for Outlook is connected to a Microsoft Exchange Server, a third address list called the Global Address List is shown in the Address Book. This list is stored on the server and contains the names of all of the mail accounts created on the server. Adding to or modifying addresses in the Global Address List is usually performed by a system administrator.

Creating a Personal Address Book

A personal address book is a file stored outside Outlook with the file name extension of PAB. You might want to create a PAB file to store personal addresses that are separate from business contacts. Complete the following steps to create a personal address book that stores addresses outside the *Contacts* folder.

1. Exit Outlook if it is currently open.
2. Right-click the *Outlook* icon on the desktop and then click P̲roperties.
3. Click the E̲-mail Accounts button in the Mail Setup – Outlook dialog box.
4. Click Add a new d̲irectory or address book and then click N̲ext.
5. Click A̲dditional Address Books and then click N̲ext.
6. Click Personal Address Book in the A̲dditional Address Book, Types list box and then click N̲ext.
7. If necessary, change the name or path for the new address book, and then click OK.
8. Click the C̲lose button to close the Mail Setup – Outlook dialog box.

When you are creating a message to someone with an entry in the Address Book, click the To or Cc buttons in the message window and the Select Names dialog box will open as shown in figure 1.4.

FIGURE

1.4 *Select Names Dialog Box*

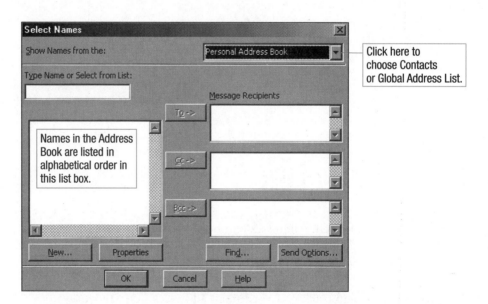

Click the name in the Name list box to whom you want to send the message, and then click To̲ →, C̲c →, or B̲cc → to enter the selected name in the M̲essage Recipients section. Click OK to close the Select Names dialog box when you are finished choosing names. The names displayed in the message window will appear underlined indicating they were selected from an address book. When you send the message, the e-mail address stored in the address book for the displayed name is used to deliver the message.

If you are working on a computer that is connected to a network or Microsoft Exchange Server, the names of the other accounts connected to the same mail server will appear when you open the Address Book under the Global Address

List. To display names that are stored in your own personal address book or the *Contacts* folder, click the down-pointing triangle next to the S̲how Names from the list box, and then click *Contacts* or *Personal Address Book*.

Adding Entries to the Address Book

New names and e-mail addresses can be added to the address book by clicking T̲ools, Address B̲ook, or clicking the *Address Book* icon on the Standard toolbar. If a message window is open, click the To button and then click the N̲ew button in the Select Names dialog box.

Address Book

By default, Outlook will store new entries to the Address Book in the *Contacts* folder. Open the Address Book, click T̲ools and then O̲ptions to change the location if you want a new entry to be stored in the Personal Address Book.

exercise 7

CREATING A PERSONAL ADDRESS BOOK

1. With the *Inbox* folder active, click F̲ile and then E̲xit to close Outlook.
2. Right-click the *Microsoft Oulook* icon on the desktop and then click Properties at the shortcut menu.
3. Create a new personal address book using the E-mail Accounts Wizard by completing the following steps:
   a. Click the E̲-mail Accounts button in the Mail Setup – Outlook dialog box.
   b. Click Add a new directory or address book and then click N̲ext.
   c. Click A̲dditional Address Books and then click N̲ext.
   d. Click *Personal Address Book* in the A̲dditional Address Book Types list box and then click N̲ext.
   e. Click OK to close the Personal Address Book dialog box.
   f. Click C̲lose to close the Mail Setup – Outlook dialog box.
4. Start Microsoft Outlook. If necessary, enter your user name and password to log back on to the mail server.

Step 2

Microsoft Oulo...

Open
Cu̲t
Create S̲hortcut
D̲elete
R̲ename
P̲roperties

E-mail Accounts

E-mail Accounts
You can change the e-mail accounts and directories that Outlook uses.

E-mail
- Add a new e̲-mail account
- V̲iew or change existing e-mail accounts

Step 3b

Directory
- Add a new directory or address book
- Vi̲ew or change existing directories or address books

Directory or Address Book Type
You can choose the type of directory or address book you'd like to add.

Step 3c

- Internet Directory Service (LDAP)
  Connect to an LDAP server to find and verify e-mail addresses and other information.
- Additional Address Books
  Connect to an address book to find and verify e-mail addresses and other information.

Outlook supports these additional address book types. Select the address book type you want to connect to and click Next.

Additional Address Book Types

Outlook Address Book
Personal Address Book

Step 3d

ADDING AN ENTRY TO THE PERSONAL ADDRESS BOOK AND SENDING A MESSAGE

1. With the *Inbox* folder active, click Tools, Address Book, or click the *Address Book* icon on the Standard toolbar.

2. Specify the Personal Address Book as the default location to store new entries to the Address Book by completing the following steps:

   a. Click Tools and then Options.

   b. Click the down-pointing triangle next to the Keep personal addresses in list box in the Addressing dialog box and then click *Personal Address Book* in the drop-down list.

   c. Click OK to close the Addressing dialog box.

   d. Click the Close button at the right end of the Address Book window Title bar.

3. Add a new entry to the Personal Address Book while creating a new message by completing the following steps:

   a. Click the New Mail Message button on the Standard toolbar.

   b. Click the To button in the Untitled - Message window.

   c. Click the down-pointing triangle next to the Show Names from the list box in the Select Names dialog box, and then click *Personal Address Book* in the drop-down list.

   d. Click the New button.

   e. Click *Internet Address* in the Select the entry type list box in the New Entry dialog box and then click OK. Click *Other Address* if Internet Address is not an option in your New Entry dialog box.

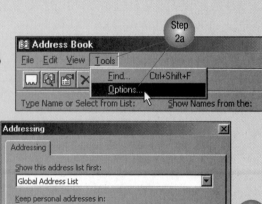

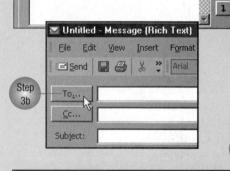

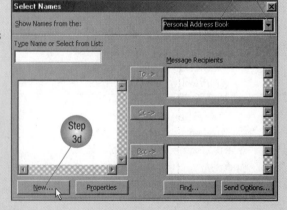

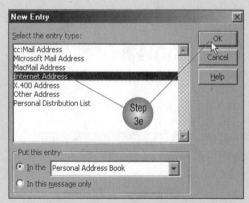

OUTLOOK

f. With the insertion point positioned in the Display name text box, key the name of the student for whom you are creating an entry.

g. Press Tab or click in the E-mail address text box and then key the full e-mail address of the student for whom you are creating an entry. If you selected *Other Address* in step 3e, you will have an additional text box labelled E-mail type in which you should key *smtp* in the text box.

h. Click OK to close the New Internet Address Properties dialog box.

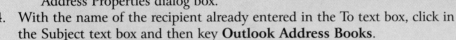
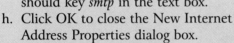

4. With the name of the recipient already entered in the To text box, click in the Subject text box and then key **Outlook Address Books**.

5. Click in the message editing window and then key the following text:

   Use a personal address book to store names and e-mail addresses for individuals that you do not want to keep track of through the Contacts folder. One suggestion is to use Contacts for business associates and a personal address book for friends and relatives.

6. Click Send.

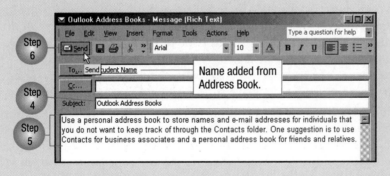

Assigning Message Options

With a message window open, click View, Options, or click the Options button on the message window toolbar to display the Message Options dialog box shown in figure 1.5. The Message Options dialog box is used to change settings, security, voting and tracking, and delivery options for the message you are creating.

Options

The Message settings section contains options for you to indicate to the recipient the message priority if it is to be treated unlike a normal message by attaching an Importance level of *High* or *Low*, and/or the Sensitivity is *Personal*, *Private*, or *Confidential*. Click the Security Settings button in the Security section to specify encryption or add a digital signature to the outgoing message.

1.5 *Message Options Dialog Box*

Voting buttons display Accept/Reject or Yes/No/Maybe buttons in the message window at the Recipient's end. These can be used to allow the recipients of your message to provide feedback on an issue described within the message. Delivery and read receipts can be attached to the message so that the sender will be notified when the message is delivered to the recipient's mailbox, and also when the recipient opens the message so that you will know they have read it.

In the Delivery options section you can direct replies to your message to someone else. For example, if you are going to be away and want a message that is replied to looked at in your absence, key an assistant's e-mail address in the Have replies sent to text box. Click the Select Names button to chose the alternate recipient from the Global Address List, Contacts, or Personal Address Book entries. Sent messages can be directed to a different folder in the Save sent messages to box. Use the Browse button to navigate to a different folder other than *Sent Items*. Use the Do not deliver before option to specify a date and time that you want the message sent if you do not want immediate delivery to take place. The message will be retained in the *Outbox* folder until the delivery date and time specified occurs. The Expires after text box can be used to enter a date and time the message will expire on. After the specified date and time, the message will no longer be available.

The Contacts button is used to display a list of contacts for which you can link the message. Later, you will be able to view the message by the Contacts name. The Categories text box is used to type in words that you want to associate the message with in order to find or group related messages.

 exercise 9

1. With the *Inbox* folder active, click the New Mail Message button on the Standard toolbar.

2. Click the To button in the Untitled - Message window to display the Select Names dialog box. Change <u>S</u>how names from the *Personal Address Book*, and then double-click the name of the student you added to the Personal Address Book in exercise 8. *Note: This moves the student's name to the T<u>o</u> list box in the <u>M</u>essage Recipients' section.*

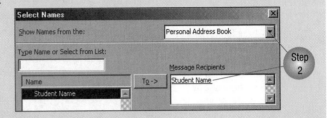

3. Click OK to close the Select Names dialog box.

4. Click in the Subject text box and then key **E-Mail Viruses**.

5. Click in the message editing window and then key the following text:

    E-mail viruses are becoming a more common occurrence. We need to be sure we are completely informed on the latest news regarding this issue and share a common strategy for protecting our systems.

6. Assign message options to the message by changing the Importance and Sensitivit<u>y</u> settings and request a read receipt by completing the following steps:

    a. Click <u>V</u>iew, Options, or click the O<u>p</u>tions button on the message window toolbar to open the Message Options dialog box.

    b. Click the down-pointing triangle next to the Importance list box in the Message settings section and then click *High* in the drop-down list.

    c. Click the down-pointing triangle next to the Sensitivit<u>y</u> list box in the Message settings section and then click *Confidential* in the drop-down list.

    d. Click the Request a <u>r</u>ead receipt for this message check box in the Voting and Tracking options section.

    e. Click the Close button at the bottom right of the Message Options dialog box.

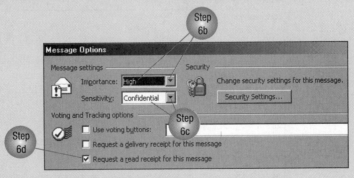

7. Click <u>S</u>end.

The recipient of a message that has the Importance High option attached to it will see a red exclamation mark in the Importance column at the left edge of the message header in the Information Viewer. When the recipient opens the message, a yellow information box displays between the toolbar and the sender's name informing the recipient of the options that have been assigned the message, as shown in figure 1.6.

1.6 *Message Options Information Box*

Information box informs reader of the options that have been assigned to the message by the sender.

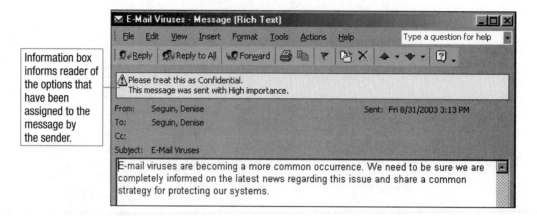

When a message has been sent with a read receipt attached to it, the sender will receive a read report message that includes the date and time the message was opened by the recipient. The read report message for the read receipt that was attached to the message sent in exercise 9 is shown in figure 1.7.

1.7 *Read Report Message*

Date and time message was opened by recipient.

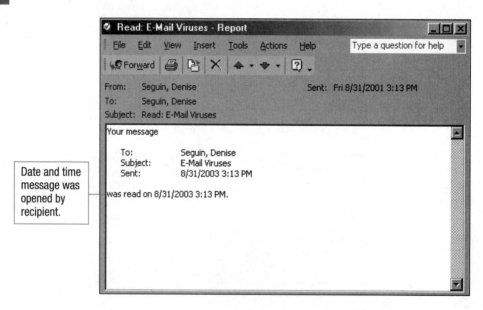

Some mail servers do not support read reports to the sender. If you do not receive a read report message after sending a message with a read receipt attached, it does not always mean that the message was not opened by the recipient. One possibility is that the recipient's mail server does not support this feature. If you are sending and receiving mail using Microsoft Outlook connected to a Microsoft Exchange Server, then the read receipt feature should be operational. Contact your system administrator if you are not sure.

Creating a Signature

A signature is a closing that you would like automatically inserted at the bottom of each message that you create. Signature text usually includes information about the sender such as name, title, department, company name, and contact numbers. Some people include additional information such as office hours, assistant's name, or alternative contact names. An advantage to creating a signature is that each message you send contains a consistent closing. Multiple signatures can be created in case you want one signature for external contacts and another one for internal business mail. Once a signature has been created, Outlook inserts the text automatically to the end of each message you create.

exercise 10

1. With the *Inbox* folder active, click <u>T</u>ools and then <u>O</u>ptions.
2. Click the Mail Format tab in the Options dialog box.
3. Click the Signatures button in the Signature section at the bottom of the Options dialog box with the Mail Format tab selected.
4. Create a new signature by completing the following steps:
   a. Click <u>N</u>ew in the Create Signature dialog box.
   b. Key **External Signature** in the Enter a na<u>m</u>e for your new signature text box in the Create New Signature dialog box.
   c. Click <u>N</u>ext.
   d. Click the <u>F</u>ont button in the Edit Signature dialog box and then change the color of the signature text by completing the following steps:
      1) Click the down-pointing triangle next to the <u>C</u>olor list box in the Font dialog box.
      2) Click *Teal* in the drop-down list.
      3) Click OK to close the Font dialog box.
   e. With the insertion point positioned in the Signature text text box, key the following signature substituting your name, school name, and address for those shown:
      Student Name
      Student
      School Name
      City, State, Zip
   f. Click <u>F</u>inish.

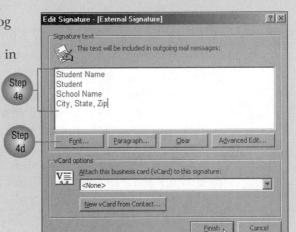

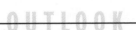

g. Click OK in the Create Signature dialog box. *External Signature* is automatically selected in the Signature for new messages list box in the Options dialog box.

h. Click OK to close the Options dialog box.

5. Create and send a new message with the external signature automatically inserted by completing the following steps:

a. Click the New Mail Message button. The external signature text is automatically inserted at the bottom of the message window.

b. Click the To button and then insert the student name from your personal address book.

c. Key **Outlook Signatures** in the Subject text box.

d. Click in the message window above the signature text and then key the following text:
A signature similar to the one inserted at the bottom of this message in the teal font color can be created in another software program such as Microsoft Word and then imported into Outlook. To do this, create the signature in a Word document. Key the Word document name in the Use this file as a template text box in the Create New Signature dialog box.

6. Click Send.

Step 5b

Untitled - Message (Rich Text)

File Edit View Insert Format

Send   Options... » Arial

To...

Cc...

Subject:

Student Name
Student
School Name
City, State, Zip

External Signature is automatically inserted at the bottom of the message.

Once a signature has been created it can be edited or deleted. To do this, display the Create Signature dialog box by completing steps 1 to 3 from exercise 10. In the Create Signature dialog box, click the signature name that you want to edit if more than one signature exists, and then click the Edit button to open the Edit Signature dialog box where you can change the content or format. Click the signature name in the Create Signature dialog box and then click the Remove button to delete the signature.

Finding a Message

Find

Once you have been sending and receiving messages for a while, the Information Viewer will be filled with a large number of messages in each of your mail folders. To locate and review a message that you sent or received in the past may be difficult. When the Information Viewer becomes filled with messages, scrolling through the list is a time-consuming process.

With the Find feature, Outlook will return a filtered list of all of the messages that contain a keyword or phrase that you specify. The messages that do not meet the search criteria are temporarily hidden from view. To begin a Find, click Tools, and then click Find, or click the Find button on the Standard toolbar to open the Find bar shown in figure 1.8.

1.8 Find Bar

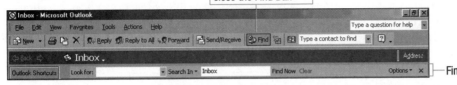

Find Bar

Key the word or phrase in the Look for text box that you want Outlook to search for within the messages. By default, the Search In list box contains the name of the current folder. Click Search In to display the drop-down list with the options *Inbox, All Mail Folders, Mail I Received, Mail I Sent,* or *Choose Folders.* The Choose Folders option will open the Select Folders dialog box where you can select which folders to search from the Folder List. Click Find Now to begin the search. Outlook will list only those messages that meet the search criteria in the Information Viewer. Click Clear to remove the filter and restore the folder to the original list.

exercise 11

FINDING A MESSAGE

1. With the *Inbox* folder active, click Tools and then Find or click the Find button on the toolbar to display the Find bar.
2. Search for messages that you sent that contain the keyword *protect* by completing the following steps:
   a. With the insertion point positioned in the Look for text box, key **protect**.
   b. Click Search In on the Find bar and then click *Mail I Sent* in the drop-down list.
   c. Click Find Now. Outlook searches through the messages in the *Sent Items* folder and displays only those that have the text string *protect* somewhere within the message.

3. Open each message in the Information Viewer and read through the message to make sure the text *protect* exists within the message. Notice in one message, the word found is *protecting*, a form of the word in the Look for text box.
4. Click Clear on the Find bar. The Information Viewer is restored to the previous list.
5. Click Tools and then Find or click the Find button on the toolbar to close the Find bar.

To use Outlook's Advanced Find feature, click the Options button on the Find bar and then click Advanced Find to open the Advanced Find dialog box shown in figure 1.9. The Messages tab of the Advanced Find dialog box contains options to locate messages by restricting the search to individual names, to search by specific fields in a message, or restrict the search to messages within a specific timeframe. To search in additional folders for the search criteria, click the Browse button to select folder names from a list. In the Folders list box, click the check boxes next to the folders that you want to search, and then click OK. The folder names will appear separated by semicolons in the In text box.

FIGURE

1.9 *Advanced Find Dialog Box with Messages Tab Selected*

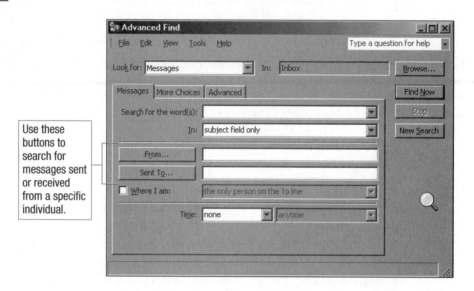

Use these buttons to search for messages sent or received from a specific individual.

The More Choices tab can be used to locate messages by the category they have been assigned, the read status, the attachments, or importance settting. The case of the text within the search string can be matched, or the messages can be filtered by the message size.

The Advanced tab can be used to enter conditional statements for which Outlook must satisfy to filter the message list.

Flagging a Message

Flag

A message that you have already received can be flagged as a reminder to follow up on an item or a message can be flagged as you are creating it to request someone else to perform an action. A red or gray flag appears next to a flagged message in the Information Viewer. A red flag indicates that the message has not yet been acted upon. A gray flag indicates that the action has been completed.

When a recipient receives a flagged message, a yellow information box appears at the top of the message with the purpose of the flag. If a reminder date has been set, the date will also appear in the information box.

To flag a message that you have already received, click the message header in the Information Viewer, click Actions on the Menu bar, and then click Follow Up. Select the type of flag you want in the Flag to list box by clicking a flag type in the drop-down list, or key your own flag in the text box. Select a due date in the Due by text box by clicking the down-pointing triangle and then selecting a date from the drop-down calendar. Click OK when you have finished setting the flag and date.

exercise 12

ATTACHING A FOLLOW UP FLAG TO A MESSAGE

1. With the *Inbox* folder active, click the New Mail Message button.
2. Click the To button and then insert the student name from your personal address book.
3. Key **Virus Protection Strategy** in the Subject text box.
4. Click in the message window above the signature text and then key the following text:
   Let's meet soon to discuss the E-Mail Virus Tips document and formalize a strategy that we can all use to protect our systems.
5. Attach a Follow Up Flag to the message by completing the following steps:
   a. Click Actions on the message window Menu bar and then click Follow Up, or click the Follow Up button on the message window toolbar.
   b. Drag across the text *None* in the Due by text box and then key **one week from today**. *(Note: This text is referred to as a natural language phrase. You can also use the down-pointing triangle to click a specific date from a drop-down calendar.)*
   c. Click OK. A yellow information box will appear between the toolbar and the recipient's name with the follow-up message.

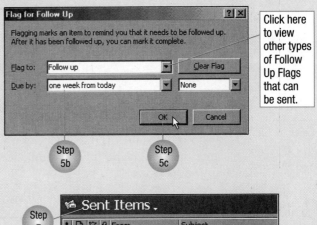

6. Click Send.
7. Display the *Sent Items* folder in the Information Viewer. The message header for the message sent in step 6 will appear with a red flag in the Flag Status column.
8. Change the active folder to the *Inbox*.

To clear a flag from a message, display the Flag for Follow Up dialog box, then click the Clear Flag button. To indicate the follow-up action has been completed, display the Flag for Follow Up dialog box and then click the Completed check box.

(Note: To complete this exercise another student must have sent you the message created in exercise 12.)

1. With *Inbox* the active folder, open the message received with the Follow Up Flag that was sent in exercise 12. A yellow information box appears between the toolbar and the sender's name with the date that the follow-up activity is due.

2. Mark the Follow Up activity as completed by completing the following steps:

    a. Click <u>A</u>ctions on the message window Menu bar and then click Follow <u>U</u>p, or click the Follow Up button on the message window toolbar. The Flag for Follow Up dialog box opens with the due date entered in the <u>D</u>ue by text box.

    b. Click the <u>C</u>ompleted check box and then click OK.

3. Look at the message header in the Information Viewer. Notice the red flag has changed to a gray flag since the Follow Up activity has been marked as completed.

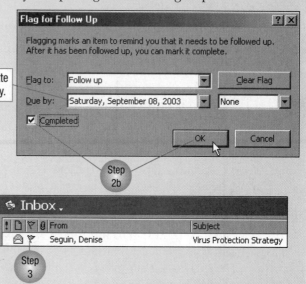

Your date will vary.

Step 2b

Step 3

Changing the View

With options on the <u>V</u>iew, Current <u>V</u>iew menu, you can change the way messages are displayed in the Information Viewer by choosing from several view options as shown in figure 1.10.

FIGURE

1.10 *Current View Options*

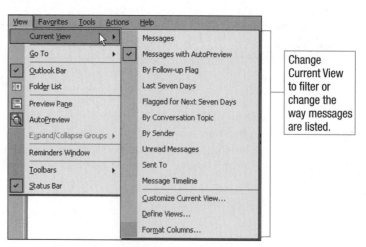

Change Current View to filter or change the way messages are listed.

The current setting displays with a check mark in a recessed box next to the menu option. *Unread Messages* acts like a filter to display only those messages with an unread status on them—messages in the current folder that have been read are not listed when this view is active. To redisplay all of the messages afterward, select Messages or Messages with AutoPreview from the Current <u>V</u>iew menu.

CHANGING THE CURRENT VIEW

1. With the *Inbox* folder active, click <u>V</u>iew and then point to Current <u>V</u>iew.
2. Click By Follow-up Flag. The messages are grouped in the Information Viewer according to the flag status.
3. Click <u>V</u>iew, point to Current View, and then click Unread Messages. Outlook will display only those messages that have not yet been opened. If you have read all of your messages, the Information Viewer will be empty as shown. Notice the message *(Filter Applied)* next to the folder name in the Folder banner.
4. Click <u>V</u>iew, point to Current View, and then click Messages with AutoPreview. All of the messages reappear in the Information Viewer.

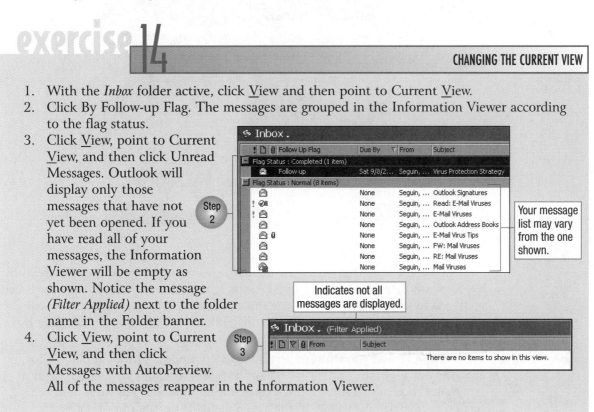

Step 2

Your message list may vary from the one shown.

Indicates not all messages are displayed.

Step 3

Organizing Messages

How you decide to organize the messages in your mail folders depends on your work environment and the types of messages you receive. For example, someone receiving messages daily with new orders may decide to organize them by the sender's name, by date received, or subject text. Outlook provides several methods for organizing messages in the Information Viewer including sorting and grouping options.

Sorting Messages

Sort the current folder contents by clicking the column heading that you want to sort by. For example, to sort the message list by the subject text, click *Subject* in the header bar between the Folder banner and the message list. A triangle will appear next to the column heading indicating the sort order is ascending (up-pointing) or descending (down-pointing).

To perform a multiple-level sort or to sort by more complex criteria, click <u>V</u>iew, point to Current <u>V</u>iew, and then click <u>C</u>ustomize Current View. Click <u>S</u>ort in the View Summary dialog box to open the Sort dialog box shown in figure 1.11.

1.11 *Sort Dialog Box*

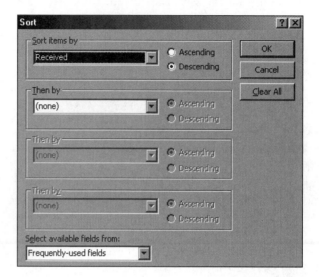

Choose the item that you want the messages arranged by in the Sort items by list box, and then click the sort order *Ascending* or *Descending*. Up to four levels can be sorted by choosing options in the three Then by sections. For example, you may want to sort the messages first by the Follow Up Flag, then by the Due By date for the flag.

If the field that you want to sort by does not appear in the drop-down list, click the down-pointing triangle next to the Select available fields from list box, and then choose a category in the drop-down list. The drop-down lists in the sections above will display all of the available fields for the category chosen.

exercise **15**

SORTING MESSAGES

(Note: If you have mail in the Outbox, click the Send/Receive button to send it to the mail server before completing this exercise.)

1. With *Inbox* the active folder, change the Information Viewer to display the contents of the *Sent Items* folder.

2. Point to the *Subject* column heading until the Tooltip displays *Sort by: Subject* and then click the left mouse button to sort the messages in *Sent Items* by the subject text in ascending order.

3. Click the *Subject* column heading again to sort the messages by subject text in descending order.

4. Sort the messages in *Sent Items* by the Importance setting and then by subject by completing the following steps:
    a. Click View, point to Current View, then click Customize Current View.
    b. Click Sort in the View Summary dialog box.

Step 2

Subject
Virus Protection Strategy
Outlook | Sort by: Subject

c. Click the down-pointing triangle next to the Sort items by list box, scroll down the list of items, and then click *Importance* in the drop-down list. The sort order will automatically be set to *Descending*.

d. Click the down-pointing triangle next to the Then by list box, scroll down the list of items, and then click *Subject* in the drop-down list. The sort order will automatically be set to *Ascending*.

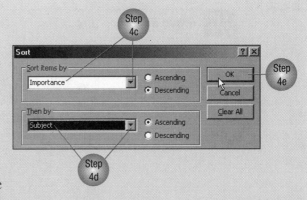

e. Click OK to close the Sort dialog box. The current settings for the Sort are displayed next to the Sort button in the View Summary dialog box.

f. Click OK to close the View Summary dialog box.

g. Review the list of messages in *Sent Items*. They should be arranged in descending order by the Importance setting and then in ascending order by the subject text.

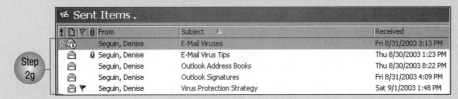

5. Clear the Sort settings to restore the Information Viewer to the default sort order by completing the following steps:

a. Click <u>V</u>iew, point to Current <u>V</u>iew, then click <u>C</u>ustomize Current View.

b. Click <u>S</u>ort in the View Summary dialog box.

c. Click the <u>C</u>lear All button in the Sort dialog box.

d. Notice <u>S</u>ort items by and <u>T</u>hen by now display *(none)*. Click OK to close the Sort dialog box.

e. Click OK to close the View Summary dialog box. The contents of *Sent Items* returns to the default sort order.

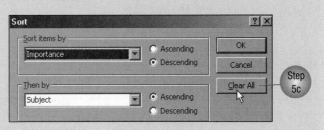

6. Display the *Inbox* folder.

Grouping Messages

The <u>G</u>roup By button in the View Summary dialog box can be used to group messages by a field such as a sender's name. The Information Viewer displays the messages in a collapsed list with an expand button. Click the expand button to display the messages within the group. The Group By dialog box is similar in structure and layout to the Sort dialog box as shown in figure 1.12.

1.12 *Group By Dialog Box*

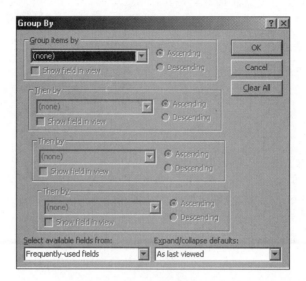

Click the down-pointing triangle next to the <u>G</u>roup items by list box and then choose the field that you want to group messages by in the drop-down list. Multiple-level grouping can be set in the Group By dialog box in a similar manner to multiple-level sorting. The difference between sorting and grouping is the way the messages are shown in the Information Viewer. All messages that have been arranged using the Sort feature are still displayed in the Information Viewer. When messages have been arranged using the Group feature, group headings display and the messages are collapsed under the group headings as shown in figure 1.13. Click the expand button (plus symbol) next to a group heading to view the messages below it.

1.13 *Grouped Message List*

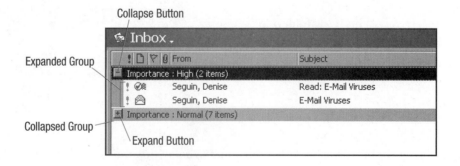

Once a group has been expanded, the expand button changes to the collapse button (minus symbol). Click the minus symbol to collapse the group.

OUTLOOK

1. With the *Inbox* folder active, group the messages in the Information Viewer by the Follow Up Flag by completing the following steps:
   a. Click <u>V</u>iew, point to Current <u>V</u>iew, and then click <u>C</u>ustomize Current View.
   b. Click <u>G</u>roup By in the View Summary dialog box.
   c. Click the down-pointing triangle next to the <u>G</u>roup items by list box, scroll down the list box and then click *Follow Up Flag* in the drop-down list. The sort order will automatically be set to *Ascending*.

   d. Click OK in the Group By dialog box. The current settings for the grouping are displayed next to the <u>G</u>roup By button in the View Summary dialog box.
   e. Click OK to close the View Summary dialog box.
2. Expand and collapse groups of messages in the Information Viewer by completing the following steps:
   a. Click the expand button (plus symbol) next to the group heading *Follow Up Flag: (none)*.
   b. Click the expand button (plus symbol) next to the group heading *Follow Up Flag: Follow up*.
   c. Click the collapse button (minus symbol) next to the group heading *Follow Up Flag: (none)*. The list of messages collapses from view and the collapse button changes to the expand button.
3. Restore the Information Viewer to the default display by completing the following steps:
   a. Click <u>V</u>iew, point to Current <u>V</u>iew, and then click <u>C</u>ustomize Current View.
   b. Click <u>G</u>roup By in the View Summary dialog box.
   c. Click the <u>C</u>lear All button in the Group By dialog box and then click OK.
   d. Click OK to close the View Summary dialog box.

If the field that you wish to group messages by is one of the column headings in the Information Viewer, right-click the column heading to display the shortcut menu and then click <u>G</u>roup By This Field. The column that is used to group the messages is displayed in the Group By Box between the Folder banner and the column headings as shown in figure 1.14. To restore the Information Viewer back to its original display, click the column button in the Group By Box and then click Don't <u>G</u>roup By This Field at the shortcut menu. The column that was used to group messages is added to the right end of the column headings. Drag the column heading back to its original position. To remove the Group By Box, right-click any column heading and then click Group <u>B</u>y Box at the shortcut menu.

1.14 *Group By Box*

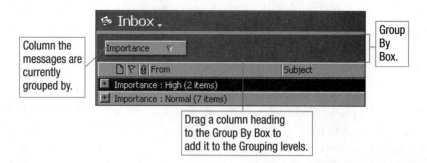

Column the messages are currently grouped by.

Group By Box.

Drag a column heading to the Group By Box to add it to the Grouping levels.

Creating and Using Mail Templates

A mail template is a message that has been saved with standard recipients, subject, and/or other text stored in the message window. If you e-mail an individual or a group of individuals frequently, consider creating a message template with the e-mail address(es) and any other standard text already keyed so that all you have to do is type the variable content for the current message. For example, if you send a monthly product update to a group of customers, you could create a template that contains the customers' e-mail addresses in the To text box and *Product News* in the Subject text box. Each month, to generate the e-mail you would open the mail template and then key the monthly update only.

By default, templates are stored in the path C:\Windows\Application Data\Microsoft\Templates for Windows ME or 98, and C:\Documents and Settings\<user names>\Application Data\Microsoft\Templates for Windows 2000 and have a file extension of *oft*. A template that you have created can be shared with others by replicating the oft file.

exercise **17**

CREATING AND USING A MAIL TEMPLATE

1. With the *Inbox* folder active, click the New Mail Message button.
2. Create a mail template for a monthly e-mail that will describe a new tip for protection against e-mail viruses by completing the following steps:
   a. Click the To button and then insert the student name from your personal address book.
   b. Key **E-Mail Virus Tip of the Month** in the Subject text box.
   c. Key the following text at the top of the message window: **E-mail virus tip for this month:**
   d. Press Enter twice after the text keyed in step 2c.
   e. Click File on the Menu bar in the message window and then click Save As.

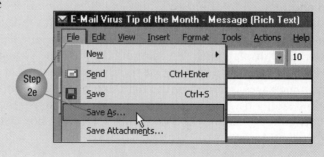

Step 2e

f. Click the down-pointing triangle next to the Save as type list box and then click *Outlook template (*.oft)* in the drop-down list.

g. Drag to select the current text in the File name text box and then key **Virus Tips xx** *(substitute your initials for* xx*).*

h. Click the Save button.

i. Close the message window. Click No when prompted to save changes. *(Since the message has already been saved as a template, there is no need to save it again.)*

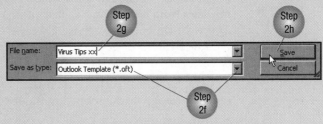

3. Create a new message using the Virus Tips xx template by completing the following steps:

a. Click File, point to New, and then click Choose Form.

b. In the Choose Form dialog box, click the down-pointing triangle next to the Look In list box and then click *User Templates in File System* in the drop-down list.

c. Double-click *Virus Tips xx* in the list box.

d. A message window will open with the stored template information inserted in the appropriate fields. Click the insertion point a double space below the text *E-mail virus tip for this month:* and then key the following text:

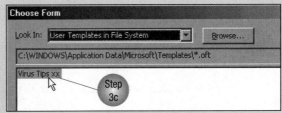

> **Macro viruses are viruses that have been embedded in document macros. Be sure to scan any Office documents that you receive by e-mail with an up-to-date virus checking program prior to opening the e-mail attachment.**

e. Click Send.

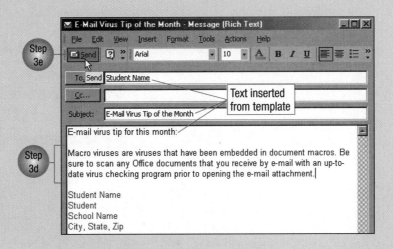

Saving a Message as a File

Occasionally you may want to save a copy of a message that you have received or sent in a file outside of your Outlook folders. For example, if you receive a message from a customer that contains important price change agreements, saving a copy of the message separately from Outlook is a good idea. A group of messages can be selected and saved as a text file. Outlook combines the content of each selected message into one file.

The Save as type list box in the Save As dialog box provides the capability to save a message in the following file formats:

- *Text Only (txt).* A text file is a file that contains the raw text only. Any formatting within the message is deleted.
- *Rich Text Format (rtf).* Any formatting within the message is retained.
- *Outlook Template (oft).* Message is saved as an Outlook template.
- *Message Format (msg).* MSG format retains all formatting and saves any attachments within the message file.
- *HTML (htm; html).* Hypertext Markup Language files can display multimedia effects for viewing within a Web browser.

The Save as type drop-down list that displays in the Save As dialog box is dependent on the message format that is currently set on the Mail Format tab of the Options dialog box. When the message format is set to Rich Text, the drop-down list does not show the HTML option. When the message format is set to HTML, the drop-down list does not show the Rich Text Format option.

exercise 18

SAVING A MESSAGE AS A TEXT FILE

1. With the *Inbox* folder active, save the message about creating Outlook signatures to a text file by completing the following steps:
   a. Click the message header for the message with the subject text *Outlook Signatures* to select the message. *(Note: If you do not have this message in your* Inbox, *choose another message to save to a file.)*
   b. Click File and then Save As.
   c. Click the down-pointing triangle next to the Save in list box and then click *3½ Floppy (A:)* in the drop-down list. *(Note: Select a different location if your student data files are stored on a drive and/or folder other than the 3½ Floppy.)*

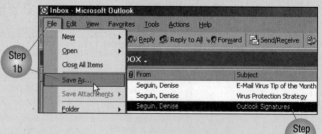

   d. Click the down-pointing triangle next to the Save as type list box and then click *Text Only (*.txt)* in the drop-down list. The File name list box defaults to the subject text of the selected message *(Outlook Signatures)* and the file extension changes automatically to match the selected file type *(txt).* If necessary you can select the text in the File name text box and key your own file name.

OUTLOOK

e. Click <u>S</u>ave.
2. A text only file can be opened in any word processing program. Open and print the text file Outlook Signatures by completing the following steps:
    a. Start Microsoft Word.
    b. Click the Open button on the Standard toolbar.
    c. Change the Look <u>i</u>n location to the 3½ Floppy (A:).
    d. Double-click the file named *Outlook Signatures*.
    e. If you receive a File Conversion dialog box similar to the one shown at the right, click <u>W</u>indows Default and then click OK. The message text appears in the document editing window.
    f. Click the Print button on the Standard toolbar.
3. Exit Microsoft Word.

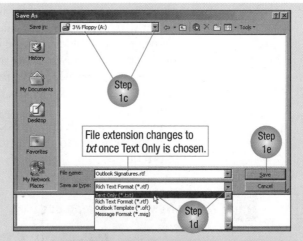

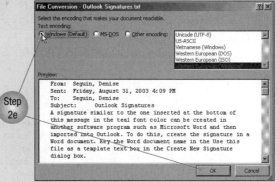

Managing Folders

Throughout this chapter you have been working with four folders set up in Outlook to organize mail messages: *Inbox* for mail that has been received; *Outbox* for mail that has been created but not yet uploaded to the mail server; *Sent Items* for messages that have been uploaded to the server and delivered to the recipient; and *Deleted Items* for messages that you have deleted. Frequently, you will want to manage the messages in your folders by organizing related items together in a separate folder with a descriptive name. For example, if you are working on a assignment and have been sending and receiving several messages about the assignment, you might want to create a folder and move all of the messages about the assignment to the folder.

Creating a Folder

The Folder List displays the names of the Outlook folders similar to a Windows Explorer folder list. A plus symbol next to a folder name in the Folder List indicates the folder contains subfolders. Click the plus symbol to expand the Folder List and view the names of the subfolders within it. Complete the following steps to create a new folder:

1. Right-click the current folder name in the Folder banner.
2. Click <u>N</u>ew Folder at the shortcut menu.
3. Key the name for the new folder in the <u>N</u>ame text box in the Create New Folder dialog box as shown in figure 1.15.

4. Click the name of the folder to place the new folder within in the Select where to place the folder list box. For example, if you are creating a new folder to store only sent messages, you could create the new folder within *Sent Items* so that it appears as a subfolder. By default, the currently active folder is the selected folder in the Select where to place the folder list box.
5. Click OK.
6. A message box will appear asking if you would like a shortcut to the new folder added to the Outlook bar. Click Yes or No to add the shortcut.

1.15 *Create New Folder Dialog Box*

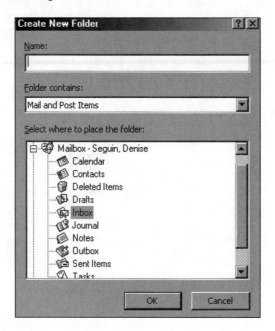

If you elect to place the new folder within an existing folder, such as *Inbox*, the new folder will appear in a hierarchial arrangement below the existing folder name. Outlook uses the standard Windows conventions of displaying the plus symbol next to collapsed lists and minus symbols next to expanded lists.

Moving Messages

Once you have created your own folders to organize messages, Outlook provides several methods for moving messages from one folder to another:

• Display the Folder List in the Information Viewer and then drag the messages from their current location to the desired folder name.
• Click to select the message in the Information Viewer; click Edit and then click Move to Folder. The Move Items list box opens with the Folder List for you to choose the destination folder.
• Right-click the message header in the Information Viewer and then click Move to Folder at the shortcut menu. The Move Items list box opens with the Folder List for you to choose the destination folder.

Multiple messages can be moved in one operation using the multiple select keys of Ctrl + click for nonadjacent messages and Shift + click for adjacent messages.

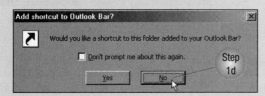

1. With *Inbox* the active folder, create a subfolder within *Inbox* by completing the following steps:
   a. Right-click *Inbox* in the Folder banner and then click <u>N</u>ew Folder at the shortcut menu.
   b. With the insertion point positioned in the <u>N</u>ame text box, key **E-Mail Viruses**.
   c. With <u>F</u>older contains already set to *Mail and Post Items* and *Inbox* already selected in the <u>S</u>elect where to place the folder list box, click OK.
   d. If the Add shortcut to Outlook Bar? message box appears, click <u>N</u>o.

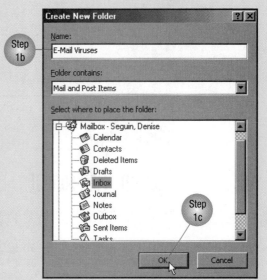

2. When the new folder is created in step 1, the Folder List automatically opens. Move messages related to e-mail viruses using the drag and drop method from the *Inbox* to *E-Mail Viruses* by completing the following steps:
   a. If the Folder List is not visible on your screen, click <u>V</u>iew and then Folder List.
   b. Click the message header for the first message received with the subject *Mail Viruses*.
   c. Hold down the Ctrl key and then click each additional message with *Mail Viruses* or *E-Mail Viruses* within the subject. If you click a message by mistake, simply click the message header a second time with the Ctrl key held down and the message will be deselected.
   d. Move the mouse pointer within the highlighted area for any of the selected messages, hold down the left mouse button, drag the mouse to the folder *E-Mail Viruses* in the Folder List, and then release the left mouse button.

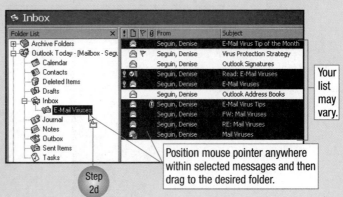

Your list may vary.

Position mouse pointer anywhere within selected messages and then drag to the desired folder.

3. Click *E-Mail Viruses* in the Folder List to view the folder contents to make sure the messages have been placed in the correct location.
4. Click *Inbox* to make *Inbox* the active folder.
5. Click the Close button in the Folder List bar to close the Folder List.

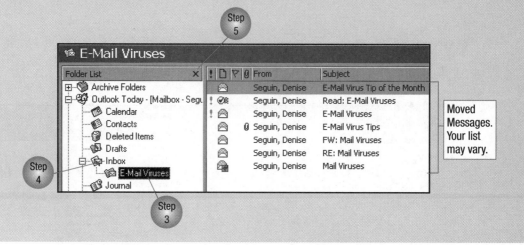

Changing Mail Format

Outlook can send messages in *Plain Text, Rich Text,* and *HTML* (Hypertext Markup Language) Format. Plain Text Format does not include any formatting; Rich Text Format displays formatting features such as font changes, text alignment, and bullets; and HTML Format displays features in addition to rich text such as backgrounds and horizontal lines commonly seen in Web pages. If many of the messages you create are sent outside your network over the Internet, consider changing the format to HTML since most popular e-mail applications support it.

You can change the mail format for an individual message using the Format menu in the message window, or change the default format for all new messages by displaying the Options dialog box with the Mail Format tab selected.

exercise 20

CHANGING TO HTML MAIL FORMAT

(Note: Skip this exercise if the Mail Format on the computer you are using is already set to HTML.)

1. With *Inbox* the active folder, change the mail format to HTML by completing the following steps:
   a. Click Tools and then Options.
   b. Click the Mail Format tab in the Options dialog box.
   c. Click the down-pointing triangle next to Compose in this message format list box, and then click *HTML*.

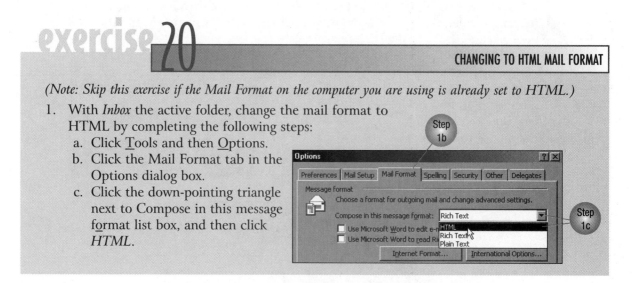

OUTLOOK

d. Click OK to close the Options dialog box.
2. Click the New Mail Message button. Notice the Title bar reads *Untitled Message – (HTML)*.
3. Close the message window.

Changing E-Mail Options

A multitude of options with respect to how Outlook processes mail that is sent and received can be changed in the E-mail Options dialog box shown in figure 1.16. The Message handling section of the E-mail Options dialog box allows you to control the actions that occur when messages are sent, received, and deleted. The On replies and forwards section provides options for how the original message text is threaded within messages that you reply to or forward to someone else.

FIGURE

1.16 *E-mail Options Dialog Box*

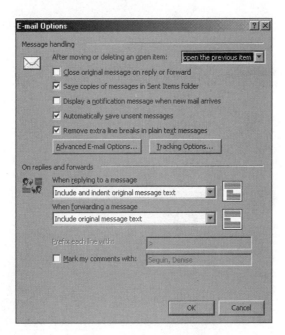

The Advanced E-mail Options button in the E-mail Options dialog box displays a dialog box with additional features for controlling the actions that occur when messages are saved, messages are received, and when messages are sent as shown in figure 1.17.

The Tracking Options button in the E-mail Options dialog box allows you to control how read receipts are processed. In this dialog box you determine how Outlook responds to requests for read receipts from other users. For example, you may want to instruct Outlook never to send a read report to someone who has attached a read receipt request to a message sent to you. By default, Outlook will display a message box when you open a message with a read receipt request giving you the opportunity to choose whether to send a report or not.

1.17 *Advanced E-mail Options Dialog Box*

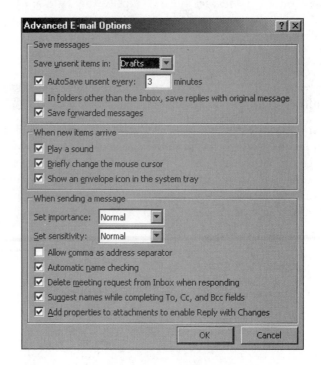

1.18 *Tracking Options Dialog Box*

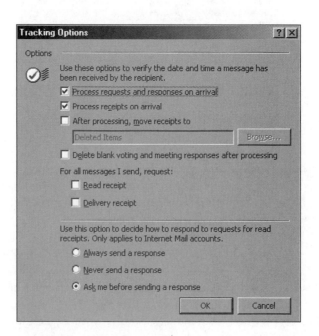

1. With *Inbox* the active folder, instruct Outlook to close the original message when you reply or forward a message by completing the following steps:
   a. Click <u>T</u>ools and then <u>O</u>ptions.
   b. Click the E-<u>m</u>ail Options button in the Options dialog box.
   c. Click the <u>C</u>lose original message on reply or forward check box. *(Note: Skip this step if this check box is already selected.)*

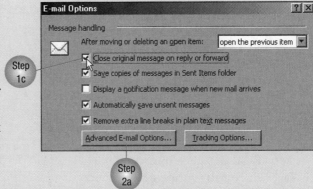

2. With the E-mail Options dialog box still open, increase the time interval that Outlook saves unsent messages in *Drafts* by completing the following steps:
   a. Click the <u>A</u>dvanced E-mail Options button in the E-mail Options dialog box.
   b. Drag across the current value in the AutoSave unsent e<u>v</u>ery [ ] minutes text box, and then key **5**. *(Note: If this box is currently empty, click the check box next to AutoSave to turn the feature on.)*
   c. Click OK to close the Advanced E-mail Options dialog box.
3. Click OK to close the E-mail Options dialog box.
4. Click OK to close the Options dialog box.

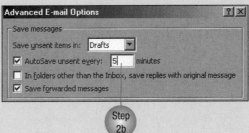

Using Help

An extensive help resource is available whenever you are working in Outlook by clicking in the Ask a Question box, keying a word or phrase related to the topic you require assistance with, and then pressing Enter. A list of Help topics that have been associated with the keyword(s) appears below the Ask a Question box. Click a topic that appears to answer your question and a Microsoft Outlook Help window opens with information about the topic. Once the Help window is open, you can show tabs to search for additional help by scrolling through the Contents list, keying a question in the Answer Wizard, or by keyword in the Index. Help topics can be printed for future reference.

> Type a question for help ▾
>
> Ask a Question box

In addition to the Help facility within Outlook, Microsoft includes an Office on the <u>W</u>eb feature on the <u>H</u>elp drop-down menu. Clicking Office on the <u>W</u>eb will start Microsoft Internet Explorer and automatically connect you to the Microsoft Office Assistance Center. From this Web site you can obtain articles about Outlook, download updates, and search for information about a problem you may be encountering with a feature.

1. With *Inbox* the active folder, search the help resources for information on how to send a message to someone without the recipient's name showing to other recipients (referred to as a *blind carbon copy*) by completing the following steps:

   a. Click in the Ask a Question box at the right end of the Menu bar, key **recipient name not shown**, and then press Enter.

   b. Click *Send a message without the recipient's name showing* in the list of topics that appears below the Ask a Question box. A Microsoft Outlook Help window will open with information about the selected topic.

   c. Read the steps presented in the Microsoft Outlook Help window. Notice that some text appears in blue indicating that the word is hyperlinked and more information can be displayed.

   d. Position the mouse pointer over the blue text *Bcc* and then click the left mouse button to expand the topic and display information about blind carbon copy. Read the definition that appears in green below the hyperlink.

   e. Position the mouse pointer over the blue text *Tip* at the bottom of the topic text and then click the mouse button. Read the information presented below the hyperlink.

2. Click the Print button on the Microsoft Outlook Help window toolbar and then click OK in the Print dialog box.

3. Click the Close button on the Microsoft Outlook Help window Title bar.

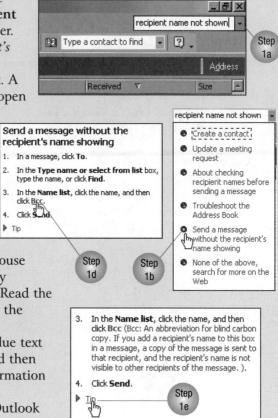

Other Help resources within Outlook are available from the Help drop-down menu shown in figure 1.19. Click Help, Microsoft Outlook Help to search for information on a feature using the animated Office Assistant. The Office Assistant appears with a yellow balloon above it where you can key a question and browse the topics found. If you prefer to work with the Office Assistant always visible, click Help and then Show the Office Assistant.

FIGURE

1.19 *Help Menu*

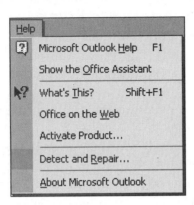

The What's This? option on the Help menu will display information about a topic that you click on after activating the feature. For example, if you are in a new message window and are wondering what a button or menu option will do, click Help, click What's This? and then click the button or menu option within the message window. A yellow information box will appear with a description of the item.

The Detect and Repair feature on the Help menu will scan the program files for errors and then automatically correct the application. About Microsoft Outlook displays a dialog box with the version of Outlook 2002 you are operating, copyright and license information, and buttons to display System Info, Tech Support, and Disabled Items.

CHAPTER summary

➤ Microsoft Outlook is an application that includes all of the tools needed to organize your work or personal environment including e-mail, calendar, contacts, tasks, notes, and a journal.

➤ Information in Outlook is organized in folders. Click a folder icon on the Outlook bar, or click the Folder banner and then click a folder name in the Folder List to view the contents of the folder in the Information Viewer.

➤ Click the New Mail Message button on the Outlook Standard toolbar to create and send an e-mail message.

➤ Messages received are placed in the *Inbox* folder. Display the contents of the *Inbox*, and then double-click a message header to open the message in a window.

➤ Print, reply to, or forward a message using buttons on the toolbar in the message window.

➤ Deleted messages are moved from the current folder to the *Deleted Items* folder where they remain until you empty the *Deleted Items* folder.

➤ Files such as Office documents can be e-mailed by attaching the file to a message.

➤ A file attachment can be opened directly from the mail server or saved to disk.

➤ Create a Personal Address Book (PAB) to store names and e-mail addresses of individuals that you do not want to store in the *Contacts* folder.

➤ Enter a name in the message window from your Address Book by opening the Select Names dialog box.

➤ The Message Options dialog box is used to assign importance levels, sensitivity, security, and delivery options.

➤ A read receipt can be sent to you indicating the date and time the recipient opens your e-mail message by tracking the message.

➤ Create a signature that is automatically added to the end of each message in the Mail Format tab of the Options dialog box.

➤ Display the Find bar to locate a message by entering search criteria.

➤ Messages can be flagged for follow-up action using the Follow Up option on the Actions menu.

➤ The Current View menu contains a variety of options for arranging messages in the Information Viewer.

➤ Click a column heading in the Information Viewer to sort the messages in ascending or descending order by the column.

➤ Messages can be sorted or grouped by up to four levels using the Sort or Group By buttons in the View Summary dialog box.

➤ Use the File, Save As command in the message window to save the message as a template. Change the Save as type option to Outlook Template (*.oft).

➤ Create a new message using a template by opening the Choose Form dialog box, changing to the user templates list box and then double-clicking the desired template name.

➤ Save a message as a file that is stored outside the Outlook folders using the File, Save As command. Outlook includes the following options for the format in which the file is saved: *Text Only (txt), Rich Text Format (rtf), Outlook Template (oft), Message Format (msg)*, and *HTML (htm, html)*.

➤ Mail messages are stored in one of four folders: *Inbox, Outbox, Sent Items*, and *Deleted Items*.

➤ Create new folders to organize related messages by opening the Create New Folder dialog box. Folders can be created in a hierarchial arrangement below existing folders. A folder created within another folder is called a subfolder.

➤ Move messages from one folder to another by dragging and dropping the message header from the current folder to the desired folder name in the Folder List.

➤ Display the Options dialog box to change the mail format or e-mail options for new mail messages.

➤ Outlook contains an extensive help resource that can be accessed by keying a word or phrase in the Ask a Question box or by displaying the Office Assistant.

➤ The Help menu in Outlook provides additional resources for finding information on features including the What's This? and Office on the Web options.

COMMANDS review

Command	Mouse/Keyboard
Attach a file	Insert, File in message window
Change mail format	Tools, Options, Mail Format tab
Change view	View, Current View
Create a new folder	File, New, Folder; or right-click folder name in Folder banner and then click New Folder at shortcut menu
Create a new mail message	File, New, Mail Message; or Actions, New Mail Message
Create a signature	Tools, Options, Mail Format, Signatures
Delete a message	Edit, Delete
Display address book	Tools, Address Book
Display e-mail options	Tools, Options, E-mail Options dialog box
Display Help dialog box	Help, Microsoft Outlook Help
Display Message Options dialog box	View, Options in message window
Find a message	Tools, Find
Flag a message	Actions, Follow Up
Forward a message	Actions, Forward in message window
Group messages	View, Current View, Customize Current View, Group By
Print a message	File, Print
Reply to a message	Actions, Reply or Reply to All
Save a template	File, Save As, change Save as type to Outlook template (*.oft)
Save a text file	File, Save As, change Save as type to Text Only (*.txt)
Send a message	Actions, Send in message window
Sort messages	Click column heading; or View, Current View, Customize Current View, Sort
Track a message	View, Options in message window

Type a question for help

Options..

Find

Forward

Reply

Send/Receive

CONCEPTS check

Completion: On a blank sheet of paper, indicate the correct term or command for each item.

1. Information in Outlook is stored in these.
2. Click an icon on this screen element to display the to-do list in *Tasks*.
3. Open a message by doing this action with the mouse while pointing at the message header.
4. When replying to or forwarding a message, this information is included and is called a thread.
5. Deleted messages are moved to this area.
6. These two actions can be done to a file attached to a message.
7. Names and e-mail addresses of individuals with whom you frequently send messages can be stored here.
8. Set the importance level of a message at this dialog box.
9. Attach this request to a message to receive a report when the recipient opens the message.
10. This feature automatically inserts stored text at the end of each message.
11. Messages can be located by keying a word or phrase that exists within the message in the Look for text box of this screen element.
12. Include a flag on a message with this option from the Actions menu.
13. Messages can be sorted or grouped by up to this many levels.
14. To restore the Information Viewer to its default order, click this button in the Sort dialog box.
15. Messages within a group that are not visible can be viewed by clicking this button next to the group heading.
16. Create a new message based on a template from this dialog box.
17. Display this dialog box to store a message in a separate file outside Outlook.
18. Move messages to a new location using the mouse by this method.
19. Change the mail format for new messages at this dialog box.
20. This feature from the Help menu will connect to the Microsoft Office XP Web site.

SKILLS check

Assessment 1

1. Create and send a new message to a student in your class as follows:
   a. Select the student's name from your personal address book.
   b. Key **More Info on E-Mail Viruses** as the subject text.
   c. Key the following text in the message window:
      I just read an article about e-mail viruses on the Web. Here is a summary of what I read.

Viruses are not replicated by means of an e-mail message since a message is based on text and text does not transmit a virus. Your computer becomes infected with a virus from a file attached to a message. You have to open the attached file for it to infect your computer. This is why it is always preferable to choose the option to save the attachment to disk and then scan the file with antivirus software prior to opening it.

    d. Print and then send the message.

Assessment 2

1. Copy the message received in your Inbox from Assessment 1 to the *E-Mail Viruses* folder and then open the message. *(Hint: To copy a message using the drag and drop method, hold down the Ctrl key while dragging.)*
2. Send a reply to the originator of the message with the following text:
   Thanks for the information. If I find any new information while browsing the Web, I will e-mail you.
3. Display the *Sent Items* folder, open the message sent in step 2, and then forward it to another student as follows:
   a. Key the following text at the top of the message:
      Are you interested in sharing information you find on e-mail viruses with us?
   b. Print and then send the message.
4. Display the *Inbox* folder and then delete the message you received from assessment 1.
5. Change the active folder to *Deleted Items* and then empty the folder.
6. Change the active folder to *Inbox*.

Assessment 3

1. Create and send a new message with a file attachment to a student in your class as follows:
   a. Select the student's name from your personal address book.
   b. Key **Picture for Political Science project** as the subject text.
   c. Key the following text in the message window:
      I have attached a picture of the White House for our project. Can you make sure to include it on the title page? Let me know if you need help with inserting the picture in Word.
   d. Attach the file named WhiteHouse.jpg from the student data disk to the message.
   e. Print and then send the message.

Assessment 4

1. Create a new message to a student in your class as follows:
   a. Select the student's name from your personal address book.
   b. Key **Security Options** as the subject text.
   c. Key the following text in the message window:
      Digital IDs or Certificates are documents that allow you to prove your identity for electronic transactions. The Security tab in the Options dialog box is where you can import or export digital IDs and set other security options.

      Have a look at this tab in the Options dialog box and let me know if you want further information on any of the other security features.

2. Assign the following message handling and tracking options to the message:
   a. Set the importance level of the message to High.
   b. Set a tracking option on the message so that you receive a read report when the recipient opens the mail message. *(Note: Remember that not all mail servers process read receipts.)*
3. Display the Flag for Follow Up dialog box. Change the flag to *For Your Information* and then click OK.
4. Print and then send the message.

Assessment 5

1. Edit the content and format of the signature named External Signature as follows:
   a. Select the text in the Edit Signature dialog box, change the font to 10-point Tahoma Regular and select Navy as the font color.
   b. Change the title *Student* to *Outlook Professional*.
   c. Delete the City, State, and Zip Code information.
2. Create a new message to a student in your class as follows:
   a. Select the student's name from your personal address book.
   b. Key **Send/Receive Options** as the subject text.
   c. Key the following text in the message window:
      If you want to change the time interval for Outlook to check for mail, open the Options dialog box and click the Mail Setup tab. Click the Send/Receive button to display the Send/Receive Groups dialog box. Options for the time interval to check for mail when you are working online and offline are available. The default is set to 5 minutes.

      Have you found anything interesting?
   d. Print and then send the message.

Assessment 6

1. Display the contents of the *Sent Items* folder.
2. Display the Find bar to filter the list of sent messages to only those that contain the word **Options** within the message.
3. Save the message with the subject *Security Options* to an HTML file on your student data disk.
4. Clear the Information Viewer so that all messages are restored in the view.
5. Change the active folder to *Inbox*.
6. Close the Find bar.
7. Start Internet Explorer and then open the HTML file saved in step 4 by completing the following steps:
   a. Click File and then Open.
   b. Click the Browse button.
   c. Change the Look in list box to the 3½ Floppy (A:).
   d. Double-click the file named *Security Options.htm*.
   e. Click OK at the Open dialog box.
8. Print the message from the Internet Explorer window.
9. Exit Internet Explorer.

Assessment 7

1. Create a new folder named *Outlook Tips* as a subfolder within the *Inbox*. Click No if prompted to add a shortcut for the new folder on the Outlook bar.

2. With the Folder List displayed, select all of the messages in the Inbox that contain information about Outlook features, and then drag the messages to the subfolder created in step 1.
3. Make *Outlook Tips* the active folder.
4. Close the Folder List.
5. Sort the message list in ascending order by the subject column.
6. Click File and then Print. Click *Table Style* in the Print style section of the Print dialog box and then click OK.
7. Make *Sent Items* the active folder.
8. Click File and then Print. Click *Table Style* in the Print style section of the Print dialog box and then click OK.
9. Make *E-Mail Viruses* the active folder.
10. Group the message list by the Subject column. Expand all of the group headings to see the messages listed below.
11. Print the message list in *Table Style* and then clear the Group settings.
12. Make *Inbox* the active folder.

Assessment 8

1. Delete the signature created in this chapter by completing the following steps:
   a. Click Tools and then Options.
   b. Click the Mail Format tab in the Options dialog box.
   c. Click the Signatures button.
   d. With *External Signature* already selected in the Create Signature dialog box, click Remove.
   e. Click Yes at the message asking if you are sure you want to permanently remove this signature.
   f. Click OK to close the Create Signature dialog box.
   g. Click OK to close the Options dialog box.

Assessment 9

(Note: This assessment assumes that templates in the computer you are using are stored in the folder C:\Windows\Application Data\Microsoft\Templates which is the default setting for Outlook on a computer running Windows ME or 98. If necessary, check with your instructor for alternate instructions in order to delete the template.)

1. Delete the mail template created in this chapter by completing the following steps:
   a. Click the Other Shortcuts button at the bottom of the Outlook bar.
   b. Click the *My Computer* icon on the Outlook bar.
   c. Double-click the icon for drive C in the Information Viewer.
   d. If necessary, scroll down the Information Viewer file list and then double-click the folder named *Windows*.
   e. Double-click the folder named *Application Data*.
   f. Double-click the folder named *Microsoft*.
   g. Double-click the folder named *Templates*. The template *Virus Tips xx.oft* should appear in the Information Viewer.
   h. Click the file named *Virus Tips xx.oft* and then press the Delete key or click the Delete button on the toolbar.
   i. Click Yes at the Confirm File Delete dialog box.
   j. Click the Outlook Shortcuts button at the top of the Outlook bar.
2. Make *Inbox* the active folder.

USING CALENDAR FOR SCHEDULING

PERFORMANCE OBJECTIVES

Upon successful completion of chapter 2, you will be able to:

- Schedule appointments and events
- Schedule recurring appointments
- Edit appointment details and move appointments
- View and print daily, weekly, and monthly calendars
- Change the current view to filter appointments and events
- Assign a category to an appointment and view appointments by category
- Apply formatting to appointments based on a keyword or category
- Schedule meetings by sending meeting requests
- Accept and decline a meeting request
- Respond to a meeting request by proposing a new time
- Find an available meeting time using the Plan a Meeting feature
- Update and cancel a meeting
- Schedule resources for a meeting
- Change calendar options

(Note: There are no student data files required for this chapter.)

The Calendar component of Outlook is used to schedule appointments, events such as conferences, and meetings. Appointments or meetings that occur on a regular basis can be created as a recurring item that needs to be entered only once. Reminders can be established to display messages and sound a chime at a set interval before the time of the appointment, event, or meeting.

Meetings are integrated with e-mail so that an individual can send a meeting request to others by e-mail and when the recipient responds to the message by accepting a meeting request, the details are automatically added in his or her calendar. The Plan a Meeting feature allows an individual who is trying to coordinate the schedules of several people to view the free/busy times of the attendees prior to sending a meeting request.

Scheduling Appointments and Events

Click the *Calendar* icon on the Outlook bar to display the contents of the *Calendar* folder in the Information Viewer as shown in figure 2.1. The default view for the Calendar is Day which is divided into three sections: *Appointment area, Date Navigator,* and *Task Pad*. The Appointment area shows the current day's appointments, events, and meetings. The Date Navigator shows the current month and the next or previous month with directional arrows to browse forward and backward. Days that have appointments, events, or meetings scheduled display in bold within the Date Navigator. The Task Pad is integrated to the *Tasks* folder and illustrates the to-do list. New items can be added to *Tasks* from the Calendar.

FIGURE

2.1 *The Calendar Window*

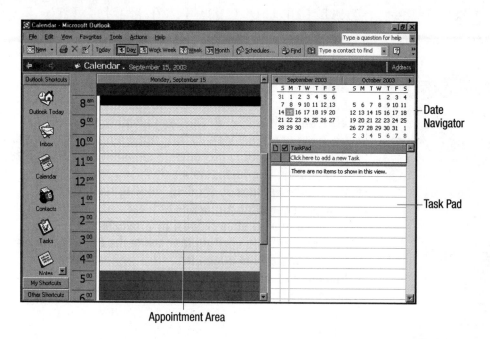

Appointment Area

New Appointment

To schedule a new appointment, click the date of the appointment in the Date Navigator, click next to the time of the appointment in the Appointment area, and then key a short description of the appointment. The appointment length will default to one-half hour. To lengthen the appointment time, point to the bottom border of the appointment box until the pointer changes to an up- and down-pointing arrow. Drag the box up or down to lengthen or shorten the appointment duration.

Display the Appointment window shown in figure 2.2 to store more detailed information about an appointment. To enter a new appointment using the Appointment window, click next to the desired time in the Appointment area and then do one of the following actions:

• Click the New Appointment button on the Standard toolbar.
• Double-click next to the appointment starting time in the Appointment area.
• Click File, point to New, and then click Appointment.
• Click Actions, New Appointment.

OUTLOOK

2.2 *Appointment Window*

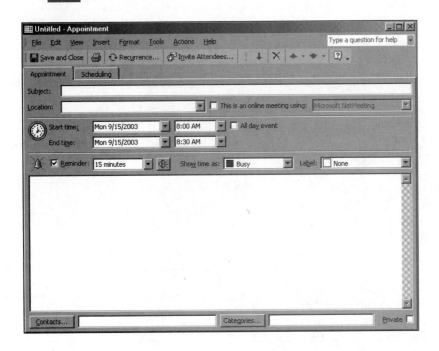

Key a description of the appointment in the Subject text box, and the location where the appointment will take place in the Location text box.

The Start time: will display the day and time that you selected in the Calendar before opening the Appointment window. You can change the start day and time by clicking the down-pointing triangle next to the day or time text box, and then clicking the correct entry. The times are displayed in half-hour blocks. If necessary, you can drag across the current time entry to select it and then key a specific time of your own such as *10:50 AM.*

Enter the end time for the appointment by clicking the down-pointing triangle next to the End time time text box, and then clicking the appropriate time from the drop-down list. The Reminder check box in figure 2.2 is set to display a reminder message and play a chime 15 minutes before the scheduled appointment.

The Show time as list box is used to assign a color code for *Busy, Free, Tentative,* or *Out of Office* in the scheduled time slot. This option displays as a colored border at the left edge of the appointment box in your calendar. When others view your calendar to plan a meeting, the time slot will appear as a colored bar dependent on the Show time as setting. The Label option allows you to color code the appointment box for quick identification when you view your calendar as to the appointment's significance. Click the down-pointing triangle next to the Label list box and then choose from the following options: *Important, Business, Personal, Vacation, Must Attend, Travel Required, Needs Preparation, Birthday, Anniversary,* or *Phone Call.* The appointment box will be shaded with the color for the associated label in the Appointment area. If you want to store additional information about the appointment, key the text in the white editing window below the Reminder check box. When all of the required entries have been made, click the Save and Close button.

1. With Outlook open and *Inbox* the active folder, click the *Calendar* icon on the Outlook bar.

2. Add a new appointment to the Calendar using the click and type method by completing the following steps:

   a. Click the right- or left-pointing triangle in the Date Navigator to scroll to the months of October and November 2003.

   b. Click Wednesday, October 15, 2003 in the Date Navigator.

   c. Click next to 10:00 am in the Appointment area. The time 10:00 to 10:30 am is selected as shown by the dark blue box.

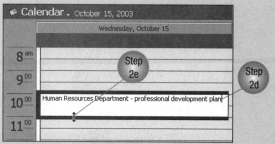

   d. Key **Human Resources Department - professional development plan**.

   e. Point at the bottom blue border of the appointment box until the pointer changes to an up- and down-pointing arrow, drag the appointment time down to the 11:00 am time boundary, and then release the left mouse button.

   f. Click in the Appointment area outside the appointment box. The appointment is displayed in a white box with a blue border at the left. Blue is the color displayed for times in the calendar that are *Busy*. By default, a reminder is set for 15 minutes prior to the appointment as shown by the bell icon next to the description.

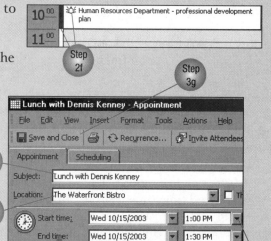

3. Add a new appointment using the Appointment window by completing the following steps:

   a. With Wednesday, October 15, 2003 the active date, click next to 1:00 pm in the Appointment area.

   b. Click the <u>N</u>ew Appointment button on the Standard toolbar (first button from left). An Untitled - Appointment window opens.

   c. With the insertion point positioned in the Subject text box, key **Lunch with Dennis Kenney**.

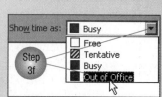

   d. Press Tab or click in the <u>L</u>ocation text box and then key **The Waterfront Bistro**.

   e. Click the down-pointing triangle next to the End ti<u>m</u>e time text box and then click *2:30 PM (1.5 hours)* in the drop-down list.

   f. Click the down-pointing triangle next to the Sho<u>w</u> time as list box and then click *Out of Office* in the drop-down list.

OUTLOOK

g. Click the Save and Close button. The appointment appears in the Appointment area with a purple border at the left of the appointment box. Purple is the color displayed for times in the calendar that are Out of Office.

4. Click the Print button on the Standard toolbar. With *Daily Style* selected in the Print style section of the Print dialog box, click OK.

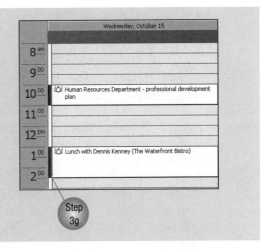

Recurring Appointments

An appointment that occurs on a regular basis at fixed intervals need only be entered once and then Outlook will automatically schedule the remainder of the appointments within the recurrence pattern. To schedule a recurring appointment, open the Appointment window and enter the details for the first appointment. Click the Recurrence button on the Appointment window toolbar to open the Appointment Recurrence dialog box shown in figure 2.3.

Recurrence

FIGURE

2.3 *Appointment Recurrence Dialog Box*

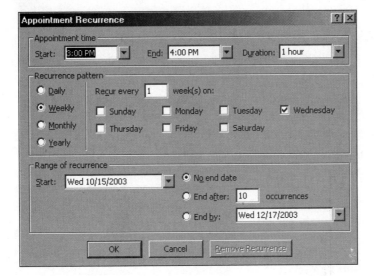

The Start, End, and Duration details in the Appointment time section will display the settings entered in the Appointment window. If necessary, change these options for the recurring appointment. Click the frequency options in the Recurrence pattern and the Range of recurrence sections and then click OK.

exercise 2

1. With the *Calendar* folder active and the date Wednesday, October 15, 2003 displayed in the Appointment area, schedule a recurring appointment by completing the following steps:

   a. Click Thursday, October 16, 2003 in the Date Navigator.

   b. Click next to 3:00 pm in the Appointment area.

   c. Click the New Appointment button on the Standard toolbar.

   d. With the insertion point positioned in the Subject text box, key **Sales update meeting**.

   e. Press Tab or click in the Location text box and then key **Conference room 101**.

   f. Click the down-pointing triangle next to the End time text box and then click *4:00 PM (1 hour)* in the drop-down list.

   g. Click the Recurrence button on the Appointment window toolbar.

   h. Drag the mouse over the value *1* in the Recur every [] week(s) on text box and then key **2**.

   i. Click OK to close the Appointment Recurrence dialog box and accept all other default settings. The current recurrence settings appear in the Appointment window below the Location text box.

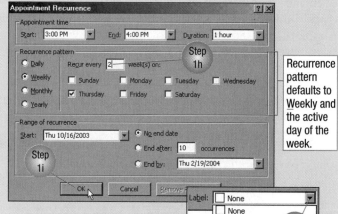

   Recurrence pattern defaults to Weekly and the active day of the week.

   j. Click the down-pointing triangle next to the Label list box and then click *Must Attend* in the drop-down list.

   k. Click the Save and Close button on the Appointment window toolbar. The appointment box in the Appointment area is shaded with the Label color for Must Attend and the recurrence icon appears below the reminder bell to indicate the appointment is a recurring item.

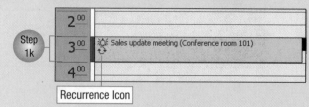

   Recurrence Icon

Scheduling Events

An event differs from an appointment in that it is an activity that lasts the entire day or longer. Examples of an event might include a seminar, training session, conference, trade show, or vacation. Other occasions that you might like to enter in the Calendar as an event are birthdays and anniversaries. An event does not occupy a time slot on the day it is scheduled. It appears in the banner for the scheduled day at the top of the Appointment area below the date.

To schedule an event, double-click the date at the top of the Appointment area, or click Actions on the Menu bar, and then New All Day Event. The Event window is similar to the Appointment window with the exception there are no text boxes for entering times.

exercise 3

ADDING AN EVENT

1. With the *Calendar* folder active and the date *Thursday, October 16, 2003* displayed in the Appointment area, schedule a one-day conference as an event by completing the following steps:
    a. Double-click the date *Thursday, October 16* at the top of the Appointment area. An Untitled - Event window opens.
    b. With the insertion point positioned in the Subject text box, key **Global Marketing Conference**.
    c. Press Tab or click in the Location text box and then key **Downtown Metro Center**.
    d. Click the Reminder check box to remove the check mark. *(Note: Skip this step if the Reminder check box is already deselected.)*
    e. Click the down-pointing triangle next to the Show time as list box and then click *Out of Office* in the drop-down list.
    f. Click the down-pointing triangle next to the Label list box and then click *Important* in the drop-down list.

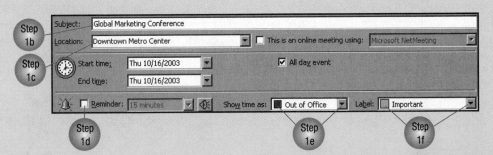

    g. Click Save and Close. The new event appears below the date at the top of the Appointment area.

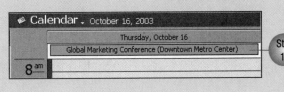

Natural Language Phrases

In day or time text boxes within Outlook's appointment or event windows you can key natural language phrases and Outlook will convert the phrase to the appropriate entry for the field. For example, in the Start time: day text box you can key *next Monday* and Outlook will automatically enter the date for the Monday following the current day. In the time text box you can key *ten o'clock am* and Outlook will automatically enter *10:00 AM*.

Editing, Deleting, and Moving Appointments

Double-click an existing appointment in the Appointment area to open the Appointment window, or right-click the appointment box and then click Open at the shortcut menu. Edit the text and/or settings as required and then click Save and Close. To delete an appointment, position the arrow pointer on the colored bar between the appointment box and the gray time slot area until the pointer changes to the four-headed arrow move icon, and then click the left mouse button. The appointment box will display with the colored bar as a border around the appointment box indicating the appointment has been selected. Press Delete or click the Delete button on the Standard toolbar. Alternatively, right-click the appointment box and then click Delete at the shortcut menu.

To move an appointment to a new time on the same day, position the arrow pointer on the colored bar between the appointment box and the time slot until the four-headed arrow move icon appears. Hold down the left mouse button and drag the appointment to the new time slot on the same day. To move an appointment to a different day, drag the appointment while the Calendar is displayed in the Week or Month view. An appointment can also be moved by opening the Appointment window and then changing the Start time: and End time settings.

exercise 4

1. With the *Calendar* folder active and the date *Thursday, October 16, 2003* displayed in the Appointment area, change the starting time for the Sales update meeting by completing the following steps:
   a. Position the arrow pointer over the shaded appointment box for the *Sales update meeting* at 3:00 pm and then double-click the left mouse button.
   b. Since the appointment is one of a recurring series of appointments, Outlook displays the Open Recurring Item dialog box asking if you want to edit this occurrence only or the entire series. Click Open the series and then click OK.

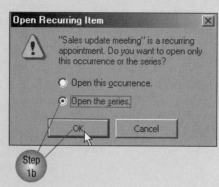

OUTLOOK

c. Click the Recurrence button on the Sales update meeting - Recurring Appointment window toolbar.

d. Click the down-pointing triangle next to the Start text box in the Appointment time section of the Appointment Recurrence dialog box and then click *5:00 PM* in the drop-down list. The End time automatically changes to 6:00 PM since the Duration is set to 1 hour.

e. Click OK to close the Appointment Recurrence dialog box.

f. Click Save and Close.

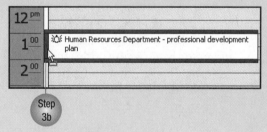

2. Delete the lunch appointment on Wednesday, October 15 by completing the following steps:

a. Click Wednesday, October 15 in the Date Navigator.

b. Position the mouse pointer on the purple colored bar at the left of the appointment box for the *Lunch with Dennis Kenney* until the pointer changes to the four-headed arrow move icon and then click the left mouse button. The appointment is selected as indicated by the purple border surrounding the appointment box.

c. Press the Delete key.

3. Move the appointment with the Human Resources Department to 1:00 pm on the same day using the drag and drop method by completing the following steps:

a. Position the mouse pointer on the blue colored bar at the left of the appointment box for the *Human Resources Department - professional development plan* until the pointer changes to the four-headed arrow move icon.

b. Hold down the left mouse button, drag the appointment to the 1:00 pm boundary, and then release the mouse. The pointer displays with a gray shaded box attached as you drag the mouse.

4. Click the Print button on the Standard toolbar. Click *Weekly Style* in the Print style section of the Print dialog box and then click OK.

Calendar Coloring

Click to select an appointment and then click the Calendar Coloring button on the Standard toolbar to assign a label to an appointment after the appointment has been created. The appointment box will be shaded with the color of the label chosen from the drop-down menu.

Calendar Coloring

Click Edit Labels from the drop-down menu to change the label text associated with a color in the menu. For example, if you prefer to use purple to shade sales appointments, click Edit Labels from the Calendar Coloring menu, drag to select the text *Birthday* in the text box next to the purple box, and then key **Sales**. Click OK to close the Edit Calendar Labels dialog box.

Changing the Calendar View

The Standard toolbar contains buttons to change the view to Wo<u>r</u>k Week, <u>W</u>eek, or <u>M</u>onth. Click <u>V</u>iew and point to Current <u>V</u>iew to display the menu shown in figure 2.4.

2.4 *Calendar Current View Menu*

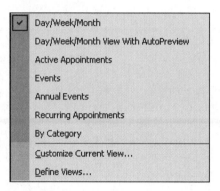

Active Appointments, Events, Annual Events, and Recurring Appointments will filter the calendar to display only the items that match the option in a table format so that all items can be viewed and printed on one page.

exercise 5

CHANGING THE CURRENT VIEW

1. With the *Calendar* folder active and the date *Wednesday, October 15, 2003* displayed in the Appointment area, change the current view to display Active Appointments only, increase the column width, and print the view by completing the following steps:
   a. Click <u>V</u>iew, point to Current <u>V</u>iew, and then click Active Appointments. The calendar displays in a table format with the appointments grouped by the recurrence pattern. Notice that the information in some columns is not entirely visible.

Step 1a
Step 1b

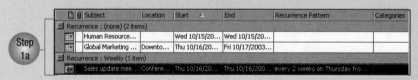

   b. Position the pointer on the column boundary to the right of the column heading *Start* until the pointer changes to a vertical line with a left- and right-pointing arrow and then double-click the left mouse button. Double-clicking the column boundary increases the column width to accommodate the longest entry in the column.

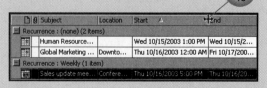

c. Position the pointer on the column boundary to the right of the column heading *End* until the pointer changes to a vertical line with a left- and right-pointing arrow and then double-click the left mouse button.

d. Position the pointer on the column boundary to the right of the column heading *Subject* until the pointer changes to a vertical line with a left- and right-pointing arrow, hold down the left mouse button, drag right approximately 1 inch, and then release the mouse button. Dragging a column boundary right or left increases or decreases the column width.

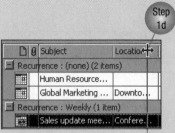

Line shows new right column boundary as you drag the mouse.

e. Click the Print button on the Standard toolbar. With *Table Style* selected in the Print style section of the Print dialog box, click OK.

2. Change the current view to examine two other formats for displaying the calendar by completing the following steps:

a. Click <u>V</u>iew, point to Current <u>V</u>iew, and then click Events. The Information Viewer displays only items that are events in table format and the message *(Filter Applied)* displays in the Folder banner to indicate that the current view is not displaying all items.

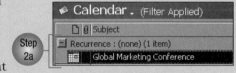

b. Click <u>V</u>iew, point to Current <u>V</u>iew, and then click Recurring Appointments. The Information Viewer displays only recurring items.

3. Click <u>V</u>iew, point to Current <u>V</u>iew, and then click Day/Week/Month to restore the Information Viewer to the default display.

4. Display a specific date in the Appointment area using the Go To Date dialog box by completing the following steps:

a. Click <u>V</u>iew, point to <u>G</u>o To, and then click Go to Da<u>t</u>e.

b. With the current date selected in the <u>D</u>ate text box, key **10/16/2003**, and then press Enter or click OK.

5. Click the <u>M</u>onth button on the Standard toolbar to view the month of October 2003.

6. Click the Print button. With *Monthly Style* selected in the Print style section of the Print dialog box, click OK. *(Note: Monthly calendars take a few moments to print. If you are sharing a printer with several other students, you may want to skip this step.)*

7. Click the Da<u>y</u> button on the Standard toolbar to return to the default view.

Assigning Categories to Appointments

Appointments can be associated with a keyword in the category list and can then be grouped, sorted, or filtered by the category. The *By Category* option on the Current <u>V</u>iew menu will group appointments by the category they have been assigned. The list of appointments can then be expanded and collapsed by category. The Categories dialog box is shown in figure 2.5. Click the Categories button in the Appointment window and then click the category check box for the category that you want to assign to the appointment. An appointment can be associated with more than one category.

FIGURE

2.5 *Categories Dialog Box*

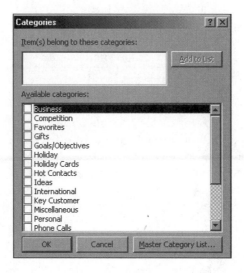

If a suitable category name for the appointment does not appear in the Available categories list, you can add your own category to the Master Category List. To do this, key the category name in the Item(s) belong to these categories text box and then click the Add to List button.

To assign a category to an existing appointment, right-click the appointment in the Appointment area and then click Categories at the shortcut menu to open the Categories dialog box.

exercise 6

ASSIGNING CATEGORIES TO APPOINTMENTS AND VIEWING APPOINTMENTS BY CATEGORY

1. With the *Calendar* folder active and the date *Thursday, October 16, 2003* displayed in the Appointment area, assign a category to existing appointments by completing the following steps:
   a. Position the mouse pointer over the *Sales update meeting* appointment box, right-click, and then click Categories at the shortcut menu.
   b. Click *Business* in the Available categories list box and then click OK.

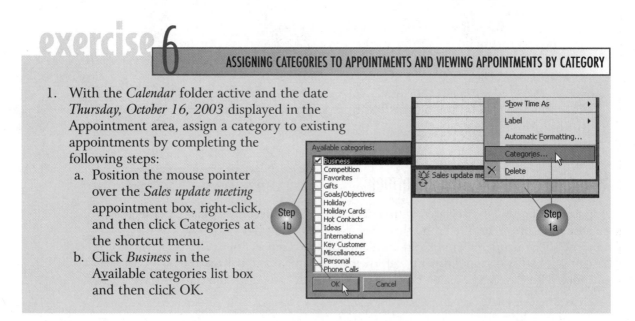

OUTLOOK

c. Click Wednesday, October 15, 2003 in the Date Navigator.

d. Position the mouse pointer over the *Human Resources Department - professional development plan* appointment box and then double-click the left mouse button.

e. Click the Categories button at the bottom of the Appointment window.

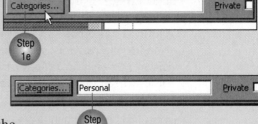

f. Click *Personal* in the A̲vailable categories list box and then click OK. The category name *Personal* appears in the Categories text box in the Appointment window.

g. Click S̲ave and Close.

2. Schedule a new appointment by dragging in the Appointment area for the time duration and assign a category by completing the following steps:

a. Click Tuesday, October 14, 2003 in the Date Navigator.

b. Position the mouse pointer next to 11:00 am in the Appointment area, hold down the left mouse button, drag to the 1:00 pm time boundary, and then release the mouse. This selects a two-hour time duration for the new appointment.

c. Key **New sales employee interviews** and then click outside the appointment box.

d. Position the mouse pointer over the *New sales employee interviews* appointment box, right-click, and then click Categori̲es at the shortcut menu.

e. Click *Business* in the A̲vailable categories list box and then click OK.

3. Display the appointments in the calendar grouped by category by completing the following steps:

a. Click V̲iew, point to Current V̲iew, and then click By Category. The appointments are collapsed below the category headings in the Information Viewer.

b. Click the expand button (plus symbol) next to the group heading *Categories : Business*. The expand button changes to the collapse button when the group is expanded.

c. Click the expand button next to the group heading *Categories: Personal*.

d. Widen column widths as necessary for the *Subject*, *Start*, and *End* column headings.

e. Click the Print button on the Standard toolbar. With *Table Style* selected in the Print style section of the Print dialog box, click OK.

4. Click V̲iew, point to Current V̲iew, and then click Day/Week/Month.

5. Display the date *Tuesday, October 14, 2003* in the Appointment area using the Go To Date dialog box by completing the following steps:

a. Click V̲iew, point to G̲o To, and then click Go to Date̲.

b. With the current date selected in the D̲ate text box, key **10/14/2003**, and then press Enter or click OK.

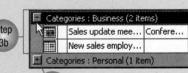

Automatic Formatting

When your Calendar becomes filled with appointments, meetings, and events, it might be desirable to format certain items based on a category or keyword to make them easily identifiable to you. Formatting can include changing the color and/or font of the text, or shading the appointment box a different color. In Outlook, automatic formatting can be applied to items in folders by creating a rule for the current view. The rules are stored with the view so that you can have different rules for different views. A *rule* is the condition you specify must exist in order for Outlook to apply the format to the item.

For example, you could instruct Outlook to automatically shade all appointments that have been assigned the category *Personal* a label color when viewing the calendar in the Day/Week/Month view. To do this, display the folder in the desired view and then open the Automatic Formatting dialog box shown in figure 2.6 by clicking View, pointing to Current View, and then clicking Customize Current View. Click the Automatic Formatting button in the View Summary dialog box. You can also display the Automatic Formatting dialog box by clicking Automatic Formatting from the drop-down menu on the Calendar Coloring button on the Standard toolbar.

FIGURE

2.6 *Automatic Formatting Dialog Box*

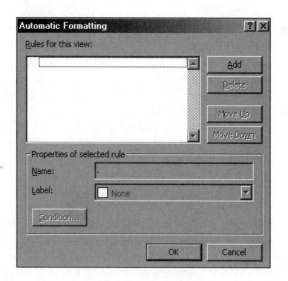

Click Add to create a new rule for the current view. Outlook will display the name *Untitled* in the Name box. Key a name to identify the rule and then click the Label button to choose the color to shade the appointment. Click Condition to open the Filter dialog box and set the criteria upon which the appointment is to be formatted. The Label list box changes to Font dependent on the active view when the Automatic Formatting dialog box is opened.

OUTLOOK

1. With the *Calendar* folder active in Day/Week/Month view and the date *Tuesday, October 14, 2003* displayed in the Appointment area, create a rule to automatically format personal appointments with a color label by completing the following steps:

   a. Click <u>V</u>iew, point to Current <u>V</u>iew, and then click <u>C</u>ustomize Current View.

   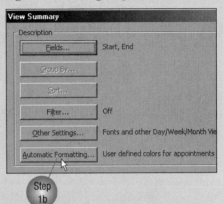

   b. Click the <u>A</u>utomatic Formatting button in the View Summary dialog box.

   c. Click the <u>A</u>dd button in the Automatic Formatting dialog box. A new rule named *Untitled* appears checked in the <u>R</u>ules for this view list box and in the <u>N</u>ame text box in the Properties of selected rule section.

   d. With the text *Untitled* already selected in the <u>N</u>ame text box, key **Personal**.

   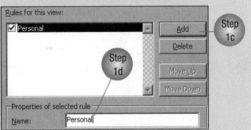

   e. Click the down-pointing triangle next to the Label list box and then click *Personal* in the drop-down list.

   f. Click the Condition button.

   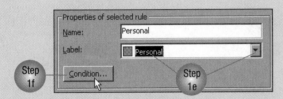

   g. Click the More Choices tab in the Filter dialog box.

   h. Click the <u>C</u>ategories button.

   i. Click *Personal* in the A<u>v</u>ailable categories list box and then click OK in the Categories dialog box.

   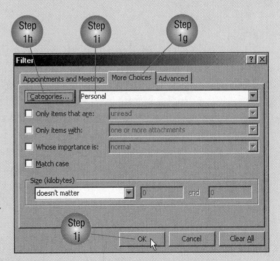

   j. Click OK to close the Filter dialog box.

   k. Click OK to close the Automatic Formatting dialog box.

   l. Click OK to close the View Summary dialog box.

2. Outlook applies the new rule once the view is activated after a rule has been created. View the automatic formatting on the personal appointment on Wednesday, October 15, 2003, by completing the following steps:

   a. Click <u>V</u>iew, point to Current <u>V</u>iew, and then click Active Appointments. You are changing the current view to reactivate Day/Week/Month view in the next step and have the new rule applied.

   b. Click <u>V</u>iew, point to Current <u>V</u>iew, and then click Day/Week/Month.

c. Press Ctrl + G to display the Go To Date dialog box, key **10/15/2003** and then press Enter. Notice the appointment scheduled at 1:00 pm is now shaded with the personal label color of green.

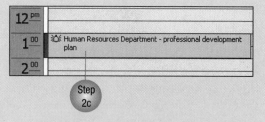

3. Schedule a new personal appointment on Monday, October 13, 2003 by completing the following steps:

   a. Click Monday, October 13, 2003 in the Date Navigator.

   b. Position the mouse pointer next to 9:00 am, hold down the left mouse button, and then drag to the 10:00 boundary.

   c. Key **Doctor's appointment** and then click outside the appointment box.

   d. Right-click the *Doctor's appointment* appointment box and then click Categories at the shortcut menu.

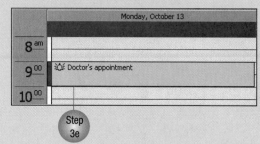

   e. Click *Personal* in the Available categories list box and then click OK in the Categories dialog box. The appointment box is automatically shaded green as the automatic formatting rule is applied to the new appointment.

4. Click the Week button on the Standard toolbar.

5. Click the Print button on the Standard toolbar. With *Weekly Style* selected in the Print style section of the Print dialog box, click OK.

6. Click the Day button on the Standard toolbar.

Scheduling Meetings and Resources

Scheduling a meeting in Outlook is essentially setting up an appointment to which you invite people by e-mail. When you create a meeting request, you identify the individuals that you want to attend, the subject, the location, and the meeting day and time. Individuals are notified of the meeting via an e-mail message. Responses to the organizer's meeting request are automatically tracked and can be viewed in the meeting window. To create a new meeting request, do one of the following actions:

- Click File, point to New, and then click Meeting Request.

- Click Actions, New Meeting Request.

- Click the down-pointing triangle on the New Appointment button and then click Meeting Request at the drop-down menu.

- Open a new Appointment window and then click the Invite Attendees button on the Appointment window toolbar.

OUTLOOK

2.7 *Meeting Window*

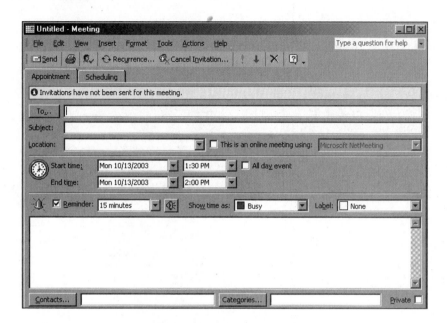

An Untitled - Meeting window will open which is similar to an Appointment window. The yellow information box displays the message *Invitations have not been sent for this meeting*, the To text box has been added above the Subject text box to include the e-mail addresses of the attendees, and the Save and Close button is replaced with the Send button to send e-mail messages for the meeting as shown in figure 2.7.

exercise 8

SCHEDULING A MEETING

(Note: In this exercise, and in several remaining exercises, you will be sending a meeting request by e-mail to the student you added to the Personal Address Book [PAB] in chapter 1. Check with your instructor if necessary for alternate instructions on to whom you should send the meeting requests.)

1. With the *Calendar* folder active and the date *Monday, October 13, 2003* displayed in the Appointment area, schedule a meeting request by completing the following steps:
   a. Click next to 3:00 pm in the Appointment area.
   b. Click File, point to New, and then click Meeting Request.
   c. Click the To button. Click the down-pointing triangle next to the Show Names from the list box in the Select Attendees and Resources dialog box and then click *Personal Address Book*.
   d. Double-click the name of the student you added to the PAB in chapter 1 to add his or her name to the Required list box.

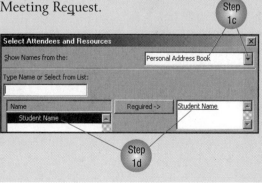

e. Click OK to close the Select Attendees and Resources dialog box.
f. Press Tab or click in the Subject text box and then key **New products information meeting**.
g. Press Tab or click in the Location text box and then key **Executive boardroom**.
h. Click the down-pointing triangle next to the End time text box and then click *4:00 PM (1 hour)* in the drop-down list.
i. Click the Reminder check box to deselect it. *(Note: Skip this step if the Reminder check box is already deselected.)*
j. Click the Send button. The meeting is scheduled in your calendar and an e-mail message is sent to the student who was selected as a required attendee.

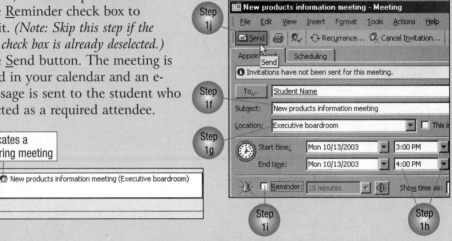

Step 1j

Step 1f

Step 1g

Icon indicates a nonrecurring meeting

Step 1j

Step 1i

Step 1h

2. View the Scheduling and Tracking information that Outlook maintains in the Meeting Request window by completing the following steps:
   a. Double-click the appointment box for the *New products information meeting* at 3:00 pm. The message *No responses have been received for this meeting* appears above the To text box.
   b. Click the Scheduling tab in the Meeting window. The window next to the Attendees list contains the calendar information for each attendee. At the bottom of the window are editing options to Add Others to the list of attendees, change the calendar Options, AutoPick different meeting times, and alter the meeting start and end times.

Step 2b

Symbol for meeting organizer

Symbol for required attendee

This shading means no information on the attendee's calendar is available. Your screen may differ.

   c. Click the Tracking tab in the Meeting window. The responses from attendees are logged on this tab.
   d. Click the Close button on the Meeting window Title bar.

Step 2c

3. View the meeting request e-mail message sent by completing the following steps:
   a. Click the *Inbox* icon on the Outlook bar.

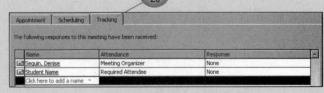

OUTLOOK

b. Click *Inbox* on the Folder banner and then click *Sent Items* in the Folder List.

c. Double-click the message header for the meeting request message sent in step 1.

d. Read the information in the message and then click the Close button on the message window Title bar.

4. Click *Sent Items* on the Folder banner and then click *Inbox* in the Folder List.

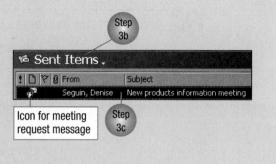

Responding to Meeting Requests

Individuals who have been invited to a meeting via a meeting request receive notification by e-mail. The message window contains buttons on the toolbar for responding to the request as shown in figure 2.8. The invitee can choose to click Accept, Tentative, Decline, or Propose New Time.

F I G U R E

2.8 *Meeting Request Message*

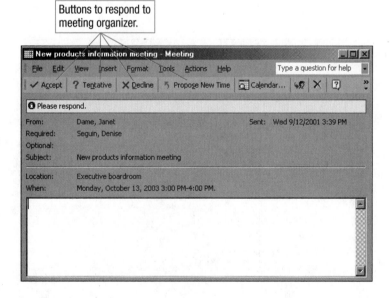

When the respondent clicks Accept, Tentative, or Decline, a Microsoft Outlook message window appears with the information that the meeting has been scheduled in the calendar for Accept or Tentative; or moved to the *Deleted Items* folder for Decline. The respondent has the option to Edit the response before sending so that a few words of explanation can be appended; Send the response now so that the meeting organizer receives the default response message of *User name has accepted*; or Don't send a response. The dialog box shown in figure 2.9 appears after clicking the Accept button.

2.9 *Accept Meeting Response Dialog Box*

The meeting organizer receives the responses from the invitees by means of e-mail messages. In addition, Outlook updates the Tracking tab of the Meeting window so that the organizer can view all invitee responses in one place.

Outlook tracks meeting request responses for users who are connected to the same Microsoft Exchange Server. If you send a meeting request to a user through an Internet mail address, Outlook exports the meeting information as an iCalendar (.ics) file attached to an e-mail message. The recipient, upon opening the message will not see the buttons shown in figure.2.8. The meeting can be imported to his or her calendar application by double-clicking the .ics file and he or she can respond to the meeting organizer using the Reply feature.

exercise 9

PROPOSING A NEW TIME TO A MEETING REQUEST

(Note: If you are not connected to a Microsoft Exchange Server, you will not be able to complete exercises 9-13. To complete this exercise another student must have sent you a meeting request from exercise 8.)

1. With the *Inbox* folder active, respond to a meeting request by proposing a new time by completing the following steps:

    a. Double-click the message header with the subject *New products information meeting*.

    b. Click the Propose New Time button on the message window toolbar.

    c. In the Propose New Time dialog box, click the down-pointing triangle next to the Meeting start time day text box (currently reads *Mon 10/13/2003*) and then click *Friday, October 17, 2003* at the drop-down calendar.

    d. Click the down-pointing triangle next to the Meeting start time time text box, scroll up the list box, and then click *11:00 AM*.

    e. Click the Propose Time button at the bottom of the Propose New Time dialog box. The Propose New Time dialog box closes and the message window displays the original meeting day and time along with the proposed meeting day and time.

f. With the insertion point positioned in the message editing window, key the following text:
   Unfortunately I may be out of town Monday, October 13. I hope that you are in agreement for Friday, October 17.

g. Click the Print button on the message window toolbar.

h. Click Send. A message is sent to the meeting organizer with the details of the proposed new day and time. It will be up to the meeting organizer to accept the proposal by opening the message and clicking Accept Proposal.

2. Display the *Calendar* folder in the Information Viewer with the active date *Monday, October 13, 2003*. By default, Outlook adds the meeting to your Calendar as Tentative. *(Note: You will have two items scheduled for 3:00 pm on Monday, October 13 if you have completed both exercises 8 and 9.)*

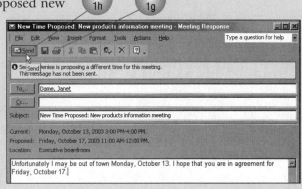

Planning a Meeting

Setting up a meeting involving more than two or three individuals, for which you have to find a common day and time when everyone is available, can be a frustrating and time-consuming process for a meeting organizer. If all of the meeting attendees schedule their appointments in Outlook's Calendar, and you have permissions to view their *Calendar* folder, then Outlook can do the work of finding free times for you. In the Plan a Meeting dialog box shown in figure 2.10, add the list of attendees required in the *All Attendees* column. As you add each attendee, Outlook displays their free/busy times in the calendar window. Use the AutoPick Next feature to have Outlook highlight the next available time slot when everyone is available and automatically update the Meeting start time.

F I G U R E

2.10 *Plan a Meeting Dialog Box*

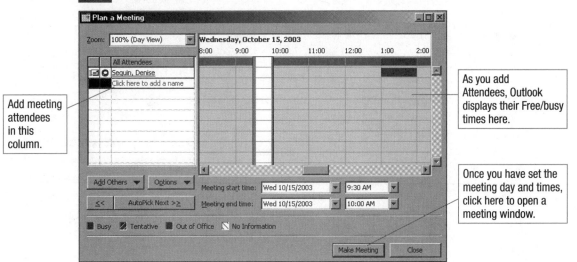

Once the meeting start and end times have been determined, click the Make Meeting button at the bottom of the Plan a Meeting dialog box to open a Meeting window where you can key the subject, location, and then send the request.

exercise 10

1. With the *Calendar* folder active and the date *Monday, October 13, 2003* displayed in the Appointment area, use the Plan a Meeting dialog box to generate a meeting request by completing the following steps:

   a. Click Wednesday, October 15, 2003 in the Date Navigator.
   b. Click next to 12:30 pm in the Appointment area.
   c. Click Actions on the Menu bar and then click Plan a Meeting.
   d. Click the Add Others button below the *All Attendees* column and then click *Add from Address Book* at the drop-down list.
   e. Click the down-pointing triangle next to the Show Names from the list box and then click *Personal Address Book* in the Select Attendees and Resources dialog box.
   f. Double-click the name of the student you added to the Personal Address Book in chapter 1 to add his or her name to the Required list box, and then click OK to close the Select Attendees and Resources dialog box.
   g. Click the AutoPick Next button. Outlook will adjust the proposed meeting time to start at 2:00 pm (after the previously scheduled appointment from 1:00 to 2:00 pm on your calendar since this time is marked as busy). Within the calendar window, the proposed start time is designated by a green border and the stop time by a red border.

   Meeting start time automatically chosen by Outlook as the next available time.

   h. Click the Make Meeting button. An Untitled - Meeting window opens with the To, Start time: and End time text boxes already completed from the Plan a Meeting dialog box.
   i. With the insertion point automatically positioned in the Subject text box, key **Review marketing plan**.
   j. Press Tab or click in the Location text box and then key **My office**.
   k. Click Send.
   l. Click the Close button in the Plan a Meeting dialog box.

2. Print the Calendar for Wednesday, October 15, 2003, in *Daily Style*.

OUTLOOK

(Note: To complete this exercise another student must have sent you a meeting request from exercise 10.)

1. With the *Calendar* folder active and the date *Wednesday, October 15, 2003* displayed in the Appointment area, accept the Review marketing plan meeting request by completing the following steps:
   a. Click *Inbox* on the Outlook bar.
   b. Double-click the message header with the subject *Review marketing plan*.
   c. Click the A̲ccept button on the message window toolbar.
   d. Click E̲dit the response before sending in the Microsoft Outlook dialog box.
   e. With the insertion point positioned in the message editing window, key the following text:

   The marketing plan has not yet been approved by the board, but is on the agenda for the next meeting. I'll let you know the outcome before this meeting.

   f. Click S̲end.
2. Click *Calendar* on the Outlook bar and then display *Wednesday, October 15, 2003* in the Appointment area.

Step 1f

Default message sent to meeting organizer.

Updating and Canceling a Meeting

From time to time meetings might need to be rescheduled, canceled, or the list of individuals attending a meeting may need to be revised. Complete the following steps to make changes to a meeting:

1. Open the Meeting window in the Calendar.
2. Change the details as required in the Meeting window.
3. Click the Sen̲d Update button.

Outlook will send an e-mail message to each attendee with the word *Updated* in the Subject line. Each attendee can then choose to accept or decline the revision. If the meeting organizer closes the Meeting window without clicking the Sen̲d Update button, Outlook will prompt the user with a message that the attendees have not been notified.

To cancel a meeting, open the Meeting window and then click A̲ctions, C̲ancel Meeting, or click to select the appointment box in the Appointment area and then press the Delete key. If you are the meeting organizer and you delete a meeting from your calendar, Outlook displays the message box shown in figure 2.11. Outlook sends each attendee an e-mail message with the word *Canceled* in the Subject line. Each attendee can then choose to open the message and remove the meeting from his or her calendar by clicking the Remove from C̲alendar button on the message window toolbar.

FIGURE

2.11 *Delete Meeting Message Box*

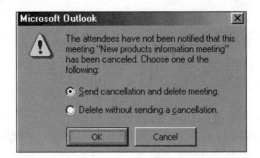

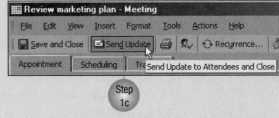

exercise 12

UPDATING AND CANCELING A MEETING

1. With the *Calendar* folder active and the date *Wednesday, October 15, 2003* displayed in the Appointment area, extend the meeting duration for the Review marketing plan meeting by completing the following steps:
   a. Double-click the *Review marketing plan* appointment box.
   b. Click the down-pointing triangle next to the End time text box and then click *3:30 PM (1.5 hours)*.
   c. Click the Send Update button on the message window toolbar. Outlook sends an e-mail message to each attendee with the updated information and automatically adjusts the appointment within your calendar.

2. Cancel the New products information meeting that you created in exercise 8 by completing the following steps:
   a. Click Monday, October 13, 2003 in the Date Navigator.
   b. Double-click the *New products information meeting* appointment box.
   c. Click Actions on the Meeting window Menu bar and then click Cancel Meeting.
   d. With Send cancellation and delete meeting already selected in the Microsoft Outlook dialog box, click OK.

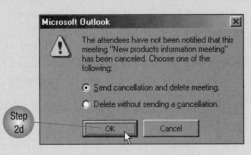

OUTLOOK

e. Click Send on the Meeting window toolbar. Outlook sends each attendee an e-mail with the High Importance option attached to it. The message *Meeting has been canceled* displays when the recipient opens the message window. The recipient can click Remove from Calendar on the message window toolbar to have Outlook remove the item from his or her calendar.

3. Print the Calendar in *Weekly Style*.

Updating Meeting Attendees and Manually Tracking Responses

If after sending a meeting request, a new attendee is to be invited to the meeting, open the Meeting window, key the e-mail address of the new attendee in the To text box, or click the Scheduling or Tracking tab. Click in the *Name* column over *Click here to add a name* and then key the name or e-mail address of the person that is being invited. To remove an attendee from the meeting, right-click the mouse over the name of the individual and then click Cut at the shortcut menu. Click Send Update to send e-mail messages to the participants advising of the changes.

If the meeting organizer closes the Meeting window without clicking Send Update, Outlook displays the message shown in figure 2.12 to remind him or her that updates should be sent. You can choose to send an update message only to the individuals who have been added or deleted, or to all of the meeting participants.

F I G U R E

2.12 *Send Update to Attendees Message Box*

Outlook tracks the responses received from attendees when they open the message and click one of the response buttons. The replies can be viewed by the meeting organizer in the *Response* column of the Tracking tab in the Meeting window. If however, an attendee contacts the meeting organizer by telephone or a subsequent e-mail with a change in their status, the meeting organizer can manually change the response status. To do this, click in the *Response* column next to the attendee's name and a down-pointing triangle appears. Click the down-pointing triangle to display the drop-down list shown in figure 2.13, and then click the new status for the attendee.

2.13 *Manually Tracking Response Options*

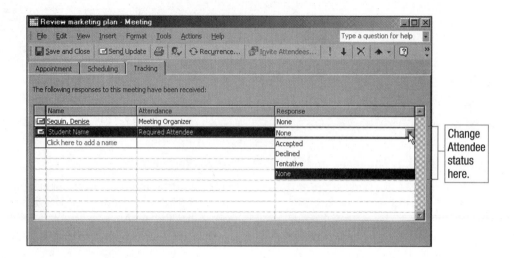

Scheduling Meeting Resources

Often a meeting organizer must also schedule resources for a meeting such as a conference room, computer, or projector. Outlook provides the ability for the organizer of a meeting to schedule resources during the creation of a meeting request while selecting the attendees in the Select Attendees and Resources dialog box as shown in figure 2.14.

2.14 *Select Attendees and Resources Dialog Box with Resource Selected*

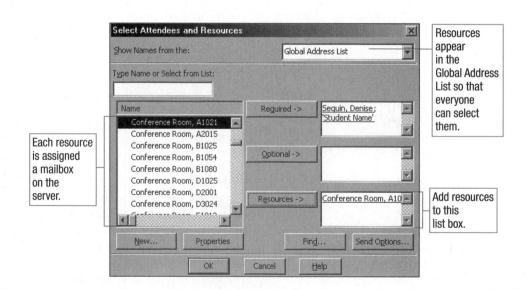

OUTLOOK

After the meeting request is sent, Outlook responds to the meeting organizer with a message about the availability of the requested resource. If the resource is available, Outlook automatically schedules it and sends a message that the resource has been successfully booked. If the resource is already scheduled at the requested meeting day and time, Outlook responds with a message that you must use another time or find another resource.

Setting Up Automatic Resource Scheduling

For Outlook to process meeting requests for resources as described above, several steps must take place beforehand to set up resource scheduling and require the assistance of the system administrator of the network. The following steps are provided for configuring resource scheduling on a Microsoft Exchange server.

1. Each resource has a mailbox and account created on the server.
2. An existing user is designated as the resource administrator and assigned full mailbox access rights to the mailbox. This step and step 1 are often completed by the network system administrator.
3. The resource administrator creates a new e-mail account and profile using the E-mail Accounts Wizard in order to access the resource mailbox.
4. The resource administrator starts Outlook. The resource's new mailbox will appear in the Folder List.
5. With the resource's mailbox active, set the resource scheduling options. To do this, display the Resource Scheduling dialog box shown in figure 2.15 and click the Automatically accept meeting requests and process cancellations check box. Select other options as desired depending on how you want meeting requests processed.
6. If other users are to have the ability to view and/or edit the resource's calendar, click the Set Permissions button. Click the Permissions tab in the Calendar Properties dialog box and then add the users and set their permission levels.
7. Exit Outlook.

The above steps need only be done once for each resource. After the resources have been configured, Outlook will automatically process meeting requests where resources have been added.

FIGURE

2.15 *Resource Scheduling Dialog Box*

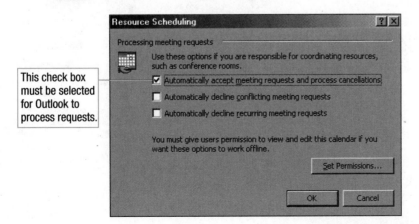

(Note: To complete this exercise, a mailbox account for a resource named Conference Room A1020 must have been set up on the server you are using. In addition, the resource's options must have been set for Outlook to automatically accept meeting requests and your account should have permissions set to allow you to send mail to the resource account. Check with your instructor before completing this exercise for possible alternate instructions. If necessary, read the steps only.)

1. With the *Calendar* folder active and the date *Monday, October 13, 2003* displayed in Day view in the Appointment area, schedule a meeting including a meeting resource by completing the following steps:

   a. Double-click next to 10:00 am in the Appointment area.

   b. Click the Invite Attendees button on the Appointment window toolbar. The Appointment window changes to a Meeting window.

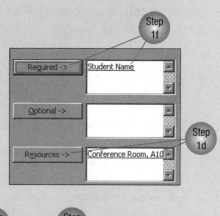

   c. Click the To button. With the *Global Address List* displayed in the Show Names from the list box in the Select Attendees and Resources dialog box, scroll down the Name list box until you see *Conference Room A1020*, and then click to select the name of the resource.

   d. Click the Resources button.

   e. Click the down-pointing triangle next to the Show Names from the list box and then click *Personal Address Book* in the drop-down list.

   f. Click the name of the student you added to the Personal Address Book in chapter 1, and then click the Required button.

   g. Click OK to close the Select Attendees and Resources dialog box.

   h. Click in the Subject text box and then key **Holiday advertising budget planning**. *(Notice the Location text box already contains the name of the conference room.)*

   i. Click the Scheduling tab and then view the list of attendees. Notice the icon next to Conference Room A1021.

   j. Click Send. *(Note: Most students will receive e-mail messages from Outlook with the text "Conference Room A1021 is already booked for the specified time. You must use another time or find another resource.")*

2. Print the Calendar for Monday, October 13, 2003, in *Daily Style*.

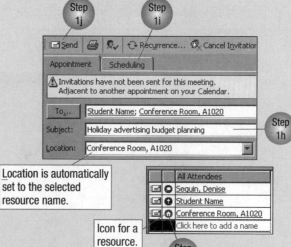

Location is automatically set to the selected resource name.

Icon for a resource.

Changing Calendar Options

You can customize the Calendar in Outlook by changing options in the Calendar Options dialog box. For example, if you work a nonstandard work week, select the days that apply to you in the Calendar work week section of the Calendar Options dialog box. Click Tools, Options, and then click the Calendar Options button in the Options dialog box to display the Calendar Options dialog box shown in figure 2.16.

FIGURE

2.16 **Calendar Options Dialog Box**

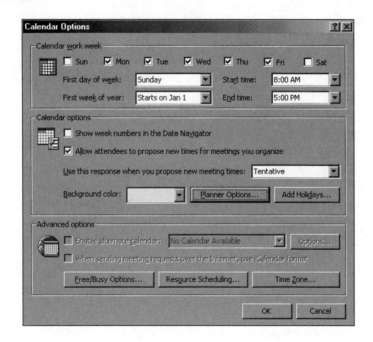

To change the way the calendar displays in the Date Navigator, change the options in the Calendar work week section. For example, if you change the First day of week entry from Sunday to Saturday, the Date Navigator will display calendars with the first day in each week as Saturday. The weeks would display in columns labeled *S S M T W T F*. Changing the Start time and End time entries will cause the Appointment area color to shorten or lengthen to reflect the length of the new workday.

The Calendar options section of the Calendar Options dialog box includes the capability to display week numbers in the Date Navigator, to provide the ability for attendees to propose alternate meeting times to your meeting requests, set the default response when proposing new meeting times, set the Appointment area Background color, change Planner Options, and Add Holidays for a specific country.

Use the Advanced options section to set Free/Busy Options, Resource Scheduling options, and change the Time Zone.

1. With the *Calendar* folder active and the date *Monday, October 13, 2003* displayed in the Appointment area, change the start and end times for the work week, show week numbers in the Date Navigator, and change the Calendar's background color by completing the following steps:

   a. Click <u>T</u>ools, <u>O</u>ptions, and then click the <u>C</u>alendar Options button in the Options dialog box.

   b. Click the down-pointing triangle next to the Sta<u>r</u>t time text box in the Calendar <u>w</u>ork week section, and then click *9:00 AM* in the drop-down list.

   c. Click the down-pointing triangle next to the E<u>n</u>d time text box in the Calendar <u>w</u>ork week section, and then click *6:00 PM* in the drop-down list.

   d. Click the Show week numbers in the Date Na<u>v</u>igator check box in the Calendar options section.

   e. Click the down-pointing triangle next to the <u>B</u>ackground color list box in the Calendar options section and then click the aqua color in the drop-down list.

   f. Click OK to close the Calendar Options dialog box.

   g. Click OK to close the Options dialog box.

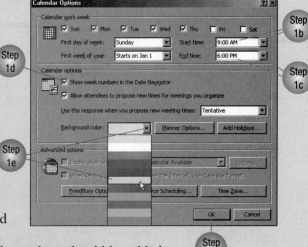

2. View the new options in the Calendar window. The background color of the Appointment area should be aqua for the new workday times between 9:00 am and 6:00 pm. Week numbers should be added to the months displayed in the Date Navigator section.

3. Change the Calendar options back to the default settings by completing the completing the following steps:

   a. Click <u>T</u>ools, <u>O</u>ptions, and then click the <u>C</u>alendar Options button in the Options dialog box.

   b. Change the Sta<u>r</u>t time to 8:00 AM and the E<u>n</u>d time to 5:00 PM.

   c. Deselect the Show week numbers in the Date Na<u>v</u>igator check box.

   d. Change the <u>B</u>ackground color to pale yellow.

   e. Click OK twice.

Week numbers in Date Navigator.

Background color is Aqua between new start and end times.

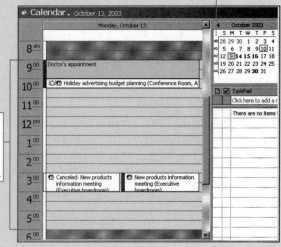

CHAPTER summary

➤ The *Calendar* folder is used to schedule appointments, events, and meetings.

➤ An event differs from an appointment in that it is an activity that lasts the entire day or longer.

➤ An appointment that occurs on an ongoing basis can be set up as a recurring appointment.

➤ Edit appointment details by double-clicking the appointment box to open the Appointment window.

➤ An appointment can be moved to another day and/or time by dragging the appointment box or by changing the start and end times.

➤ The Standard toolbar contains buttons to change the view from Day to Work Week, Week, or Month.

➤ The Current View menu contains options such as Active Appointments and Events that will filter the calendar and display the items in a table format.

➤ Appointments can be grouped by a keyword in the category list and can then be expanded or collapsed in groups in table format using the By Category option on the Current View.

➤ Outlook can apply automatic formatting to appointments, meetings, or events that can include changing the color and/or font of the text, or shading the appointment box. Formatting is applied based on a rule that is stored with the current view.

➤ Scheduling a meeting in Outlook is similar to setting up an appointment, with the exception that you identify the meeting attendees that you want to attend. Attendees are notified of the meeting via an e-mail message.

➤ The attendee can choose to click Accept, Tentative, Decline, or Propose New Time in the meeting request e-mail message.

➤ Responses to the organizer's meeting request are automatically tracked by Outlook for users connected to a Microsoft Exchange Server.

➤ In the Plan a Meeting dialog box, Outlook will highlight available free times for the meeting attendees using the AutoPick feature.

➤ Open the Meeting window and edit the details to reschedule or change the attendees. Click the Send Update button to notify the meeting attendees of the changes that have been made.

➤ To cancel a meeting, open the Meeting window and then click Actions, Cancel Meeting.

➤ Responses to meeting requests can be manually changed on the Tracking tab in the Meeting window.

➤ Resources for a meeting can be scheduled during the creation of a meeting request while selecting the attendees in the Select Attendees and Resources dialog box.

➤ Outlook automatically responds to the meeting organizer with a message indicating whether or not the resource has been successfully booked.

➤ You can customize the Calendar in Outlook by changing options in the Calendar Options dialog box.

COMMANDS review

Command	Mouse/Keyboard	
Cancel meeting	Actions, Cancel Meeting in Meeting window	
Change current view	View, Current View	
Create a meeting request	File, New, Meeting Request; or Actions, New Meeting Request	
Create an appointment	File, New, Appointment; or Actions, New Appointment	🗒 New
Create an event	Actions, New All Day Event; or double-click date in banner at top of Appointment area	
Delete appointment	Edit, Delete	✕
Display Automatic Formatting dialog box	View, Current View, Customize Current View, Automatic Formatting	
Display Calendar Options	Tools, Options, Calendar Options dialog box	
Display Plan a Meeting dialog box	Actions, Plan a Meeting	

CONCEPTS check

Completion: On a blank sheet of paper, indicate the correct term, symbol, or command for each item.

1. The Day view in the *Calendar* folder divides the Information Viewer into these three sections.
2. Double-click here to create an event.
3. Click this button in the Appointment window to create an appointment that occurs on an ongoing basis at fixed intervals.
4. Do this action with the mouse over an appointment box to open the Appointment window.
5. The Standard toolbar contains four buttons to change the current view: Day, Week, Month, and this button.
6. Click this menu sequence to display the current appointments in a table format.

OUTLOOK

7. Associate an appointment with a keyword in this dialog box that will allow you to view appointments grouped by the keyword.
8. Automatic formatting of items is applied based on a condition created in this for the current view.
9. To view the free/busy times of meeting attendees, click this tab in the Meeting window.
10. Use this feature to assist you with generating a meeting request where there are several attendees with many appointments already booked.
11. An attendee can click this button in the message window to suggest an alternative meeting day and/or time.
12. Click this button in the Meeting window after making changes to the meeting details to ensure the attendees are informed that something has changed.
13. Use this tab in the Meeting window to manually change a response from an attendee to a meeting request.
14. A resource can be scheduled for a meeting in this dialog box while creating the meeting request.
15. This section of the Calendar Options dialog box is where you set the normal start and end times of your workday.

SKILLS check

Assessment 1

1. With the *Calendar* folder active in Day view, schedule an appointment at 10:00 am on Monday, November 10, 2003, as follows:

    Subject **Budget planning**
    Location **Accounting conference room**
    1-hour duration
    No reminder
    Show time as Out of Office

2. Schedule a recurring appointment at 2:30 pm on Monday, November 10, 2003, as follows:

    Subject **Review sales**
    Location **My office**
    ½ hour duration
    Reminder at 5 minutes
    Recurs monthly on the second Monday of every month

3. Print the Calendar in *Daily Style*.

Assessment 2

1. With the *Calendar* folder active and the date *Monday, November 10, 2003* displayed, schedule the following events:
    a. A two-day E-learning conference in San Diego starting Tuesday, November 11, 2003. Deselect the Reminder option if it is active, show the time as Out of Office, and assign the label *Travel Required*.
    b. A vacation day on Friday, November 14, 2003. Deselect the Reminder option if it is active, and assign the event to the *Personal* category.

2. Display the Calendar in <u>W</u>eek view.
3. Move the budget planning appointment at 10:00 am on Monday, November 10, 2003, to Thursday, November 13, 2003.
4. Print the Calendar in *Weekly Style*.
5. Change the current view to display only events.
6. Adjust column widths as necessary to view the event details.
7. Print the events in *Table Style*.
8. Restore the current view to the Da<u>y</u> view for *Monday, November 10, 2003*.

Assessment 3

1. With the *Calendar* folder active and the date Monday, November 10, 2003 displayed, create and send a meeting request at 9:00 am as follows:

Attendee	Student from Personal Address Book
Subject	**Sales training**
Location	**My office**
1-hour duration	
10 minute reminder	

2. Print the Calendar in *Daily Style*.

Assessment 4

(Note: To complete this assessment you must be connected to a Microsoft Exchange Server, and another student must have sent you the Sales training meeting request from Assessment 3.)

1. Display the *Inbox* folder.
2. Open the Sales training meeting request message.
3. Decline the meeting with the following text keyed in the response message:

    I have a personal appointment outside the office on this day. Please reschedule this meeting at your convenience.

4. Print and then send the response.
5. Display the *Calendar* folder for the date *Monday, November 10, 2003*.

Assessment 5

1. With the *Calendar* folder active and the date Monday, November 10, 2003 displayed in Da<u>y</u> view, add a new rule for automatic formatting of items as follows:
    a. Name the rule *Sales appointments and meetings*.
    b. Assign the label *Important*.
    c. Key the word **Sales** in the Sear<u>c</u>h for the word(s) text box of the Appointments and Meetings tab in the Filter dialog box.
2. Open the recurring series for the Sales update meeting appointment on Thursday, November 13, 2003, and change the La<u>b</u>el in the Appointment window to *None*.
3. Display the Calendar in the Week view.
4. Print the Calendar in *Weekly Style*.
5. Display the Calendar in Da<u>y</u> view.

Assessment 6

1. With the *Calendar* folder active and the date *Thursday, November 13, 2003* displayed, create and send a meeting request at noon as follows:

Attendee	Student from Personal Address Book
Subject	**Meeting with client**
Location	**Client's office**
1½-hour duration	

No reminder

Show time as Out of Office

2. Open the Meeting window for the meeting scheduled in step 1 and then edit the meeting as follows:
    a. Change the location to The Waterfront Bistro.
    b. Change the duration of the meeting to 2 hours.
3. Send the update message.
4. Print the Calendar in *Daily Style*.

Assessment 7

1. With the *Calendar* folder active and the date *Thursday, November 13, 2003* displayed, change the calendar options as follows:
    a. Change the start time for the workday to 8:30 AM.
    b. Change the end time for the workday to 4:30 PM.
    c. Display week numbers in the Date Navigator.
    d. Change the background color for the Appointment area to White.
2. Print the Calendar in *Daily Style*.
3. Change the Calendar Options back to the default settings as follows:
    a. Start time of 8:00 AM and end time of 5:00 PM.
    b. No week numbers in the Date Navigator.
    c. Pale yellow background color.

MANAGING CONTACTS

PERFORMANCE OBJECTIVES

Upon successful completion of chapter 3, you will be able to:
- Add, edit, and delete contacts
- Add a new contact from an existing contact
- Flag a contact for follow-up
- Sort and filter contacts
- Group contacts into categories
- Find a contact
- Change the current view
- Print contacts in card, booklet, and phone directory style
- Change contact options
- Send an e-mail message from the *Contacts* folder
- Schedule an appointment from the *Contacts* folder
- Create a letter from the *Contacts* folder
- Perform a mail merge using the Contacts list

(Note: There are no student data files to copy for this chapter however you will require a data disk to save files for some exercises and assessments.)

The *Contacts* folder can be used to maintain all of the information you need about the individuals or companies with whom you regularly communicate by e-mail, fax, letters, or telephone. The information you store can go beyond addresses and telephone numbers to include additional details such as manager's name, assistant's name, spouse's name, children's names, birthday, or anniversary. Outlook provides several methods for viewing contacts by sorting, filtering, and grouping related records.

Any Outlook item such as an e-mail message, appointment, or meeting can be linked to a contact and all activities related to the contact viewed in one window. The information in the *Contacts* folder can be used to print mailing labels, and send bulk e-mail messages, letters, or faxes.

Adding Contacts

Visualize the *Contacts* folder as an electronic Rolodex or address book—names, addresses, telephone numbers, and e-mail addresses for individuals with whom you communicate. The *Contacts* folder is a database, with each contact occupying a *record* in the folder and each unit of information about an individual within the record, such as a telephone number, referred to as a *field*. Approximately 140 fields are available for storing information about a contact including three different addresses, three different e-mail addresses, and up to nineteen contact numbers. The information can be viewed and printed in a variety of formats and order.

When you click Contacts on the Outlook bar, the Contacts window appears as shown in figure 3.1.

FIGURE

3.1 **Contacts Window**

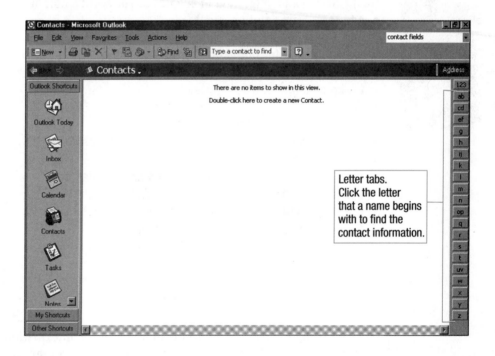

Letter tabs.
Click the letter
that a name begins
with to find the
contact information.

New Contact

To open the Contact window with the General tab selected shown in figure 3.2, click the New Contact button on the Standard toolbar; click File, point to New, and then click Contact; or click Actions, New Contact. The General tab is used to group the most frequently used fields such as job title, company name, address, telephone numbers, e-mail, Web, and instant messaging addresses.

OUTLOOK

3.2 New Contact Window with General Tab Selected

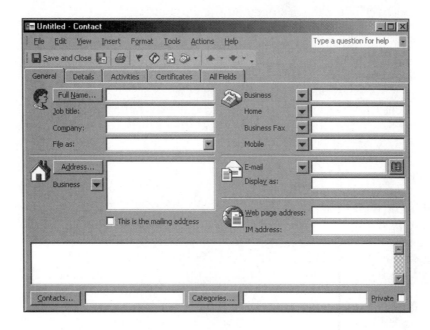

The Details tab contains fields to enter the Department, Office, Profession, Manager's name, and Assistant's name for the contact's business. If you have personal information about the contact that you would like to keep track of, key entries in the *Nickname*, *Spouse's name*, *Birthday*, or *Anniversary* fields. If the contact will be participating in online meetings or sharing calendar information, the server and directory address settings are entered in the Details tab.

Use the Activities tab to view details for the various Outlook actions that are related to the selected contact. For example, you can use the Activities tab to view e-mail messages sent or received to the active contact. The Certificates tab is used to import or export digital IDs that can be used to encrypt mail sent to the contact. Use the All Fields tab to view a group of related fields. For example, you can choose to view only the telephone numbers entered for the contact in the All Fields window.

Additional fields not shown in the previous tabs can be viewed from the All Fields tab by selecting a category of fields from the Select from drop-down list. The *All Contact fields* option from the Select from drop-down list will show all of the fields in one window for the active contact.

1. With Outlook open, click the *Contacts* icon on the Outlook bar.
2. Add a new record to the *Contacts* folder by completing the following steps:
   a. Click the New Contact button on the Standard toolbar.
   b. With the insertion point positioned in the Full N̲ame text box, key **Mrs. Carla McWilliams**. The Fil̲e as text box automatically enters the name with the last name first for sorting purposes when you move to the next field.
   c. Press Tab or click in the J̲ob title text box, and then key **Sales Manager**.
   d. Press Tab or click in the Co̲mpany text box and then key **Worldwide Enterprises**.
   e. Click in the A̲ddress text box and then key the following street address, city, state, and Zip Code as you would normally key them on a letter or envelope.

   P.O. Box 99A
   1453 Airport Road
   Middleton, WI 53562

   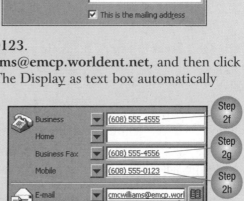

   f. Click in the Business text box in the Telephone section and then key **608 555 4555**. After you click in the next field, Outlook converts the telephone number to (608) 555-4555

   g. Click in the Business Fax text box in the Telephone section and then key **608 555 4556**.

   h. Click in the Mobile text box in the Telephone section and then key **608 555 0123**.

   i. Click in the E-mail text box, key **cmcwilliams@emcp.worldent.net**, and then click in a blank text box to complete the entry. The Display̲ as text box automatically converts the e-mail entry to *Carla McWilliams (cmcwilliams@emcp.worldent.net)*.

   j. Click the S̲ave and Close button on the Contact window toolbar.

3. By default, the contact displays in the Information Viewer as an Address Card with the name, address, telephone numbers, and e-mail address visible. Review the text entered for Carla McWilliams in step 2.

4. Add a new record to the *Contacts* folder using the Check Full Name and Check Address dialog boxes in the Contacts window by completing the following steps:
   a. Click the New Contact button on the Standard toolbar.
   b. With the insertion point positioned in the Full N̲ame text box, click the Full N̲ame button to open the Check Full Name dialog box.

c. With the insertion point positioned in the <u>T</u>itle text box in the Name details section, key **Mr.** and then press Tab or click in the <u>F</u>irst text box.

d. Key **Jorge** in the <u>F</u>irst text box and then press Tab twice or click in the <u>L</u>ast text box.

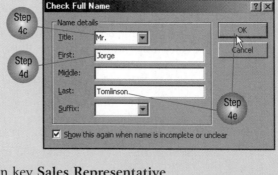

e. Key **Tomlinson** in the <u>L</u>ast text box and then press Enter or click OK.

f. Click in the <u>J</u>ob title text box and then key **Sales Representative**.

g. Press Tab or click in the Co<u>m</u>pany text box and then key **Globalware Distributors**.

h. Click the A<u>d</u>dress button to open the Check Address dialog box.

i. With the insertion point positioned in the <u>S</u>treet text box in the Address details section, key **4532 Dundas Street West** and then press Tab or click in the <u>C</u>ity text box.

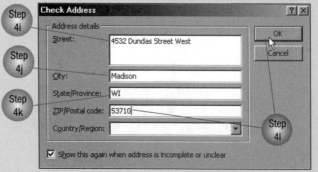

j. Key **Madison** and then press Tab or click in the S<u>t</u>ate/Province text box.

k. Key **WI** and then press Tab or click in the <u>Z</u>IP/Postal code text box.

l. Key **53710** and then press Enter or click OK.

m. Key the following telephone numbers in the fields noted:

Business   **608 555 2199**
Business Fax   **608 555 2200**
Mobile   **608 555 4975**

n. Key the following text in the *E-mail* field:
   jtomlinson@emcp.globalware.net

o. Click the <u>S</u>ave and Close button on the Contact window toolbar.

5. Change the current view to add the job title and company fields by clicking <u>V</u>iew, pointing to Current <u>V</u>iew, and then clicking Detailed Address Cards.

6. Click the Print button on the Standard toolbar. With *Card Style* already selected in the Print style section, click OK.

In exercise 1, step 2, you keyed text directly into the Full <u>N</u>ame and A<u>d</u>dress text boxes while in step 4, you keyed text into the individual fields that comprise the name and address using the Check Full Name and Check Address dialog boxes. Outlook inserts text into the corresponding fields based on the input unless it cannot recognize the entry, in which case the Check Full Name and Check Address dialog boxes will open automatically. Outlook recognizes the titles *Dr., Miss, Mr., Mrs., Ms.,* and *Prof.* Use the Check Full Name dialog box if the person for which you are creating a contact record has a title other than those in the list.

Editing Contacts

Maintaining contact records involves activities such as changing an address, telephone number, or e-mail address as individuals move or change companies, adding information to fields not previously completed, or deleting contacts for which you no longer require a record in the *Contacts* folder.

Double-click a contact name in the Information Viewer to open the Contact window. Edit the fields as required and then click the Save and Close button. If the data you need to change is visible in the current view, click the insertion point within the field and make the necessary changes directly within the Information Viewer. Editing in the Information Viewer is allowed in all fields except the name in the contact record banner.

To delete a contact record, click to select the contact name in the banner for the record and then press Delete or click the Delete button on the Standard toolbar.

exercise 2

1. With Outlook open and the *Contacts* folder active in Detailed Address Cards view, add a new contact by completing the following steps:
   a. Click Actions on the Menu bar and then click New Contact.
   b. With the insertion point positioned in the Full Name text box, key **Miss Guiseppina D'Allario**.
   c. Press Tab or click in the Job title text box, and then key **Regional Sales Manager**.
   d. Press Tab or click in the Company text box and then key **Eastern Industries**.
   e. Click in the Address text box and then key the following text:
      44 Queen Street North
      Madison WI 53562
   f. Click in the Business text box in the Telephone section and then key **608 555 4968**.
   g. Click in the Business Fax text box in the Telephone section and then key **608 555 4702**.
   h. Click in the Mobile text box in the Telephone section and then key **608 555 3795**.
   i. Click in the E-mail text box and then key **dallario@emcp.easternind.net**.
   j. Click Save and Close.

OUTLOOK

2. Edit the telephone numbers for Jorge Tomlinson in the Information Viewer by completing the following steps:

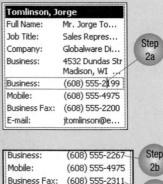

a. Position the I-beam pointer [I] in the *Business* telephone number field between 2 and 1 in the record for Tomlinson, Jorge, and then click the left mouse button. A dotted box appears around the field and an insertion point is placed between 2 and 1.

b. Press the Delete key three times to remove *199*, key **267**, and then press Enter.

c. Click the mouse at the end of the *Business Fax* field (after the last zero), press Backspace four times to delete *2200*, key **2311**, and then press Enter.

3. Change the street address for Carla McWilliams in the Contact window by completing the following steps:

a. Position the mouse pointer over the name banner for *McWilliams, Carla*, and then double-click the left mouse button.

b. Position the I-beam pointer in the Address text box at the beginning of the second line, hold down the left mouse button, and then drag to select the street address *1453 Airport Road*.

c. Key **18 Forsythia Avenue**.

d. Click Save and Close.

4. Click the Print button on the Standard toolbar. With *Card Style* already selected in the Print style section, click OK.

Adding New Contacts from Existing Contacts

When there is more than one person from the same company that you communicate with, you can quickly add the second or third record by basing a new record on an existing one. Outlook inserts the company name and address in the Contact window so that you don't have to rekey it. This not only avoids duplication of effort, but also ensures that records are consistent and reduces the chance of keying errors.

Once one of the contacts has been created for the company, the remaining contacts for the same company can be quickly added by selecting the record, clicking Actions, and then clicking New Contact from Same Company.

1. With Outlook open and the *Contacts* folder active in Detailed Address Cards view, add a new contact by basing the record on an existing contact by completing the following steps:

    a. Position the mouse pointer over the name banner for *McWilliams, Carla*, and then click the left mouse button. This selects the record as indicated by the dotted box surrounding the fields.

    b. Click <u>A</u>ctions, then New <u>C</u>ontact from Same Company.

    c. With the insertion point positioned in the Full <u>N</u>ame text box, key **Mr. Vladimir Keildov**.

    d. Press Tab or click in the <u>J</u>ob title text box and then key **Sales Manager, European Division**.

    e. Click in the E-mail text box and then key **vkeildov@emcp.worldent.net**.

    f. Click <u>S</u>ave and Close.

2. Click the Print button on the Standard toolbar. With *Card Style* already selected in the Print style section, click OK.

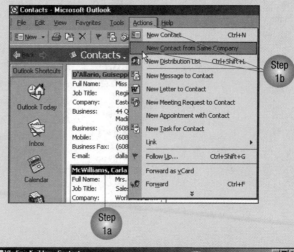

Fields already completed based on information in Carla McWilliams' record.

Using the Details and All Fields Tabs

Approximately 140 fields are available for storing information about a contact including four user-defined fields. The Details tab in the Contact window shown in figure 3.3 groups fields related to the contact's business and personal relationships. The bottom of the Details tab contains the settings required to participate in online meetings using Microsoft NetMeeting and for sharing calendar information over the Internet.

The All Fields tab provides the ability to view subsets of related fields or all of the contact fields in a table format.

3.3 *Contact Window with Details Tab Selected*

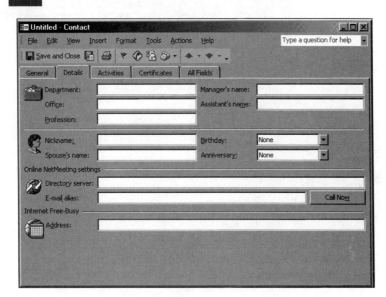

exercise 4

ADDING INFORMATION IN DETAILS AND ALL FIELDS TABS

1. With Outlook open and the *Contacts* folder active in Detailed Address Cards view, add a new contact with information in the Details tab by completing the following steps:
   a. Click the New Contact button on the Standard toolbar.
   b. Key the following information in the General tab of the Contact window.

Full Name	**Dr. Tina Nunez**
Job title	**Director, Marketing and Sales**
Company	**Globe Products**
Address	**393 Brentwood Road**
	Madison, WI 53562
Business	**608 555 2689**
Business Fax	**608 555 2458**
Mobile	**608 555 1598**
E-mail	**nunez@emcp.globeproducts.net**

   c. Click the Details tab in the Contact window.
   d. With the insertion point positioned in the Department text box, key **Marketing** and then press Tab.
   e. With the insertion point positioned in the Manager's name text box, key **Kyle Winston** and then click in the Assistant's name text box.

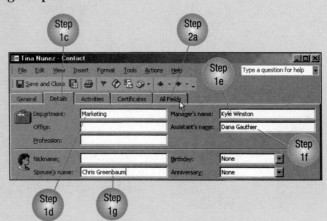

f. Key **Dana Gauthier** and then click in the Spouse's name text box.

g. Key **Chris Greenbaum**.

2. View all of the contact fields and add the names of the children for the contact by completing the following steps:

a. Click the All Fields tab in the Contact window.

b. Click the down-pointing triangle next to Select from, scroll down the list box, and then click *All Contact fields*.

c. Scroll down the list box and examine all of the contact fields that are available for storing information about contacts.

d. Scroll up the list box until you can see the field named *Children*.

e. Position the arrow pointer in the column labeled *Value* beside the field named *Children* and then click the left mouse button. The field is selected with an insertion point positioned inside a dotted text box.

f. Key **Brooke, Dustin, Jamie**.

g. Click Save and Close.

3. Add the birthday information for an existing contact by completing the following steps:

a. Double-click the *McWilliams, Carla* name banner.

b. Click the Details tab in the Contact window.

c. Drag to select the text *None* in the Birthday field.

d. Key **October 15, 1979**.

e. Click Save and Close.

4. Click the Print button on the Standard toolbar. With *Card Style* already selected in the Print style section, click OK.

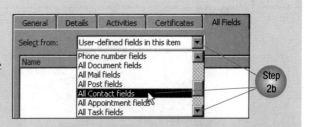

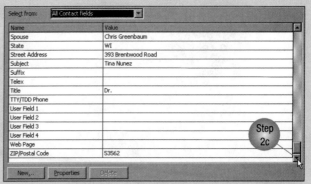

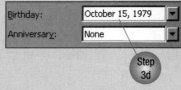

Flagging a Contact for Follow-up

Flag

A reminder to follow up on an outstanding issue with a contact can be set by flagging the contact's record. To do this, select the contact record that you want to mark with a flag, click Actions, and then click Follow Up to open the Flag for Follow Up dialog box. Click the down-pointing triangle next to the Flag to list box, and then click the type of flag that you want to set, or type your own flag name in the Flag to text box. Figure 3.4 shows the flags available in the Flag to drop-down list.

OUTLOOK

To enter a due date for the follow-up activity, key a date in the <u>D</u>ue by text box or click the down-pointing triangle to select a date from the drop-down calendar. The text box next to the date (currently reads *None*) can be used to enter a time that the activity must be completed by.

FIGURE

3.4 *Flag for Follow-up Dialog Box with Flag to Drop-Down List*

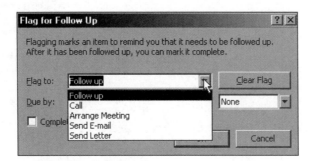

exercise 5

FLAGGING CONTACTS FOR FOLLOW-UP

1. With Outlook open and the *Contacts* folder active in Detailed Address Cards view, attach a Follow Up flag to a contact record that will remind you to schedule a meeting by completing the following steps:

   a. Position the mouse pointer over the name banner for *Tomlinson, Jorge,* and then click the left mouse button.

   b. Click <u>A</u>ctions, and then Follow <u>U</u>p; or click the Follow Up button on the Standard toolbar.

   c. Click the down-pointing triangle next to <u>F</u>lag to and then click *Arrange Meeting* at the drop-down list.

   d. Drag to select *None* in the <u>D</u>ue by text box and then key **one week from today**. (Outlook allows dates to be entered using natural language phrases. The <u>D</u>ue by date will be set to one week from the current date.)

   e. Click OK. The Follow Up information appears in the Information Viewer below the name banner for the contact record.

2. Double-click the name banner for *Tomlinson, Jorge* to view the Follow Up flag message inside the Contact window.

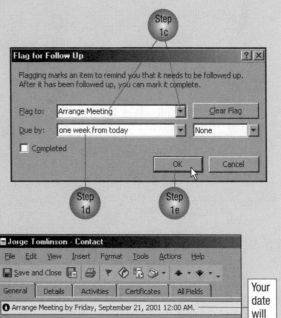

3. Add a Follow Up flag to the contact record for *McWilliams, Carla* by completing the following steps:
   a. Click the name banner for *McWilliams, Carla*.
   b. Click the Follow Up button on the Standard toolbar.
   c. Click the down-pointing triangle next to <u>F</u>lag to and then click *Send Letter*.
   d. Click the down-pointing triangle next to <u>D</u>ue by and then click the date that is two weeks from today in the drop-down calendar.
   e. Click OK.
4. Change the current view to display the contact records in table format grouped by Follow Up Flags by completing the following steps:
   a. Click <u>V</u>iew, point to Current <u>V</u>iew, and then click By Follow-up Flag.
   b. Double-click the miniature card icon in the first column of the row in the table for Mrs. Carla McWilliams to open the Contact window with the flag message displayed.
   c. Click the Close button on the Contact window Title bar.
   d. Double-click the right column boundary for the *Follow Up Flag* column heading to expand the column width to the length of the longest entry.
5. Click the Print button on the Standard toolbar. With *Table Style* already selected in the Print style section, click OK.
6. Click <u>V</u>iew, point to Current <u>V</u>iew, and then click Detailed Address Cards.

A red flag displayed in the *Flag* column indicates the flag is still active. Once the contact activity has been completed, select the contact, display the Flag for Follow Up dialog box, and then click the C<u>o</u>mpleted check box. The flag color changes to gray and will appear in a group labeled Flag Status: Completed.

To remove a flag from a contact record, select the contact, display the Flag for Follow Up dialog box, and then click the <u>C</u>lear Flag button.

A Follow Up flag that becomes overdue displays in red in the Information Viewer. For example, if you set a due date for a reminder to arrange a meeting for a contact and the due date passes without the flag being cleared or marked as completed, the data in the contact record will display in red.

Sorting Contacts

Contacts are initially displayed in the Information Viewer alphabetically sorted in ascending order by the *File As* field which defaults to the contact's last name followed by first name. In the Sort dialog box shown in figure 3.5 you can specify up to four fields by which to sort the contact list.

FIGURE

| 3.5 | *Sort Dialog Box*

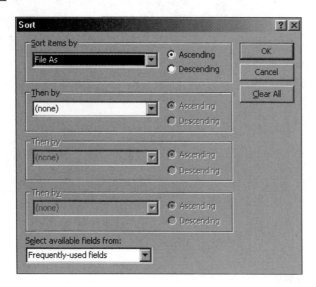

The drop-down list of fields for <u>S</u>ort items by and <u>T</u>hen by defaults to *Frequently-used fields*. Click the down-pointing triangle next to the S<u>e</u>lect available fields from list box to change to any of the subsets of related fields or all of the contact fields.

To begin a sort, click <u>V</u>iew, point to Current <u>V</u>iew, and then click <u>C</u>ustomize Current View. Click the <u>S</u>ort button in the View Summary dialog box and then define the sort criteria in the Sort dialog box.

exercise 6

SORTING CONTACTS AND EXPANDING COLUMN WIDTHS

1. With Outlook open and the *Contacts* folder active in Detailed Address Cards view, sort the contact list by company name and then by last name by completing the following steps:
    a. Click <u>V</u>iew, point to Current <u>V</u>iew, and then click <u>C</u>ustomize Current View.
    b. Click the <u>S</u>ort button in the View Summary dialog box.
    c. Click the down-pointing triangle next to <u>S</u>ort items by, scroll up the list box, and then click *Company*. The sort order defaults to Ascending.
    d. Click the down-pointing triangle next to <u>T</u>hen by, scroll down the list box, and then click *Last Name*. The sort order defaults to Ascending.

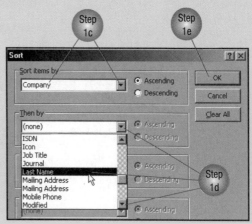

e. Click OK to close the Sort dialog box. A message box displays informing you that the field *Last Name* is not shown in the current view and asking if you want to show it.

f. Click N̲o. You do not need to display the *Last Name* field since the name banner for the address card displays the *File As* field which defaults to last name followed by first name.

g. With the current sort settings displayed next to the S̲ort button in the View Summary dialog box, click OK.

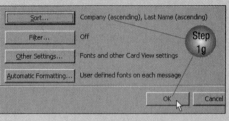

h. Examine the order of the records in the Information Viewer. Notice that for the two contacts at Worldwide Enterprises, the first record displayed is Vladimir Keildov followed by Carla McWilliams.

2. Expand the column widths to display more data in the Information Viewer by completing the following steps:

a. Position the arrow pointer on the vertical line between the first and second columns until the pointer displays as a left- and right-pointing arrow.

b. Hold down the left mouse button, drag the pointer right approximately 1 inch, and then release the left mouse button. Notice the column boundary between columns 2 and 3 moves simultaneously.

3. Add the following contact by basing the record on an existing contact by completing the following steps:

a. Select the record for Tina Nunez.

b. Click A̲ctions, and then click New C̲ontact from Same Company.

c. Key the following information in the fields noted:
   Full N̲ame   **Mr. Cal Fillmore**
   J̲ob title   **Sales Manager**
   Mobile   **608 555 2146**
   E-mail   **fillmore@emcp.globeproducts.net**

d. Click S̲ave and Close.

e. Notice the new record is inserted maintaining the current order of sorting first by company and then by last name within the company.

f. Print the contact list in *Card Style*.

4. Restore the sort order to the default setting by completing the following steps:

a. Click V̲iew, point to Current V̲iew, and then click C̲ustomize Current View.

b. Click the S̲ort button in the View Summary dialog box.

OUTLOOK

c. Click the Clear All button in the Sort dialog box.

d. Click the down-pointing triangle next to Sort items by, scroll down the list box, and then click *File As*. The sort order defaults to Ascending.

e. Click OK to close the Sort dialog box and then click OK to close the View Summary dialog box.

f. Scroll the window left if necessary to view the first record in the contact list.

5. Expand the column width to view all data within the fields in the Information Viewer by completing the following steps:

a. Position the arrow pointer on the vertical line between the first and second columns until the pointer displays as a left- and right-pointing arrow.

b. Double-click the left mouse button.

Filtering Contacts

A filtered contact list is a subset of contact records that has been selected based on a criterion specified in the Filter dialog box. Records that do not meet the condition are temporarily removed from the Information Viewer. The message *Filter Applied* appears in the Status bar next to the total number of records to indicate to the user that not all of the records are currently displayed.

To specify the condition upon which to display records, click View, point to Current View, and then click Customize Current View. Click the Filter button in the View Summary dialog box and then specify which records to display in the Filter dialog box with the Contacts tab selected as shown in figure 3.6.

FIGURE

3.6 *Filter Dialog Box with Contacts Tab Selected*

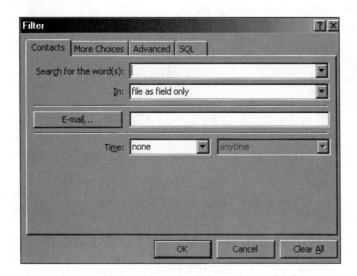

View and print the filtered list as necessary and then restore all records to the Information Viewer by completing the following steps:

1. Click View, point to Current View, and then click Customize Current View.
2. Click the Filter button in the View Summary dialog box.
3. Click the Clear All button in the Filter dialog box.
4. Click OK twice.

exercise 7

FILTERING CONTACTS

1. With Outlook open and the *Contacts* folder active in Detailed Address Cards view, filter the contact list to display only those records for Globe Products by completing the following steps:
   a. Click View, point to Current View, and then click Customize Current View.
   b. Click the Filter button in the View Summary dialog box.
   c. With the insertion point positioned in the Search for the word(s) text box, key **Globe Products**.
   d. Click the down-pointing triangle next to In and then click *company field only*.
   e. Click OK to close the Filter dialog box.
   f. With the current filter settings displayed next to the Filter button in the View Summary dialog box, click OK. Only two records are displayed in the Information Viewer and the message *Filter Applied* displays at the left edge of the Status bar.

2. Print the filtered list in Phone Directory style by completing the following steps:
   a. Click the Print button on the Standard toolbar.
   b. Scroll down the Print style list box and then click *Phone Directory Style*.
   c. Click OK.

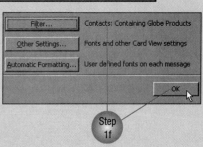

3. Restore the Information Viewer to display all contacts by completing the following steps:
   a. Click View, point to Current View, and then click Customize Current View.
   b. Click the Filter button in the View Summary dialog box.
   c. Click the Clear All button in the Filter dialog box.
   d. Click OK twice.

Grouping Contacts into Categories

Contacts can be associated with a keyword in the category list and can then be grouped or filtered by the category to produce different lists of contacts. The *By Category* option on the Current View menu will group contacts by the catgeory they have been assigned. The list of contacts can then be expanded and collapsed

OUTLOOK

as required. The list of categories in the A̲vailable categories list box in the Categories dialog box is the same list as was used for appointments in the previous chapter. A contact can be associated with more than one category so that his or her name will appear on more than one list.

To create your own category name, key the category name in the I̲tem(s) belong to these categories text box and then click the A̲dd to List button.

To assign a category to an existing contact, right-click the contact name in the Information Viewer and then click Categor̲ies at the shortcut menu to open the Categories dialog box; or select the contact and then click E̲dit, Categor̲ies.

exercise 8

CREATING CATEGORIES, ASSIGNING CONTACTS TO CATEGORIES, & VIEWING CONTACTS IN CATEGORIES

1. With Outlook open and the *Contacts* folder active in Detailed Address Cards view, create a new category and assign a contact to the new category by completing the following steps:
   a. Right-click the contact name *D'Allario, Guiseppina*.
   b. Click Categor̲ies at the shortcut menu.
   c. Click the insertion point inside the I̲tem(s) belong to these categories text box, and then key **Association Member**.
   d. Click A̲dd to List.
   e. Look at the list in the A̲vailable categories list box to view the new category added in step 1d. Notice the category is automatically checked for the current contact. Click OK.

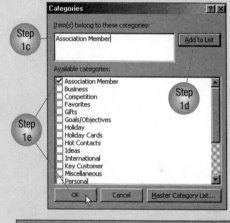

2. Assign categories to the remaining contacts by completing the following steps:
   a. Double-click *Fillmore, Carl*.
   b. Click the Categories button at the bottom of the Contact window.
   c. Click *Association Member, Business,* and *Holiday Cards* in the A̲vailable categories list box and then click OK.
   d. Click S̲ave and Close.
   e. Click *Keildov, Vladimir* and then click E̲dit, Categor̲ies.
   f. Click *Business* and *International* in the A̲vailable categories list box and then click OK.
   g. Assign categories to contacts as follows using any of the previous methods:
      McWilliams, Carla   Association Member, Holiday Cards
      Nunez, Tina   Personal
      Tomlinson, Jorge   Key Customer

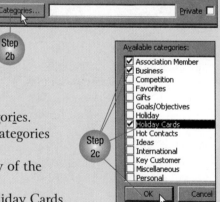

3. View the contacts by category in the Information Viewer by completing the following steps:
   a. Click V̲iew, point to Current V̲iew, and then click By Category.

b. The contacts are grouped according to the categories to which they were assigned in a collapsed list. Click the plus symbol next to *Categories: Association Member* to expand the list. The plus symbol changes to a minus symbol (collapse button).

c. Click the plus symbol next to *Categories: Business* to expand the list. Notice that *Mr. Cal Fillmore* is shown under both of the expanded categories.

d. Expand the remaining category lists.

4. Print the contact list in *Table Style*.

5. Click <u>V</u>iew, point to Current <u>V</u>iew, and then click Detailed Address Cards.

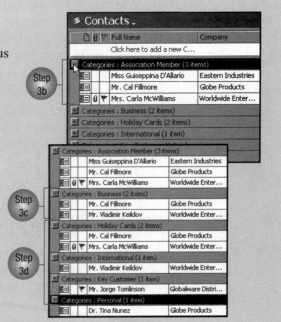

Step 3b

Step 3c

Step 3d

exercise 9

ASSIGNING CATEGORIES WHILE CREATING A CONTACT

1. With Outlook open and the *Contacts* folder active in Detailed Address Cards view, assign a category while adding a new contact by completing the following steps:

a. Scroll right if necessary and then click *Tomlinson, Jorge*.

b. Click <u>A</u>ctions and then click New <u>C</u>ontact from Same Company.

c. Key the following information in the fields noted:

Full <u>N</u>ame	**Mrs. Bernice Atvar**
<u>J</u>ob title	**District Sales Manager**
Mobile	**608 555 1158**
E-mail	**batvar@emcp.globalware.net**

d. Click the Categories button.

e. Click *Association Member, Holiday Cards,* and *Key Customer* in the A<u>v</u>ailable categories list box and then click OK.

f. Click the Print button on the Contact window toolbar.

g. Click <u>S</u>ave and Close.

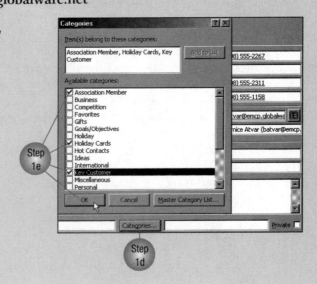

Step 1e

Step 1d

OUTLOOK

exercise 10

1. With Outlook open and the *Contacts* folder active in Detailed Address Cards view, filter the contact list to produce a list of only those contacts in the *Association Member* category by completing the following steps:

   a. Click <u>V</u>iew, point to Current <u>V</u>iew, and then click <u>C</u>ustomize Current View.

   b. Click the Fi<u>l</u>ter button in the View Summary dialog box.

   c. Click the More Choices tab in the Filter dialog box.

   d. Click the <u>C</u>ategories button.

   e. Click *Association Member* in the A<u>v</u>ailable categories list box and then click OK.

   f. Click OK to close the Filter dialog box.

   g. Click OK to close the View Summary dialog box. Only four records are displayed in the Information Viewer. The message *Filter Applied* appears at the left edge of the Status bar.

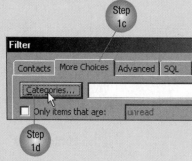

Step 1c

Step 1d

2. Print the filtered list in Small Booklet style by completing the following steps:

   a. Click the Print button on the Standard toolbar.

   b. Click *Small Booklet Style* in the Print style section of the Print dialog box.

   c. Click OK.

   d. Click <u>Y</u>es at the message box saying booklets should be printed double-sided and instructing you to select the double-sided printing options in the Properties dialog box for the printer. *(Note: Small booklet style will still print on a regular 8-1/2 x 11 page without the double-sided option set on the printer.)*

Step 1g

Contacts . Atv - McW	
Atvar, Bernice	**Fillmore, Cal**
Full Name: Mrs. Bernice Atvar	Full Name: Mr. Cal Fillmore
Job Title: District Sales Manager	Job Title: Sales Manager
Company: Globalware Distributors	Company: Globe Products
Business: 4532 Dundas Street West Madison, WI 53710	Business: 393 Brentwood Road Madison, WI 53562
Business: (608) 555-2267	Business: (608) 555-2689
Mobile: (608) 555-1158	Mobile: (608) 555-2146
Business Fax: (608) 555-2311	Business Fax: (608) 555-2458
E-mail: batvar@emcp.globalware.net	E-mail: fillmore@emcp.globeproducts.net
Categories: Association Member, Holiday Cards, K...	Categories: Association Member, Business, Holida...
D'Allario, Guiseppina	**McWilliams, Carla**
Full Name: Miss Guiseppina D'Allario	Follow Up Flag: Send Letter
Job Title: Regional Sales Manager	Full Name: Mrs. Carla McWilliams
Company: Eastern Industries	Job Title: Sales Manager
Business: 44 Queen Street North Madison WI 53562	Company: Worldwide Enterprises
	Business: P. O. Box 99A 18 Forsythia Avenue Middleton, WI 53562
Business: (608) 555-4968	
Mobile: (608) 555-3795	Business: (608) 555-4555
Business Fax: (608) 555-4702	Mobile: (608) 555-0123
E-mail: dallario@emcp.easternind.net	Business Fax: (608) 555-4556
Categories: Association Member	E-mail: cmcwilliams@emcp.worldent.net
	Categories: Association Member, Holiday Cards

3. Restore the Information Viewer to display all contacts by completing the following steps:

   a. Click <u>V</u>iew, point to Current <u>V</u>iew, and then click <u>C</u>ustomize Current View.

   b. Click the Fi<u>l</u>ter button in the View Summary dialog box.

   c. Click the Clear <u>A</u>ll button in the Filter dialog box.

   d. Click OK twice.

Finding a Contact

Once a *Contacts* folder contains a lot of records, browsing through the folder to find a contact record may not be feasible. Outlook provides the following three features to assist with locating a record quickly:

- The Find a Contact box on the Standard toolbar
- The Find bar
- The Advanced Find dialog box

In addition to the three features listed above, the Letter tabs along the right side of the Information Viewer can be used to scroll quickly to the first record that begins with the letter. For example, to move the selected record to the first contact whose last name begins with *w*, click the *w* letter tab.

Find a Contact Box

Type a contact to find

Find a Contact

To locate a contact record, click in the Find a Contact box on the Standard toolbar (currently displays *Type a contact to find*), key the name of the individual whose record you want to see, and then press Enter. Outlook can locate records based on a partial entry such as *Joe Sm*, a first name only, a last name only, an e-mail alias, or a company name. Once you have used the Find a Contact box, clicking the down-pointing triangle to the right of the box will display previously searched for entries so that you can repeat a search.

exercise 11

LOCATING CONTACTS USING LETTER TABS AND FIND A CONTACT BOX

1. With Outlook open and the *Contacts* folder active in Detailed Address Cards view, locate and select records using the letter tabs by completing the following steps:
    a. Click the *t* letter tab along the right side of the Information Viewer. The screen scrolls right and the contact record for *Tomlinson, Jorge* is selected.
    b. Click the *ab* letter tab. The screen scrolls left and the contact record for *Atvar, Bernice* is selected.
    c. Click the *n* letter tab. The screen scrolls right and the contact record for *Nunez, Tina* is selected.

    Step 1a

2. Locate and select records using the Find a Contact box by completing the following steps:
    a. Click the *ab* letter tab to return to the first record in the *Contacts* folder.
    b. Click the insertion point inside the Find a Contact box (currently reads *Type a contact to find*). The text *Type a contact to find* disappears and a blinking insertion point is positioned inside the box.
    c. Key **jorge** and then press Enter.

    jorge

    Step 2c

    d. The contact window for *Jorge Tomlinson* opens. Review the information in the window and then click the Close button on the Contact window Title bar.
    e. Click the insertion point inside the Find a Contact box. The recently searched for contact name *Mr. Jorge Tomlinson* is selected.
    f. Key **Worldwide** and then press Enter. Since more than one record exists for Worldwide Enterprises, Outlook opens the Choose Contact dialog box. The Contacts list box contains a list of all records within the folder that have *Worldwide* within them.

OUTLOOK

g. Click *Mrs. Carla McWilliams* in the Contacts list box in the Choose Contact dialog box and then click OK.

h. Review the information in the *Carla McWilliams* Contact window and then click the Close button on the Title bar.

i. Click the down-pointing triangle next to the Find a Contact box. A drop-down list of previously searched for entries appears.

j. Click *Mr. Jorge Tomlinson* in the drop-down list.

k. Close the *Jorge Tomlinson* Contact window.

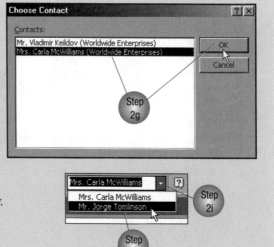

Find Bar

With the F<u>i</u>nd feature, Outlook returns a filtered list of all contacts that contain the name or other keyword specified in the Look for text box. The contact records that do not meet the search criteria are temporarily hidden from view. To begin a Find, click <u>T</u>ools, and then click F<u>i</u>nd, or click the F<u>i</u>nd button on the Standard toolbar to open the Find bar shown in figure 3.7.

Find

F I G U R E

3.7 *Find Bar*

Contacts ▾ Atv - Kei				Address
Look for:	▾ Search In ▾	Contacts	Find Now Clear	Options ▾ X

The Find bar for contacts is used in the same manner as described for finding messages in chapter 1. Key the name or keyword that you want Outlook to search for within the contact records in the Look for text box. By default, the Search In list box contains the name of the current folder. Click Find Now to begin the search. Outlook will list only those records that meet the search criteria in the Information Viewer. Click Clear to remove the filter and restore all of the contact records to the Information Viewer.

1. With Outlook open and the *Contacts* folder active in Detailed Address Cards view, locate records for contacts from Globe Products using the Find bar by completing the following steps:
   a. Click Tools and then Find, or click the Find button on the Standard toolbar to display the Find bar.
   b. With the insertion point positioned in the Look for text box, key **Globe Products**.
   c. Click Find Now. Outlook displays the records for the two contacts that meet the search criteria— *Fillmore, Cal*, and *Nunez, Tina*.
   d. Print the contact list in *Card Style*.

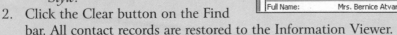
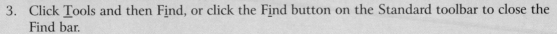

2. Click the Clear button on the Find bar. All contact records are restored to the Information Viewer.
3. Click Tools and then Find, or click the Find button on the Standard toolbar to close the Find bar.

Advanced Find

Click the Options button on the Find bar and then click Advanced Find to open the Advanced Find dialog box with the Contacts tab selected as shown in figure 3.8. The Contacts tab contains options to locate records by keying a word that exists within the record such as a name, telephone number, or e-mail name; to search within a set of related fields such as address fields; or to restrict the search to records within a specific timeframe.

FIGURE

3.8 *Advanced Find Dialog Box with Contacts Tab Selected*

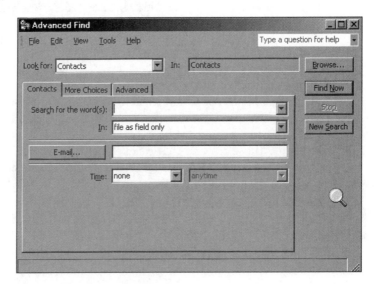

Use the More Choices tab to locate contact records by the category to which they have been assigned, and the Advanced tab to enter conditional statements for a field that Outlook must satisfy to filter the message list.

1. With Outlook open and the *Contacts* folder active in Detailed Address Cards view, locate records that have been assigned the category *Holiday Cards* using the Advanced Find dialog box by completing the following steps:
    a. Click <u>T</u>ools and then F<u>i</u>nd, or click the F<u>i</u>nd button on the Standard toolbar to display the Find bar.
    b. Click Options on the Find bar.
    c. Click Advanced Find at the drop-down menu.
    d. Click the More Choices tab in the Advanced Find dialog box.
    e. Click in the <u>C</u>ategories text box and then key **holiday cards**.
    f. Click Find <u>N</u>ow.
2. The Advanced Find dialog box expands and the records that match the search criteria are displayed in table format at the bottom of the dialog box. The Status bar at the bottom of the dialog box displays a message with the number of records found. Click <u>F</u>ile on the Advanced Find Menu bar and then click <u>P</u>rint. With *Table Style* already selected in the Print style section, click OK.
3. Click the Close button on the Advanced Find window Title bar.
4. Click <u>T</u>ools and then F<u>i</u>nd, or click the F<u>i</u>nd button on the Standard toolbar to close the Find bar.

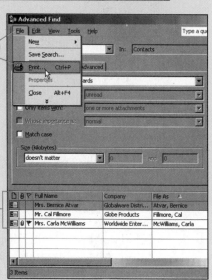

Records found that match search criteria.

Changing the Current View

The <u>V</u>iew, Current <u>V</u>iew menu provides several options for displaying contact information. The Address Cards and Detailed Address Cards view display the contacts in a columnar arrangement. Select Phone List from the Current <u>V</u>iew menu to display the contacts in rows with the *Full Name, Company, File As*, and *telephone number* fields as the column headings. The By Category, By Company, By Location, and By Follow-up Flag will automatically group related contacts together and display the results in rows of a table that you can expand or collapse.

Fields can be added or removed from the current view by right-clicking a column heading and then choosing Remove This Column from the shortcut menu to delete the column from the current view, or Field Chooser to display a list of fields from which you can add to the view.

exercise 14

1. With Outlook open and the *Contacts* folder active in Detailed Address Cards view, change the current view to Phone List and then delete columns from the view by completing the following steps:
    a. Click <u>V</u>iew, point to Current <u>V</u>iew, and then click Phone List.
    b. Scroll right to view all of the columns that are in the current view. Notice the *Home Phone* column is included in the view but contains no information.
    c. Right-click the column heading *Home Phone*.
    d. Click <u>R</u>emove This Column at the shortcut menu.
    e. Remove the following columns from the current view by completing steps similar to those in steps 1c and 1d.
        File As
        Journal
        Categories

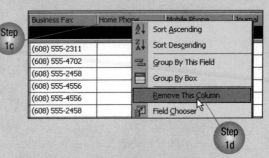

2. Position the arrow pointer on the right column boundary for the *Company* field until the pointer changes to a vertical line with a left- and right-pointing arrow and then double-click the left mouse button. This expands the width of the column to the length of the longest entry within the column.
3. Add a field to the current view and then expand the column width by completing the following steps:
    a. Position the arrow pointer on any of the column headings and then right-click to display the shortcut menu.
    b. Click Field <u>C</u>hooser. A Field Chooser list box appears with the field set *Frequently-used fields* initially displayed.
    c. Scroll down the Field list box until you see the field named *Job Title*.
    d. Position the mouse pointer over *Job Title* in the Field Chooser list box, hold down the left mouse button, drag the field to the column header row between *Company* and *Business Phone*, and then release the mouse button. As you drag the field, red arrows appear in the column header row indicating the position where the new field will be placed.

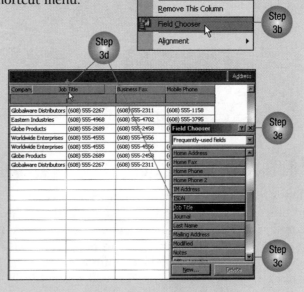

OUTLOOK

e. Click the Close button on the Field Chooser Title bar.

f. Double-click the right column boundary for the *Job Title* field to expand the column to the length of the longest entry.

4. Print the contact list in *Table Style* in landscape orientation by completing the following steps:

a. Click the Print button on the Standard toolbar.

b. Click the Page Setup button in the Print dialog box.

c. Click the Paper tab in the Page Setup: Table Style dialog box.

d. Click Landscape in the Orientation section and then click OK.

e. Click OK in the Print dialog box.

5. Click View, point to Current View, and then click Address Cards to restore the Information Viewer to the default display for the *Contacts* folder.

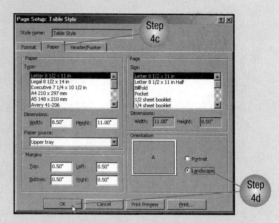

Changing Contact Options

Open the Contact Options dialog box shown in figure 3.9 to change the fields upon which records are created, sorted, and displayed by clicking Tools, Options, and then clicking the Contact Options button in the Options dialog box. The default order that Outlook uses to interpret the name that is being keyed in the Full Name text box as a new record is added is first name followed by middle name and then last name. Click the down-pointing triangle next to the Default "Full Name" order list box in the Contact Options dialog box to choose *Last First*, or *First Last1 Last2*.

The Default "File As" order list box allows you to choose the field(s) that Outlook uses to organize the contact records. The File As setting is the default sort order for records displayed in the Information Viewer. Click the down-pointing triangle next to Default "File As" order to choose to organize by last name, first name, or company name. The drop-down list contains the following options:

- *First Last*
- *Company*
- *Last, First (Company)*
- *Company (Last, First)*

3.9 *Contact Options Dialog Box*

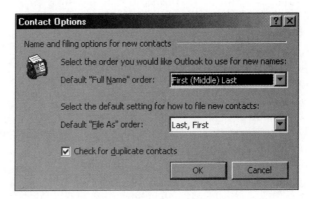

If you do not want Outlook to prompt you when adding a new record with a name that is the same as in a record that already exists in the folder, deselect the Check for duplicate contacts check box. By default, Outlook displays the Duplicate Contact Detected dialog box shown in figure 3.10 when a name is keyed in the Full Name text box that already exists in another record. You have the option of adding the new contact record anyway or updating the information in the current record. If you deselect the check box, Outlook defaults to adding the new record anyway.

3.10 *Duplicate Contact Detected Dialog Box*

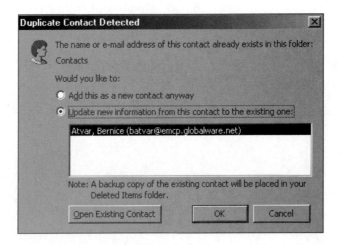

OUTLOOK

Sending E-Mail Messages to Contacts

You can create an e-mail message to a contact without leaving the *Contacts* folder and displaying the Inbox. To do this, select the contact record for the person to whom you want to send an e-mail and then do one of the following actions:

New Message
to Contact

- Click File, point to New, and then click Mail Message.
- Click Actions, New Message to Contact.
- Click the New Message to Contact button on the Standard toolbar. The New Message to Contact button is also on the toolbar inside an individual Contact window.

exercise 15

SENDING AN E-MAIL MESSAGE TO A CONTACT; REVIEWING ACTIVITIES FOR A CONTACT

1. With Outlook open and the *Contacts* folder active in Address Cards view, create and send an e-mail message to a contact by completing the following steps:
   a. Click the name banner for *Tomlinson, Jorge*.
   b. Click the New Message to Contact button on the Standard toolbar. A message window will open with the e-mail address for Jorge Tomlinson already entered in the To. . . text box.
   c. With the insertion point positioned in the Subject text box, key **Meeting next week**.
   d. Press Tab or click in the message editing window and then key the following text: **I would like to arrange a meeting with you sometime next week to review the new product lines. Please let me know what day and time work best for you.**
   e. Click the Print button on the message window toolbar.
   f. Click Send. The message window closes and you are returned to the Information Viewer.

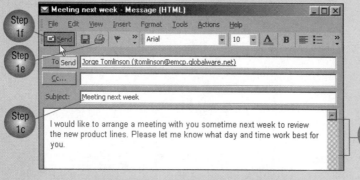

2. View the message created for the contact from the *Contacts* folder by completing the following steps:

   a. Double-click *Tomlinson, Jorge* to open the Contact window.
   b. Click the Activities tab.

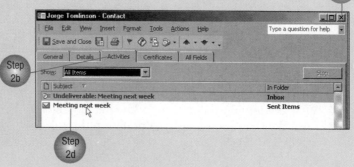

c. Two items should appear within the Contact window: the message header for the message sent in step 1, and an undeliverable message in the *Inbox* from the mail server stating the message was not delivered. *(Since the e-mail address for Jorge Tomlinson is fictitious, the server will not be able to deliver the message created in step 1. If the undeliverable message does not appear, it may be because the mail server has not processed it yet.)*

d. Double-click the message header for the message created in step 1. The message window opens for you to review the content of what was sent to the contact.

e. Click the Close button on the message window Title bar.

f. Close the Jorge Tomlinson - Contact window.

Scheduling Appointments from Contacts

An appointment with a contact can be scheduled without leaving the *Contacts* folder and displaying the Calendar. If you already know that you are available on the required day and time, there is no need to display your Calendar to complete the scheduling. Select the contact, click File, point to New, and then click Appointment; or click Actions, New Appointment with Contact.

exercise 16

SCHEDULING AN APPOINTMENT FROM CONTACTS; VIEWING ACTIVITIES FOR A CONTACT

1. With Outlook open and the *Contacts* folder active in Address Cards view, schedule an appointment for a meeting with a contact by completing the following steps:

a. If necessary, click the name banner for *Tomlinson, Jorge*.

b. Click Actions and then click New Appointment with Contact. An Appointment window opens with the contact's name automatically entered in the Contacts text box.

c. With the insertion point positioned in the Subject text box, key **New products review meeting**.

d. Press Tab or click in the Location text box and then key **Globalware Distributor's office**.

e. Drag to select the current text in the Start time text box and then key **one week from today**.

f. Drag to select the current time in the Start time text box and then key **noon**.

g. Click the down-pointing triangle next to the End time time text box and then click *1:30 PM (1.5 hours)* in the drop-down list.

h. Click Save and Close. The Appointment window closes and you are returned to the Information Viewer.

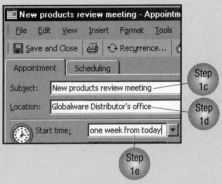

2. View the appointment created for the contact from the *Contacts* folder by completing the following steps:

a. Double-click *Tomlinson, Jorge* to open the Contact window.

OUTLOOK

b. Click the Activities tab.

c. Three items should appear within the Contact window with the appointment at the top of the list.

d. Double-click the appointment header for the appointment scheduled in step 1. The Appointment window opens for you to review the subject, location, day, and time of the appointment.

e. Click the Close button on the Appointment window Title bar.

f. Close the Jorge Tomlinson - Contact window.

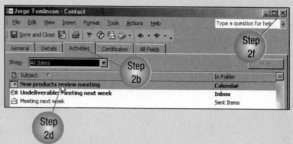

Creating a Letter to a Contact

A letter can be generated to a contact within the *Contacts* folder using the Letter Wizard that is available in Microsoft Word. Select the contact record for which you want to send a letter, click Actions, and then click New Letter to Contact. Microsoft Word will automatically open with the Letter Wizard Step 1 of 4 dialog box open. The Letter Wizard walks you through the process of creating the letter by choosing the letter format, inserting recipient information, including letter elements such as an attention line, and keying the sender information.

When the Letter Wizard is complete, the selected contact's name and address will be automatically inserted in the inside address section of the letter. Key the body of the letter in the document, save, print, and then exit Word to return to the *Contacts* folder in Outlook.

INTEGRATED

exercise 17

CREATING A LETTER TO A CONTACT

1. With Outlook open and the *Contacts* folder active in Address Cards view, start a letter to a contact by completing the following steps:

   a. Click the name banner for *Keildov, Vladimir*.

   b. Click Actions, and then click New Letter to Contact. Microsoft Word will automatically open with the Letter Wizard started. (*Note: If Microsoft Word does not automatically open, look on the Taskbar for the Word document button. Clicking the Word button on the Taskbar will switch to Microsoft Word where you can complete the exercise.*)

2. Finish the letter in Microsoft Word by completing the following steps:

   a. In the Microsoft Word Letter Wizard Step 1 of 4 dialog box with the Letter Format tab selected, complete the following steps:

   1) Click the Date line check box. The current date appears in the text box next to Date line.

   2) Click the down-pointing triangle next to the Choose a page design list box, and then click *Contemporary Letter* in the drop-down list. (*Note: See next page for screen image.*)

   3) Click Next.

b. Click at the beginning of the first line of text in the <u>D</u>elivery address text box in the Letter Wizard Step 2 of 4 dialog box with the Recipient Info tab selected, and then delete the title *Sales Manager, European Division.*

c. Click B<u>u</u>siness in the <u>S</u>alutation section of the Letter Wizard Step 2 of 4 dialog box with the Recipient Info tab selected, and then click <u>N</u>ext. *(Note: See screen image below.)*

d. Click <u>N</u>ext at the Letter Wizard Step 3 of 4 dialog box with the Other Elements tab selected.

e. Enter the sender information in the Letter Wizard Step 4 of 4 dialog box with the Sender Info tab selected by completing the following steps:

1) Key your first and last name in the <u>S</u>ender's name text box.

2) Key the address of your school in the <u>R</u>eturn address text box.

3) Click the down-pointing triangle next to the Complimentar<u>y</u> closing text box, and then click *Sincerely yours,* in the drop-down list. *(Note: If no options display in the drop-down list, click in the Complimentar<u>y</u> closing text box and then key* **Sincerely yours,***.)*

4) Key your initials in the <u>W</u>riter/typist initials text box.

5) Click <u>F</u>inish.

Your date will vary.

Step 2a1

Step 2a2

Step 2a3

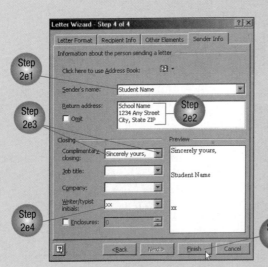

Step 2e1

Step 2e2

Step 2e3

Step 2e4

Step 2e5

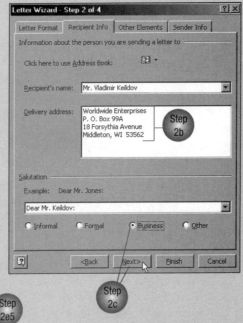

Step 2b

Step 2c

OUTLOOK

f. Key the following text as the body of the letter. *(Note: The letter is formatted to double space between paragraphs automatically. You will need to press Enter only once between paragraphs.)*

We are now finished with the implementation of our new order processing system for the new product lines we presented at our last meeting.

Products are in inventory and ready to ship to Europe. We encourage you to advise your representatives in the European division to proceed with entering orders into our system.

With our streamlined process, we anticipate shipments within your specified timeframes and fewer returns for errors and omissions. Thank you for your feedback and assistance during this setup time.

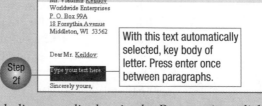

g. Click File, Page Setup and then click the Layout tab in the Page Setup dialog box. Click the down-pointing triangle next to the Vertical alignment list box in the Page section, click *Center* in the drop-down list, and then click OK. This will vertically center the letter on the page.

3. Click the Save button on the Standard toolbar. Change the Save in list box to 3½ Floppy (A:), key **Ch03 Ex17** in the File name text box, and then click Save. *(Note: Select a different drive and/or folder if you save student files in a location other than the floppy disk drive.)*

4. Click the Print button on the Standard toolbar.

5. Exit Microsoft Word. *(Note: Click No if prompted to save changes to Ch03 Ex17 when exiting.)*

Creating a Standard Letter to Multiple Contacts

You can filter or sort data in a *Contacts* folder in Outlook, and then use the data as the data source in a mail merge in Microsoft Word. A *mail merge* is the term used when a list of names and addresses from one file, called the *data source*, is used to create form letters, mailing labels, or envelopes. A second file, called the *main document*, contains the standard text for each letter. Formatting instructions and field codes that instruct Word as to the placement of the name and address fields is also included in the main document.

The contact information for the selected contacts is sent to a temporary mail merge file while the main document is created in Word. Save the data source file in Word if you want to use the same contact data for future merges.

Performing a mail merge using Outlook and Word requires completion of the following three steps:

1. Export the contact data as a data source from Outlook.
2. Create the main document in Word by keying standard text and inserting the merge fields as required.
3. Merge the data source with the main document to a new document screen or directly to the printer.

Exporting Data from *Contacts* to Create a Data Source

Complete the following steps to create a data source from the *Contacts* folder:

1. Change to the view that contains the fields you want to merge and then sort or filter the data in the *Contacts* folder in the order you want the letters generated. If you do not want a letter, label, or envelope generated to each record, select the records to include in the merge. For example, use Ctrl + click to select nonadjacent records, or click the first record and then Shift + click the last record to select adjacent contacts.

2. Click Tools and then click Mail Merge to open the Mail Merge Contacts dialog box shown in figure 3.11. All contacts in current view is automatically selected in the Contacts section. If you had selected multiple contact records before opening the Mail Merge Contacts dialog box, the Only selected contacts option would be active instead.

3. Click Contact fields in current view in the Fields to merge section. The default option of All contact fields will send all contact data to the data source file. In most cases, it is unnecessary to include all of the fields in contact records for generating a letter.

4. Click New document in the Document file section, or click Existing document and then browse to the folder and file name of the existing data source.

5. If you want to save the exported contact information permanently for future mail merges, click the Permanent file check box. Click Browse to specify the folder in which to store the file and then enter a file name.

6. Select the type of main document that you will be creating in Word in the Document type drop-down list. You can choose *Form Letters, Mailing Labels, Envelopes,* or *Catalog.*

7. Select where the merged records are to be sent in the Merge to drop-down list. The data can be merged to *New Document, Printer,* or *E-mail.*

8. Click OK.

9. Microsoft Word will open when the data is finished exporting.

3.11 *Mail Merge Contacts Dialog Box*

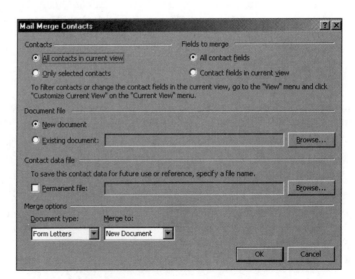

Completing the Merge in Word

When the data from the *Contacts* folder has finished exporting from Outlook as a data source, you will be at a Microsoft Word clear document screen with the Mail Merge toolbar automatically opened. Insert the required fields and text to complete the letters, and then click the Merge to New Document or Merge to Printer button on the Mail Merge toolbar. Microsoft Word will generate an individual letter to each record in the data source.

To create the main document, key the text in the form letter to the point where you need to insert the recipient's name and address. Click the Insert Merge Field button on the Mail Merge toolbar, and then click the required field in the drop-down list. Press Enter or insert spaces or other punctuation as required between the fields. Continue inserting merge fields and keying text until the form letter is complete.

Save the main document and data source records if you want to use them for future merges. An example of a main document with merge fields inserted for the name and address from a *Contacts* folder is shown in figure 3.12.

FIGURE

3.12 *Main Document in Word*

Mail Merge Toolbar

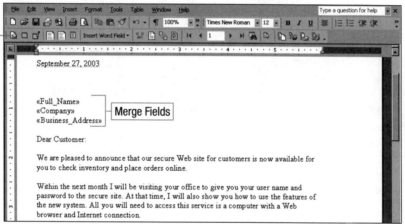

INTEGRATED exercise 18

CREATING A FORM LETTER TO CONTACTS

1. With Outlook open and the *Contacts* folder active in Address Cards view, start a mail merge to create a standard letter to all contacts by completing the following steps:
   a. Click <u>V</u>iew, point to Current <u>V</u>iew, and then click Detailed Address Cards.
   b. Click <u>T</u>ools and then click Mail Merge.

c. Click Contact fields in current <u>v</u>iew in the Fields to merge section in the Mail Merge Contacts dialog box.

d. With <u>A</u>ll contacts in current view selected in the Contacts section, <u>N</u>ew document selected in the Document file section, *Form Letters* as the <u>D</u>ocument type, and *New Document* selected for <u>M</u>erge to in the Merge options section, click OK.

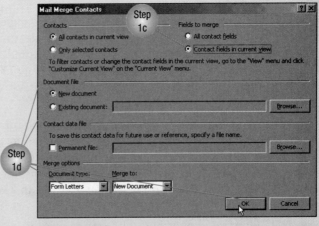

2. Outlook exports the records to a data source file in Microsoft Word. Microsoft Word opens with a clear document screen and the Mail Merge toolbar below the Standard and Formatting toolbars. Create the main document for the form letters in Word by completing the following steps:

a. Key your name and school address at the top of the letter as the return address and then press Enter four times.

b. Key the current date and then press Enter four times.

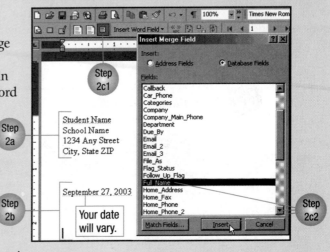

c. Insert the inside address for the letter by completing the following steps:

1) Click the Insert Merge Fields button 📧 on the Mail Merge toolbar.

2) Scroll down the <u>F</u>ields list box in the Insert Merge Field dialog box, click *Full_Name*, and then click <u>I</u>nsert.

3) Click the Close button in the Insert Merge Field dialog box and then press Enter.

4) Click the Insert Merge Fields button, click *Company* in the <u>F</u>ields list box, and then click <u>I</u>nsert.

5) Click Close and then press Enter.

6) Click the Insert Merge Fields button, click *Business_Address* in the <u>F</u>ields list box, click <u>I</u>nsert, click Close, and then press Enter twice.

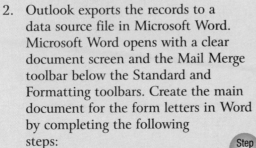

d. Key **Dear Customer:** as the salutation and then press Enter twice.

e. Key the following text as the body of the form letter in the main document:
We are pleased to announce that our secure Web site for customers is now available for you to check inventory and place orders online.

Within the next month I will be visiting your office to give you your user name and password to the secure site. At that time, I will also show you how to use the features of the new system. All you will need to access this service is a computer with a Web browser and Internet connection.

OUTLOOK

> We are looking forward to improved customer service and faster order processing with this system. Please feel free to contact me anytime with your feedback.

    f. Key an appropriate closing for the letter with your name as the signatory a double space below the last paragraph in the letter.

    g. Key your initials a double space below the closing as the writer/typist initials.

    h. Center the letter vertically on the page. Refer to exercise 17, step 2g if you need assistance with vertical centering.

3. Merge the main document with the data source exported from Outlook by completing the following steps:

    a. Click the Merge to New Document button on the Mail Merge toolbar.

    b. With <u>A</u>ll selected in the Merge records section in the Merge to New Document dialog box, click OK.

    c. Word completes the merge in a new document screen. The first letter is currently visible as shown by the Status bar which displays *Page 1 Sec 1 1/7*. Notice the Title bar for the new document is *Letters1*. Scroll the Letters1 document to view all seven of the merged letters.

    d. Click the Print button on the Standard toolbar. *(Note: Check with your instructor before completing this step. He or she may prefer that you print only the first letter rather than all seven.)*

    e. Close the Letters1 document without saving the changes. You are returned to the main document in Word.

4. Click the Save button on the Standard toolbar. Change the Save <u>i</u>n list box to 3½ Floppy (A:), key **Ch03 Ex18 Main Document** in the File <u>n</u>ame text box, and then click <u>S</u>ave. *(Note: Select a different drive and/or folder if you save student files in a location other than the floppy disk drive.)*

5. Click the Print button on the Standard toolbar.

6. Exit Microsoft Word. *(Note: Click <u>N</u>o if prompted to save changes to Ch03 Ex18 when exiting.)*

CHAPTER summary

➤ The *Contacts* folder is used to store information you need about the individuals or companies with whom you communicate by e-mail, fax, letters, or telephone.

➤ The *Contacts* folder is a database, with the information for each individual occupying a record in the folder and each unit of information within the record, such as an e-mail address referred to as a field.

➤ Add a new contact by opening a new Contact window and then keying information into the General, Details, Activities, and All Fields tabs.

➤ Outlook inserts text into the name and address fields based on the way in which the text is keyed unless it cannot recognize the entry, in which case the Check Full Name and Check Address dialog boxes will open automatically for you to complete the entry.

➤ Double-click a contact name in the Information Viewer to open the Contact window to edit information within the fields.

- To delete a contact record, select the contact and then press Delete or click the Delete button on the Standard toolbar.

- When there is more than one person from the same company, you can add the second or third record by basing a new record on an existing one. Select the existing record, click Actions, and then click New Contact from Same Company.

- A Follow Up flag is a reminder to follow up on an outstanding issue with a contact. Display the Flag for Follow Up dialog box and then choose the type of reminder flag and a due date.

- By default, contacts are displayed alphabetically sorted in ascending order by the *File As* field which is the contact's last name followed by first name.

- Display the Sort dialog box to sort the records by up to four fields in ascending or descending order.

- A filter is a subset of contacts that has been selected based on a condition specified in the Filter dialog box. Records that do not meet the condition are temporarily removed and the message *Filter Applied* appears in the Status bar.

- A category can be assigned to a contact record so that the contact list can then be grouped or filtered by the category names to produce different lists of contacts.

- Letter tabs along the right side of the Information Viewer can be used to scroll quickly to the first record that begins with the letter.

- To quickly locate and select a contact record, click in the Find a Contact box, key the name of the individual, and then press Enter.

- Use the Find feature to display a filtered list of all contacts that contain the name or other keyword specified in the Look for text box in the Find bar. The Find bar is displayed by clicking Tools and then Find, or by clicking the Find button.

- Open the Advanced Find dialog box with the Contacts tab active to locate records by keying a word that exists within the record such as a name, telephone number, or e-mail name.

- The More Choices tab in the Advanced Find dialog box can be used to locate contact records by the category to which they have been assigned.

- The View, Current View menu provides several options for displaying contact information such as Address Cards and Detailed Address Cards that display contacts in a columnar arrangement; Phone List that displays in a table format; By Category, By Company, By Location, and By Follow-up Flag that group related contacts together and display the results in a table.

- Fields can be removed from or added to the current view by right-clicking a column heading and then choosing Remove This Column or Field Chooser.

- Open the Contact Options dialog box by clicking Tools, Options, and then clicking the Contact Options button in the Options dialog box, to change the fields upon which records are created, sorted, and displayed.

- You can create an e-mail message, schedule an appointment, or create a letter to a selected contact directly from the *Contacts* folder.

- You can filter or sort data in *Contacts*, and then use the data as the data source in a mail merge that is completed within Microsoft Word.

- A list of names, addresses, and other contact fields, called the data source, is exported to a temporary file to create form letters, mailing labels, or envelopes.

- A second file, called the main document, contains the standard text for each letter and is created in Word.

- Once the main document is created in Word, click the Merge to New Document button to produce a complete letter to each contact record.

OUTLOOK

COMMANDS review

Command	Mouse/Keyboard	
Add a contact	File, New, Contact; or Actions, New Contact	New
Add contact from existing contact	Actions, New Contact from Same Company	
Assign categories	Edit, Categories	
Change current view	View, Current View	
Create letter to a contact	Actions, New Letter to Contact	
Delete a contact	Edit, Delete	✕
Display Contact Options dialog box	Tools, Options, Contact Options	
Filter contacts	View, Current View, Customize Current View, Filter	
Find contacts	Tools, Find	Find
Flag a contact	Actions, Follow Up	⚑
Mail merge contacts	Tools, Mail Merge	
Schedule appointment with a contact	File, New, Appointment; or Actions, New Appointment with Contact	
Send e-mail to a contact	File, New, Mail Message; or Actions, New Message to Contact	
Sort contacts	View, Current View, Customize Current View, Sort	

CONCEPTS check

Completion: On a blank sheet of paper, indicate the correct term or command for each item.

1. Click this button in the Contact window to key the name of the contact in separate fields such as *Title*, *First*, and so on.
2. Click this tab in the Contact window to view a list of e-mail messages, appointments, or other items related to the contact.
3. Click this menu sequence to create a new contact record by basing fields upon an existing record.
4. A Follow Up flag displays in this color if the flag is still active.
5. Click this menu sequence to sort the list of contacts.
6. When some contact records are temporarily removed from the Information Viewer, this message displays in the Status bar.
7. Click this button next to a category name in the By Category view to expand the list.
8. Key a contact name in this box on the Standard toolbar to quickly locate a record.
9. Open this bar to filter the list of contacts by a name or other keyword that is entered in the Look for text box.
10. Open this dialog box to search for a contact by keying the category to which the contact has been assigned.
11. An e-mail message can be sent to a selected contact by clicking File, New, Mail Message, or this menu sequence.
12. Open an Appointment window for a selected contact in the *Contacts* folder by clicking either of these menu sequences.
13. A letter to a selected contact is completed in Microsoft Word with the assistance of a series of dialog boxes referred to as this.
14. A mail merge requires two files, one of which is referred to as a data source and another one which is called this.
15. Outlook exports the contact records to a temporary location where they are used in Word as this file in the mail merge.

SKILLS check

Assessment 1

1. With the *Contacts* folder active in Detailed Address Cards view, add the following records to the appropriate fields:

Mr. Leung Wong	Miss Heather Lyman
Sales Manager, North America	Sales Representative
VSI International	Worldover Enterprises
398 Oxford Street W.	982 Highbury Avenue
Harrisburg, PA 17101	Harrisburg, PA 17124
Bus: 717-555-5891	Bus: 717-555-6598
Fax: 717-555-5892	Fax: 717-555-6599

Mobile: 717-555-3126   Mobile: 717-555-3485
lwong@emcp.vsi.net   hlyman@emcp.worldover.net

Ms. Jan Gorsky   Miss Edna Nadira
Sales Manager   District Manager
Worldwide Marketing   Horizon Sales
231 Forest Avenue   65 Bradley Avenue
Harrisburg, PA 17112   Harrisburg, PA 17101
Bus: 717-555-6588   Bus: 717-555-3256
Fax: 717-555-6589   Fax: 717-555-3257
Mobile: 717-555-2389   Mobile: 717-555-1279
jgorsky@emcp.wwmarketing.net   ednan@emcp.horizonsales.net

2. Change the current view to Address Cards.
3. Print the contact list in *Card Style*.

Assessment 2

1. With the *Contacts* folder active in Address Cards view, edit the contact records as follows:
   Wong, Leung—change street address to: 12-9874 Church Street
   Nadira, Edna—change e-mail address to: ednanadira@emcp.horizonsales.net
   Lyman, Heather—change job title to: Eastern Region Sales Manager
2. Delete the record for *D'Allario, Guiseppina*.
3. Add the following two contacts for VSI International by basing them on the record for *Wong, Leung*:
   Mr. Kenneth McTague   Mrs. Meredith Abruzzi
   Sales Representative   Sales Manager, Europe
   Mobile: 717-555-1495   Mobile: 717-555-6987
   kmctague@emcp.vsi.net   mabruzzi@emcp.vsi.net
4. Print the contact list in *Small Booklet Style*. Click Yes if prompted to proceed with printing with the double-sided settings.

Assessment 3

1. With the *Contacts* folder active in Address Cards view, add Follow Up flags to contact records as follows:
   Nadira, Edna—Follow up with a call; due two weeks from today
   Abruzzi, Meredith—Arrange a meeting; due one month from today
2. Mark the Arrange Meeting flag on *Jorge Tomlinson's* record as completed.
3. Clear the Send Letter flag on *Carla McWilliam's* record.
4. Change the current view to display the records by Follow Up flag.
5. Remove the *File As*, *Business Fax*, *Home Phone,* and *Categories* columns in the By Follow-up Flag view.
6. Print the contact list in *Table Style* in portrait orientation.

Assessment 4

1. With the *Contacts* folder active in the By Follow-up Flag view, change the current view to Detailed Address Cards.
2. Assign the following categories to existing contacts:
   Mr. Leung Wong   Key Customer, Holiday Cards
   Miss Heather Lyman   Association Member, Business

Ms. Jan Gorsky	Association Member, Business
Miss Edna Nadira	Key Customer, Holiday Cards
Mr. Kenneth McTague	Association Member, Business
Mrs. Meredith Abruzzi	Business, International

3. Use the Advanced Find feature to locate all of the records of the contacts who have been assigned the *Association Member* category. When the find is complete, click File in the Advanced Find dialog box, and then click Print. Click OK to print the Association member contact list in *Table Style*.

4. Close the Advanced Find dialog box.

5. Change the current view to display the contact list grouped by category.

6. Expand all categories so that all names are visible below each category heading.

7. Remove the *File As*, *Business Fax*, and *Home Phone* columns in the By Category view.

8. Expand the width of the *Company* column to accommodate the width of the longest entry.

9. Print the contact list in *Table Style*.

10. Change the current view to Detailed Address Cards.

Assessment 5

1. With the *Contacts* folder active in Detailed Address Cards view, change the current view to Address Cards.

2. Sort the contact list first by *Company* in ascending order, then by *Last Name* in ascending order. Click Yes to show the *Company* field and then click No to show the *Last Name* field in the current view.

3. Print the contact list in *Card Style*.

4. Restore the sort order to sort items by *File As* in ascending order.

5. Use the Filter or Find feature to list only those contacts that are employees of VSI International.

6. Print the filtered list in *Phone Directory Style*.

7. Clear the filter so that all records are restored to the Information Viewer.

Assessment 6

1. With the *Contacts* folder active in Address Cards view, create an e-mail message to *Leung, Wong* from Contacts as follows:

    Subject   **New Price List**

    Message

    A new price list has been sent today to reflect a 2% increase in all products. We will continue to honor the old prices for one week only.

2. Print and then send the message.

3. Select the record for *Lyman, Heather* and then schedule the following appointment:

    | *Subject* | **Advertising Campaign** |
    | *Location* | **Conference Room A1021** |
    | *Start time* | two weeks from today at 10:00 AM |
    | *Duration* | 1.5 hours |
    | *Reminder* | 10 minutes |
    | *Label* | Needs Preparation |

4. Display the *Calendar* folder for two weeks from today and then print the Calendar in *Daily Style*.

5. Display the *Contacts* folder.

Assessment 7

1. With the *Contacts* folder active in Address Cards view, create a letter to *Jan Gorsky* using the Letter Wizard as follows.
   a. Include the current date and choose the Professional Letter page design.
   b. Choose the For<u>m</u>al salutation.
   c. Click <u>N</u>ext at the Letter Wizard Step 3 of 4 dialog box to add no other elements to the letter.
   d. Key your first and last name as the <u>S</u>ender's name.
   e. Key your school name and address as the <u>R</u>eturn address.
   f. Choose an appropriate closing for the letter.
   g. Key your initials as the <u>W</u>riter/typist initials.
   h. Key the following text as the body of the letter.
      Our new product line is now available for shipping and we have launched an extensive advertising campaign to coincide with the holiday season.

      The advertising campaign is both print and Web-based including a toll free number to our call center where we have customer service representatives available 24/7.

      If you have any questions about the new products, please feel free to call or e-mail me at any time.
   i. Center the letter vertically on the page.
   j. Print the letter.
   k. Save the letter and name it Ch03 SC07.
2. Exit Microsoft Word.

Assessment 8

1. With the *Contacts* folder active in Address Cards view, perform a mail merge to contacts as follows:
   a. Change the current view to Detailed Address Cards.
   b. Filter the list of contacts to display only those contacts who have been assigned the category *Association Member*.
   c. Display the Mail Merge Contacts dialog box and then click the Contacts fields in current <u>v</u>iew option in the Fields to merge section.
   d. With all other options in the Mail Merge Contacts dialog box at the default settings, click OK to export the contact records to Microsoft Word.
   e. In Microsoft Word, create the main document as follows:
      1) Key your name and school address at the top of the letter as the return address.
      2) Key the current date four lines below the return address.
      3) Insert the merge fields required for the inside address four lines below the date.
      4) Key **Dear Association Member:** as the salutation two lines below the inside address.
      5) Key the following text as the body of the letter:
         The next meeting of the Sales Association will be hosted by VSI International at their Harrisburg office.

         The guest speaker will be Mr. William Neudorf, a leading authority on global marketing and exporting issues.

The cost for the dinner is $22.00 per person payable in advance. Each member is allowed to bring up to three guests. Please let me know within two weeks whether you will be attending and if you will be bringing guests.

      6) Key an appropriate closing to the letter a double space below the last paragraph with your name as the signatory and your title as *Sales Association Events Manager*.

      7) Key your initials as the writer's initials a double space below the closing.

      8) Center the letter vertically on the page.

    f. Merge the main document with the data source to a new document screen.

2. Print the merged letters and then close the document without saving the changes.
3. Save the main document and name it Ch03 SC08 Main Document.
4. Print and then close Ch03 SC08 Main Document.
5. Exit Microsoft Word.

Assessment 9

1. Delete the *Association Member* category name from the Master Category List by completing the following steps:
   a. Click Edit and then click Categories.
   b. Click the Master Category List button in the Categories dialog box.
   c. Click *Association Member* in the list box and then click the Delete button.
   d. Click OK to close the Master Category List dialog box.
   e. Click OK to close the Categories dialog box.
2. The category name will no longer appear in the Available categories list box; however, existing records with the category name associated with them retain the category.

CREATING TASKS, NOTES, AND JOURNAL ENTRIES

PERFORMANCE OBJECTIVES

Upon successful completion of chapter 4, you will be able to:
- Create, update, print, and delete tasks
- Create a recurring task
- Assign a task to someone else
- Respond to a task request
- View and track assigned tasks
- Send task information to other users
- Change the view to create task lists including customizing a filter for a view
- Change task options
- Create, edit, and delete notes
- Assign a category to a note
- Change note options
- Change the note view
- Change journal options to automatically record activities to contacts
- Create, edit, view, and print journal entries including manual entries
- Change the Journal entry view

Outlook Chapter 4

(Note: There are two student data files to copy for this chapter.)

Working in *Tasks* is similar to maintaining a to-do list. Outlook includes the capability to track information about a job such as how much of the task is completed, the priority that has been assigned, and the due date for the task. A task request can be sent via e-mail to someone else so that you can assign him or her responsibility for completing the task.

Use the *Notes* folder to enter small, unstructured text reminders for tasks you want to pursue. For example, you may have an idea for a new project that you do not want to forget. Keying a short description in a note will store the idea for you to follow up at a later time. Notes can be created so that they appear on the desktop, which places these reminders in a prominent location.

With entries created in the *Journal* folder, you can account for time spent on a document or project, or record particulars of a telephone discussion for future reference. The *Journal* can be set up to automatically track certain activities, such as e-mail messages or appointments related to a client in the *Contacts* folder.

Creating and Updating Tasks

Adding activities in *Tasks* is similar to jotting down a list of jobs in a to-do list on your desk. Add tasks in the Information Viewer in the Tasks window shown in figure 4.1, or the TaskPad in the Calendar window. New tasks are added by clicking the mouse over the text *Click here to add a new Task*, keying a short description of the job or activity, and then pressing Enter. If you want to assign a date by which the task must be completed, click in the *Due Date* column, and then key a date or select the date from the drop-down calendar that displays by clicking the down-pointing triangle. A task that is still active after a due date has expired displays in red.

FIGURE

4.1 *The Tasks Folder*

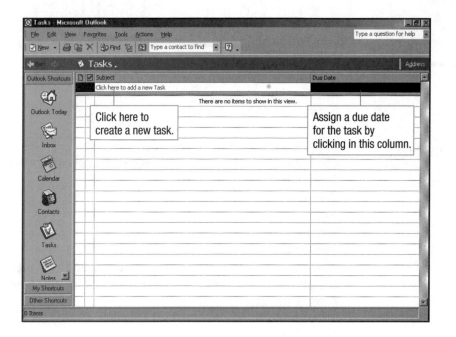

exercise 1

CREATING TASKS

1. With Outlook open, click the Tasks icon on the Outlook bar.
2. Add a new task to the *Tasks* folder by completing the following steps:
   a. Click over the text *Click here to add a new Task* just below the Folder banner.
   b. With the insertion point positioned in a blank text box in the Subject column, key **Assemble research on anti-virus software.**
   c. Press Tab or click in the *Due Date* column and then key **two weeks from today.**

OUTLOOK

d. Press Enter. The task entry moves into the Task table and the insertion point appears inside another blank text box in the *Subject* column.

3. Add a task using the TaskPad in the *Calendar* folder by completing the following steps:

   a. Click the *Calendar* icon on the Outlook bar.
   b. Click over the text *Click here to add a new Task* in the TaskPad.
   c. With the insertion point positioned in a blank text box in the *TaskPad* column, key **Purchase extra toner for printer** and then press Enter.

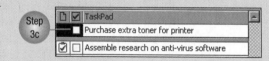

4. Click the *Tasks* icon on the Outlook bar.
5. Click the Print button on the Standard toolbar. With *Table Style* already selected in the Print style section, click OK.

Tasks can also be created in the Task window shown in figure 4.2 by clicking <u>F</u>ile, pointing to Ne<u>w</u>, and then clicking <u>T</u>ask; clicking <u>A</u>ctions and then clicking New Ta<u>s</u>k; or by clicking the New Task button on the Standard toolbar. Key a description of the task in the Subject text box, change other fields as required, and then click the <u>S</u>ave and Close button on the Task window toolbar.

New Task

FIGURE

4.2 *Task Window with Task Tab Selected*

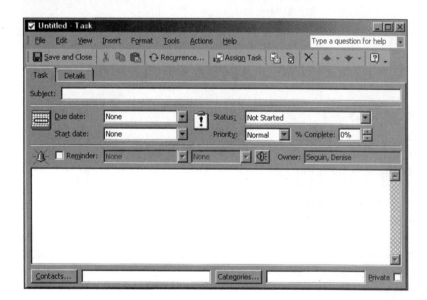

The default status for a new task is *Not Started*. Enter a different status by clicking the down-pointing triangle next to the Status<u>:</u> list box and then choosing from *In Progress, Completed, Waiting on someone else*, or *Deferred*. The default Priority of *Normal* can be changed to *Low* or *High*.

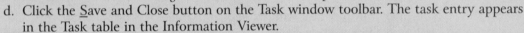

exercise 2

1. With Outlook open and the *Tasks* folder active, add a new task in the Task window by completing the following steps:
   a. Click the New Task button on the Standard toolbar.
   b. With the insertion point positioned in the Subject text box, key **Start budget preparation for next year**.
   c. Click the down-pointing triangle next to the Status: list box and then click *Waiting on someone else* in the drop-down list.
   d. Click the Save and Close button on the Task window toolbar. The task entry appears in the Task table in the Information Viewer.

2. Print only the task entry added in step 1 by completing the following steps:
   a. Click in the *Subject* column for the entry *Start budget preparation for next year*. This selects the entry as indicated by the dotted box surrounding the row and the blue highlighting.
   b. Click the Print button on the Standard toolbar.
   c. Click *Memo Style* in the Print style section of the Print dialog box.
   d. Click OK.

Updating Tasks

Updating tasks can include activities such as changing the Due date, Start date, Status:, Priority, or the % Complete. When a task is finished, you can either delete the task from the Task table, or change the task status to *Completed*. To do this, open the Task window and change the *Status:* field to *Completed*, or click the white check box to the left of the task in the Task table. A completed task displays with a line drawn through dimmed task text.

Delete a task by selecting it and then pressing the Delete key; by clicking the Delete button on the Standard toolbar; or by clicking Edit on the Menu bar and then clicking Delete. The due date can be changed in the Task table by clicking in the *Due Date* column for the task and then keying a new date or selecting one from the drop-down calendar.

Double-click a task in the Task table to open the Task window for the entry and then make changes to the task details as required. To edit the subject text only for a task, position the mouse pointer over the task entry in the Task table and then click the left mouse button. The task will be selected as indicated by a dotted box around the text and an insertion point will appear at the position where the pointer was located. Insert or delete text as required and then click in the table outside the task entry.

OUTLOOK

1. With Outlook open and the *Tasks* folder active, change the status for the task entry *Assemble research on anti-virus software* by completing the following steps:
   a. Position the mouse pointer over the task entry *Assemble research on anti-virus software*, and then double-click the left mouse button to open the Task window.
   b. Click the down-pointing triangle next to the Status: list box and then click *In Progress* in the drop-down list.
   c. Drag to select *0%* in the % Complete text box and then key **40**. *(Note: The spin buttons at the right of the % Complete text box increment the value by 25s.)*
   d. Click the Save and Close button on the Task window toolbar.

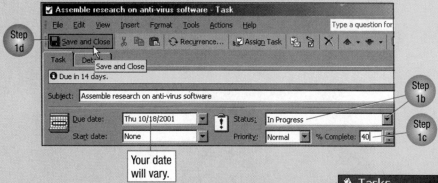

2. Change the status for the task entry *Purchase extra toner for printer* to completed by clicking the white check box to the left of the task in the Task table. A line is drawn through the entry.

3. Change the current view and expand a column width by completing the following steps:
   a. Click View, point to Current View, and then click Detailed List. The Detailed List view adds the *Status*, *% Complete*, and *Categories* columns to the Task table.
   b. Position the mouse pointer on the right column boundary for the *Status* column until the pointer changes to a vertical line with a left-and right-pointing arrow.
   c. Double-click to expand the column to the width of the longest entry.

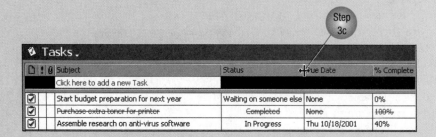

4. Click the Print button on the Standard toolbar. With *Table Style* already selected in the Print style section, click OK.

Creating a Recurring Task

Recurrence

A task that you perform on a regular basis can be set up in a manner similar to a recurring appointment. Recurring tasks appear one at a time in the task list. When you change the status for one occurrence of the task to *Completed*, Outlook automatically generates the next occurrence in the task list. To create a recurring task, open the Task window, key a description of the task in the Subject text box, click Actions on the Task window toolbar and then click Recurrence, or click the Recurrence button on the toolbar. Select the options as required in the Recurrence pattern and Range of recurrence sections of the Task Recurrence dialog box shown in figure 4.3, and then click OK.

FIGURE

4.3 Task Recurrence Dialog Box

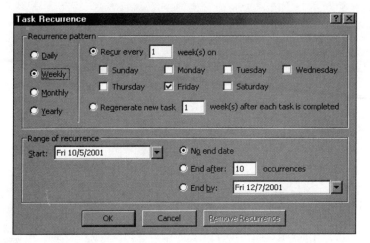

exercise 4

CREATING A RECURRING TASK

1. With Outlook open and the *Tasks* folder active in Detailed List view, add a recurring task to the task list by completing the following steps:
   a. Click File, point to New, and then click Task.
   b. With the insertion point positioned in the Subject text box, key **Prepare month end sales reports**.
   c. Click the Recurrence button on the toolbar in the Task window.
   d. Click Monthly in the Recurrence pattern section.
   e. Click The. The current day of the week displays in the day text box next to The. If necessary, click the down-pointing triangle next to the occurrence list box and select *first*. Then click the down-pointing triangle next to the current day of the week and select *Thursday* so that the Recurrence pattern becomes *The first Thursday of every 1 month(s)*.

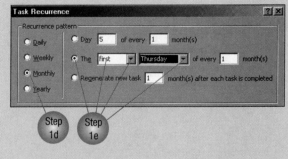

Step 1d   Step 1e

f. Click OK to close the Task Recurrence dialog box. The yellow information box in the Task window above the Subject text box displays the recurrence pattern details.

g. Click Save and Close. The first recurring task is added to the Task table. Notice the icon for the recurring task in the first column of the Task table.

2. Click View, point to Current View, and then click Simple List.

3. Click the Print button on the Standard toolbar. With *Table Style* already selected in the Print style section, click OK.

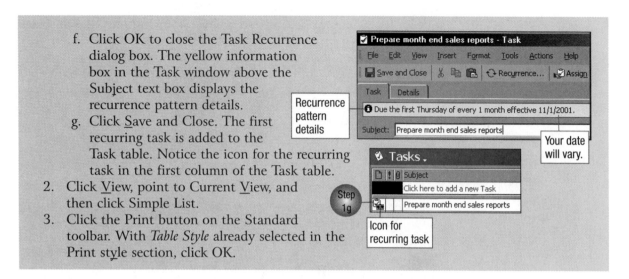

Recurrence pattern details

Step 1g

Icon for recurring task

Your date will vary.

If you created a recurring task with no end date and then want to stop the task from recurring, complete the following steps to stop the automatic generation of the next task entry:

1. Double-click the current recurring entry in the Task table to open the Task window.

2. Click the Recurrence button on the Task window toolbar.

3. Click the Remove Recurrence button at the bottom of the Task Recurrence dialog box. The Task Recurrence dialog box closes and the yellow information box with the recurrence pattern details is removed from the Task window.

4. Click Save and Close in the Task window.

Assigning a Task to Someone Else

You can assign a task to someone else by e-mailing the individual a task request. The recipient of the task request can choose to accept the task, decline the task, or assign the task to someone else. When the recipient accepts the task, the task is automatically added to his or her task list.

If you accept the task, you become the *owner* of the task. The owner is the only person who can make changes to the task details. By default, if the owner updates the task, Outlook sends a copy of the revision to the task originator, and when the owner changes the status of the task to *Completed*, a status report is automatically sent to the task originator.

If you decline the task, you can provide a reason why you are declining, and then the task is returned to the originator of the task request so that he or she can assign the task to someone else. To create a task request, do one of the following actions:

• Click File, point to New, and then click Task Request.
• Click Actions, New Task Request.
• Click the down-pointing triangle on the New Task button and then click Task Request at the drop-down menu.
• Open a new Task window and then click the Assign Task button on the Task window toolbar.

An Untitled - Task window opens with a yellow information box that displays *This message has not been sent* as shown in figure 4.4. The To text box is added above the Subject text box to key the e-mail address of the person to whom you are assigning the task. Two check boxes below the date section are selected by default that instruct Outlook to send updates and completed status reports to the task originator. The <u>S</u>ave and Close button is replaced with the <u>S</u>end button to send the task request via e-mail.

FIGURE

| 4.4 | *Task Request* |

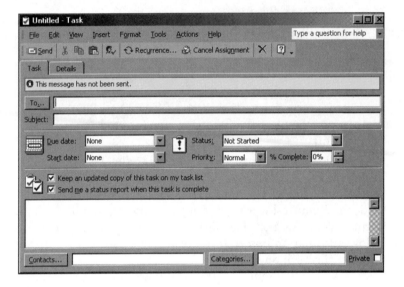

exercise 5

ASSIGNING A TASK TO SOMEONE ELSE

(Note: In this exercise you will be sending a task request by e-mail to the student that you added to your Personal Address Book [PAB] in chapter 1. Check with your instructor if necessary for alternate instructions on to whom you should send the task request.)

1. With Outlook open and the *Tasks* folder active in Simple List view, assign a task to someone else by completing the following steps:
   a. Click <u>A</u>ctions and then click New Task Request.
   b. Click the To button. Click the down-pointing triangle next to the <u>S</u>how Names from the list box in the Select Task Recipient dialog box and then click *Personal Address Book.*
   c. Double-click the name of the student you added to the PAB in chapter 1 to add his or her name to the T<u>o</u> list box.
   d. Click OK to close the Select Task Recipient dialog box.

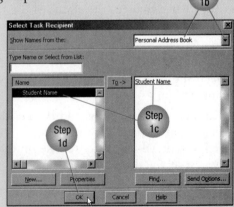

OUTLOOK

 e. Click in the Subject text box and then key **Research anti-virus software**.

 f. Drag to select *None* in the <u>D</u>ue date text box and then key **one week from today**.

 g. Click the down-pointing triangle to the right of the Priorit<u>y</u> list box and then click *High* in the drop-down list. *(Notice that as soon as you click in another field, Outlook automatically converts* one week from today *to a specific date in the* <u>D</u>ue date *field.)*

 h. Click <u>S</u>end. The task is added to the Task table and an e-mail message is sent to the task recipient. The task icon in the first column of the Task table portrays a hand holding a clipboard to indicate the task has been assigned to someone else.

2. Double-click the entry in the Task table for the task assigned to someone else in step 1. The Task window opens with a message indicating the status of the task request. Notice the task *Owner* section shows the e-mail name of the person to whom you sent the task request.

Your date will vary.

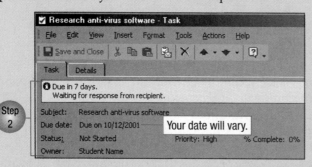

Your date will vary.

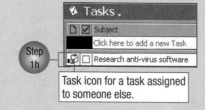

Task icon for a task assigned to someone else.

3. Click the Close button on the right end of the Task window Title bar.

4. View and print the e-mail message to the task recipient by completing the following steps:

 a. Click *Tasks* on the Folder banner.

 b. Click *Sent Items* in the Folder List. *(Note: Click* Outbox *instead of* Sent Items *if the message does not appear in the* Sent Items *folder.)*

 c. Double-click the message header for the task request message sent in step 1.

 d. Read the information in the message window.

 e. Click <u>F</u>ile and then click <u>P</u>rint.

 f. With *Memo Style* selected in the Print style section, click OK.

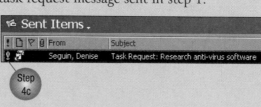

 g. Click the Close button on the message window Title bar.

5. Click *Sent Items* (or *Outbox*) on the Folder banner and then click *Inbox* in the Folder List.

Responding to a Task Request

The recipient of the task will receive a task request message in his or her *Inbox* similar to the one shown in figure 4.5. Upon opening the message, he or she can click Accept, Decline, or Assign Task if he or she wants to delegate the task to someone else. If the task recipient is not connected to a Microsoft Exchange Server, the message will appear slightly different.

FIGURE

4.5 *Task Request Message to Task Recipient*

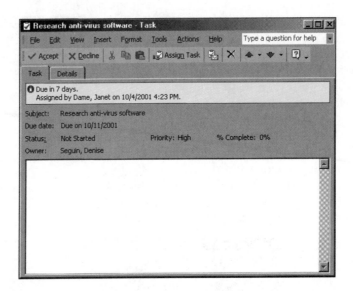

When the recipient clicks Accept or Decline, a message window appears with the information that the task will be accepted and moved into the *Tasks* folder for Accept; or moved to the *Deleted Items* folder for Decline. The recipient has the option to Edit the response before sending so that a few words of explanation can be appended, or Send the response now so that the task originator receives the default response message of *User name has accepted*. The dialog box shown in figure 4.6 appears after clicking the Accept button.

If the recipient clicks Assign Task, the message window changes to a new task request window in which the recipient can then reassign the task to someone else.

FIGURE

4.6 *Accepting Task Dialog Box*

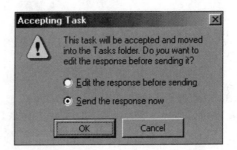

OUTLOOK

Once a task recipient accepts or declines a task, Outlook automatically deletes the task request message from the *Inbox* folder. A copy of the message sent to the task originator is, however, retained in *Sent Items*.

exercise 6

(Note: To complete this exercise another student must have sent you a task request from exercise 5. If you are using Outlook 2002 connected to a server that is <u>not</u> running Microsoft Exchange Server, the task request message will function differently. Wherever possible, alternate instructions have been included. If necessary, check with your instructor for assistance if your screen does not match the instructions.)

1. With Outlook open and the *Inbox* folder active, open the task request message and accept the task by completing the following steps:

   a. Double-click the message header with the subject *Task Request: Research anti-virus software*.

   b. Click A<u>c</u>cept. *(Click Reply if A<u>c</u>cept does not appear in your message window.)*

   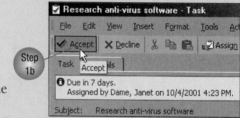

   Step 1b

   c. Click <u>E</u>dit the response before sending in the Accepting Task dialog box and then click OK. *(Skip this step if you clicked Reply in the previous step.)*

   d. With the insertion point positioned in the message editing window, key the following text:

   Preliminary discussions with IT staff indicate that two companies offer attractive site licensing agreements. I will send a report as soon as I have completed the research.

   e. Click <u>S</u>end.

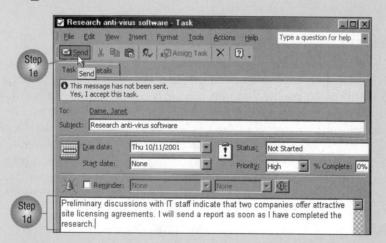

2. Click the *Tasks* icon on the Outlook bar.
3. When you accepted the task request in step 1, Outlook automatically added the task to your Task table. *(Note: If you clicked Reply in step 1b, the task may not appear in your list. If that is the case, you will not be able to complete the instructions that follow in step 3—proceed to step 4.)* Open the Task window and view the entry by completing the following steps:

   a. Double-click the entry in the Task table to open the Task window. *(Note: You will have two tasks in the Task table for* Research anti-virus software *if you have completed both exercises 5 and 6, step 1. Notice the icons are different for a task that you have assigned to someone else and a task that has been assigned to you and accepted.)*

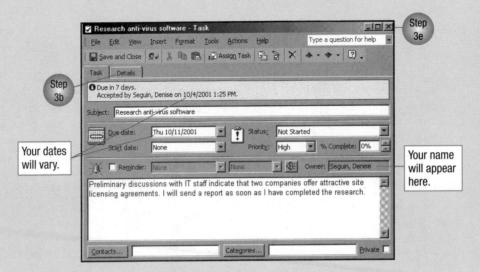

Step 3e

Step 3b

Your dates will vary.

Your name will appear here.

   b. Click the Details tab in the Task window. Notice the name that appears next to Update list is the name of the task originator.

   c. Click File on the Task window Menu bar and then click Print.

   d. With *Memo Style* selected in the Print style section of the Print dialog box, click OK.

   e. Click the Close button on the Task window Title bar.

4. Click the Print button on the Standard toolbar. With *Table Style* already selected in the Print style section, click OK.

Viewing and Tracking Assigned Tasks

By default *Keep an updated copy of this task on my task list*, and *Send me a status report when this task is complete* is active in the Task Request window. Leaving these options turned on means that you can automatically track the status of the task. When the task owner changes any task details, Outlook will generate an update and send it to the name(s) in the Update list on the Details tab. Generally, the update list contains only the name of the task originator, however, if a task request was sent to someone who then delegated the task to someone else, both names in the task request chain will be included. When you open and read the task status message, Outlook updates your copy of the task in the *Tasks* folder and then deletes the status message in the *Inbox*.

When the task owner changes the status of an assigned task to *Completed*, Outlook sends a task completed message back to the task originator. When you open the message, the task status in your folder is also changed to *Completed*. Completed status messages are not deleted from the *Inbox*.

Click View on the Menu bar, point to Current View, and then click Assignment to view a filtered list of tasks that have been assigned to others. The Current View menu option By Person Responsible will display the tasks grouped by the task owner's name which can then be expanded and collapsed as required.

OUTLOOK

(Note: If you clicked Reply in Exercise 6, step 1b, and the assigned task does not appear in your Task table, you will not be able to complete step 1 of this exercise – proceed to step 2.)

1. With Outlook open and the *Tasks* folder active in Simple List view, update the task that was assigned to you by completing the following steps:

   a. Double-click the entry in the Task table for the assigned task that you accepted. *Be careful to double-click the correct Research anti-virus software task – the yellow information box should display the date that you accepted the task.*

   b. Click the down-pointing triangle next to Status: and then click *In Progress* in the drop-down list.

   c. Drag to select *0%* in the % Complete text box and then key **55%**.

   d. Click Save and Close.

2. View and print the Task table in a filtered list of tasks assigned to other users by completing the following steps:

   a. Click View, point to Current View, and then click Assignment. The Task table displays a filtered list of only those tasks that have been assigned to other users. The list is sorted by the owner's name in ascending order and then by the due date in ascending order.

   b. Click the Print button on the Standard toolbar. With *Table Style* selected in the Print style section of the Print dialog box, click OK.

Your date will vary.

3. View and print the Task table in groups by the task owner by completing the following steps:

   a. Click View, point to Current View, and then click By Person Responsible. The Task table displays a group heading for each owner of tasks in the table. The task entries are collapsed below the group headings. The list is sorted by the owner's name in ascending order and then by the due date in ascending order.

   b. Click the expand button (plus symbol) next to the group heading *Owner : Student Name* (where your name is *Student Name*).

   c. Click the expand button (plus symbol) next to the group heading *Owner : Student Name* (where *Student Name* is the name of the person to whom you assigned a task).

Your order may be different. Task list is sorted by owner's name in ascending order and then by due date in ascending order.

    d. If necessary, adjust column widths so that data in all columns is visible within the Information Viewer.

    e. Click the Print button on the Standard toolbar. With *Table Style* selected in the Print style section of the Print dialog box, click OK.

4. Click View, point to Current View, and then click Simple List.

Sending Task Information to Other Users

If you want to e-mail comments about a task to other users, or report the status of the task to the task originator, open the Task window, click Actions on the Task window Menu bar, and then click Send Status Report. A Task Status Report message window will open similar to the one shown in figure 4.7. If the active task is one that was assigned to you by someone else, the name(s) of the task originator(s) in the Update list from the Details tab will automatically be inserted in the To text box. If necessary, key additional e-mail addresses in the To and Cc text boxes. Key the message text in the editing window and then click Send.

FIGURE

4.7 *Task Status Report Message Window*

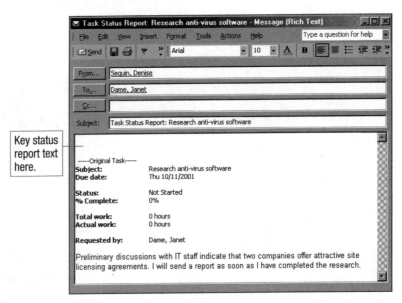

To send a copy of the task to another user, open the Task window, click Actions on the Menu bar, and then click Forward. A message window similar to the one shown in figure 4.8 opens with the task subject automatically inserted in the Subject text box after *FW:*. A copy of the Task window is inserted in the message as a file attachment. Key the e-mail address of the person to whom you want to send the task information in the To text box, key an explanatory message in the editing window, and then click Send. The recipient will receive an e-mail message and can view the task details by double-clicking the attached task name in the message window.

OUTLOOK

4.8 *Forwarded Task Message Window*

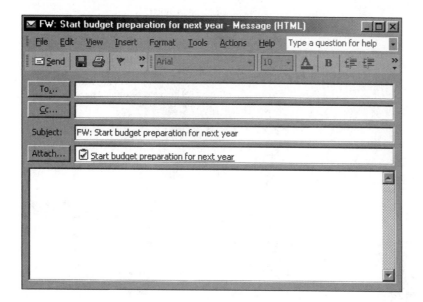

exercise 8

UPDATING AND SENDING TASK INFORMATION TO ANOTHER USER

(Note: In this exercise you will be sending task details by e-mail to the student that you added to your Personal Address Book [PAB] in chapter 1. Check with your instructor if necessary for alternate instructions on to whom you should send the task information.)

1. With Outlook open and the *Tasks* folder active in Simple List view, update the *Start budget preparation for next year* task by completing the following steps:

   a. Double-click the task entry with the subject *Start budget preparation for next year* to open the Task window.

   b. Click the down-pointing triangle next to Priority and then click *High* in the drop-down list.

   c. Click in the editing window and then key the following text:
   Need to create a spreadsheet with last year's budget organized by division and then project a 3% increase in operating funds for next year.

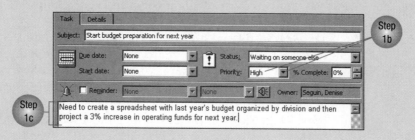

2. With the Start budget preparation for next year Task window still open, send the task information to another user by completing the following steps:
   a. Click Actions on the Task window Menu bar and then click Forward. Click OK at the message that the original action must be saved first.
   b. Click the To button in the message window.
   c. Click the down-pointing triangle next to the Show Names from the list box in the Select Names dialog box and then click *Personal Address Book*.
   d. Double-click the name of the student you added to the PAB in chapter 1 to add his or her name to the To list box in the Message Recipients section.
   e. Click OK to close the Select Names dialog box.
   f. Click in the message editing window and then key the following text:
      I need your help to prepare the budget for next year. The task details with instructions are attached to this message.
   g. Click the Print button on the message window toolbar.
   h. Click Send.

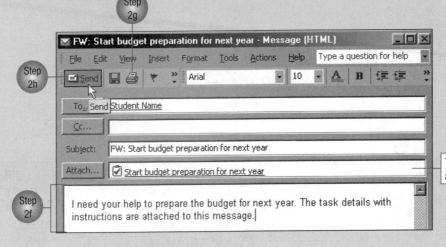

Changing the Task View to Create Task Lists

In exercise 7 you changed the view to create a list of tasks that were assigned to others and a list of tasks grouped by task owner. In addition to these options and the Detailed List view, the Current View menu provides the ability to create the following task lists:

- *Active tasks.* A filtered list of all tasks not marked as complete and sorted in ascending order by the due date.
- *Next Seven Days.* A filtered list of all tasks with a due date that is within the next seven days and sorted in ascending order by the due date.
- *Overdue Tasks.* A filtered list of all tasks that are not marked as complete and are past the due date. The list is sorted in ascending order by due date and then in descending order by priority status.
- *By Category.* The task list is organized by groups according to the category to which they have been assigned. The list is sorted by categories in ascending order and then by due date in ascending order.

OUTLOOK

- *Completed Tasks*. A filtered list of only those tasks where the status has been changed to complete. The list is sorted in descending order by the due date.
- *Task Timeline*. The tasks are displayed in a linear calendar format with the task appearing below its respective due date.

Open the View Summary dialog box to change the sort or filter settings if the available views are not suited to your needs. Click <u>V</u>iew, point to Current <u>V</u>iew, and then click <u>C</u>ustomize Current View to display the View Summary dialog box and change sort or filter settings as required. The Sort and Filter dialog boxes are similar to those used in previous chapters. In exercise 9 you will create a customized task list by adding a criterion to the filter settings for a view..

exercise 9

CREATING TASK LISTS AND CUSTOMIZING A FILTER

1. With Outlook open and the *Tasks* folder active in Simple List view, create and print task lists on the Current <u>V</u>iew menu by completing the following steps:
   a. Click <u>V</u>iew, point to Current <u>V</u>iew, and then click Active Tasks.
   b. Right-click the *Categories* column heading and then click <u>R</u>emove This Column at the shortcut menu.
   c. If necessary, adjust column widths so that data in all columns is visible within the Information Viewer.
   d. Click the Print button on the Standard toolbar. With *Table Style* selected in the Print style section of the Print dialog box, click OK.
   e. Click <u>V</u>iew, point to Current <u>V</u>iew, and then click Next Seven Days.
2. Create and print a customized list of active tasks where you are the task owner by adding an additional criterion to the filter settings for the Active Tasks view by completing the following steps:
   a. Click <u>V</u>iew, point to Current <u>V</u>iew, and then click Active Tasks.
   b. Click <u>V</u>iew, point to Current <u>V</u>iew, and then click <u>C</u>ustomize Current View.
   c. Click the Fi<u>l</u>ter button in the View Summary dialog box.
   d. Click the Advanced tab in the Filter dialog box. The current filter settings are displayed in the Find items that <u>m</u>atch these criteria list box. Notice that the current view is filtered by statuses that indicate a task is still active.
   e. Click the F<u>i</u>eld button in the Define more criteria section of the Filter dialog box.

Step 1b

Current view is filtered by these criteria.

Step 2d

Step 2e

f. Point to *All Task Fields* in the drop-down list of fields and then click *Owner* in the cascading side menu. The field name *Owner* is inserted in the F̲ield text box and the C̲ondition text box automatically inserts the condition *contains*.

g. Click in the Val̲ue text box and then key your last name, a comma, and then your first name as it appears in the *Owner* field in the Task windows that you have viewed. For example *Smith, John*.

h. Click the A̲dd to List button. The criterion is added to the bottom of the Find items that m̲atch these criteria list box.

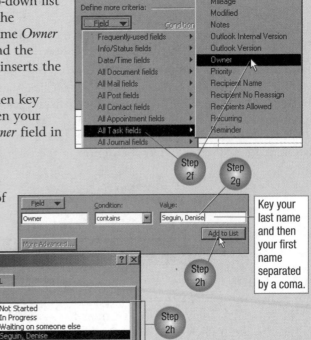

Step 2f

Step 2g

Step 2h

Key your last name and then your first name separated by a coma.

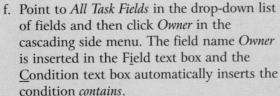

Step 2h

Criterion is added to list box.

Your name should appear here.

i. Click OK to close the Filter dialog box.

j. Click OK to close the View Summary dialog box. The current view now displays only those active tasks that are assigned to you. The task that was assigned in exercise 5 is removed from the list since you are not the owner of the task. The message Filter Applied appears on the Folder banner.

k. If necessary, adjust column widths so that data in all columns is visible within the Information Viewer.

l. Click the Print button on the Standard toolbar. With *Table Style* selected in the Print style section of the Print dialog box, click OK.

3. With the Active Tasks view still active, remove the additional criterion added to the filter by completing the following steps:

a. Click V̲iew, point to Current V̲iew, and then click C̲ustomize Current View.

b. Click the Fi̲lter button in the View Summary dialog box.

c. Click the Advanced tab in the Filter dialog box.

d. Click the criterion added to the Find items that m̲atch these criteria list box beginning with *Owner* that was added to the list in step 2.

e. Click the R̲emove button.

f. Click OK to close the Filter dialog box.

g. Click OK to close the View Summary dialog box. The current view is now filtered by all active tasks.

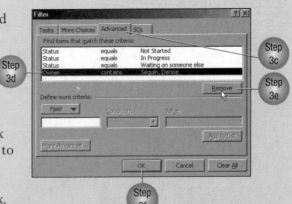

Step 3d

Step 3c

Step 3e

Step 3f

4. Click V̲iew, point to Current V̲iew, and then click Simple List.

OUTLOOK

Changing Task Options

Open the Task Options dialog box shown in figure 4.9 to change the color that overdue and completed tasks are displayed, or to deselect the default options for tracking assigned tasks and setting reminders. Click <u>T</u>ools, <u>O</u>ptions, and then click the <u>T</u>ask Options button in the Options dialog box.

FIGURE

| 4.9 | *Task Options Dialog Box* |

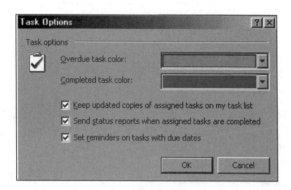

Creating and Editing Notes

A note in Outlook contains a small amount of text that is not structured in any way but is meant to act as a reminder or placeholder to store thoughts, ideas, or other types of messages that you would like to be reminded of or pursue at a later date. Notes can be copied to other folders or placed on the desktop in a location where they will be easily seen.

New Note

To create a new note, activate the *Notes* folder, and then do one of the following actions:

- Click <u>F</u>ile, point to Ne<u>w</u>, and then click <u>N</u>ote
- Click <u>A</u>ctions and then click <u>N</u>ew Note.
- Click the New Note button on the Standard toolbar.
- Right-click in the Information Viewer and then click <u>N</u>ew Note at the shortcut menu.
- Double-click in any unused space within the *Notes* folder.

A yellow note window similar to the one shown in figure 4.10 opens where you key the text that you would like to store. The note window is small, since notes are meant to store short reminders or ideas. The text to the first hard return, or Enter, is used as the Note title and is displayed below the note icon in Icons view, or as a note header in Notes List view. Double-click a note icon to view the remaining text inside the Note if additional text is included. Click the Close button at the right end of the Note Title bar to close the Note window.

4.10 *New Note Window*

Current day and time display at the bottom of the window. —— 10/6/2001 3:21 PM

exercise 10

CREATING NOTES

1. With Outlook open, click the *Notes* icon on the Outlook bar. *(Note: If the* Note *icon is not visible on the Outlook bar, click the down-pointing triangle at the bottom of the Outlook bar to scroll down.)*

2. Create a new note using the toolbar by completing the following steps:
   a. Click the New Note button on the Standard toolbar.
   b. With the insertion point positioned in a Note window, key **Buy Birthday Present for Mom**.
   c. Click the Close button at the right end of the Note Title bar. A note icon appears in the Information Viewer, with the note text below the icon.

Step 2b

Step 2c

3. Create a new note using the mouse by completing the following steps:
   a. Position the mouse pointer in any white area of the Information Viewer and then double-click the left mouse button.
   b. With the insertion point positioned in a Note window, key **New Project Idea**, and then press Enter twice.
   c. Key **Research market potential in the European Union**, and then click the Close button.
   d. Notice the text below the note icon contains only the first line of text that you keyed in the Note window.

Step 2c

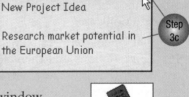

Step 3b

Step 3c

Step 3d

4. Print the two notes created in this exercise by completing the following steps:
   a. With the *New Project Idea* note currently selected, hold down the Ctrl key and then click the *Buy Birthday Present for Mom* note next to it. This selects both notes.
   b. Click the Print button on the Standard toolbar.
   c. With *Memo Style* selected in the Print style section of the Print dialog box, click OK. *(Each note will print on a separate page.)*
   d. Click in any white area in the Information Viewer to deselect the two notes.

Step 4a

OUTLOOK

Editing and Deleting Notes

The content of a note can be edited by double-clicking the note icon to open the Note window. Insert and delete text as required and then click the Close button. A selected note can be deleted by clicking the Delete button on the Standard toolbar or pressing the Delete key.

Delete

exercise 11

CREATING, EDITING, AND DELETING NOTES

1. With Outlook open and the *Notes* folder active, create a new note by completing the following steps:
   a. Click Actions and then click New Note.
   b. With the insertion point positioned in a Note window, key **Renew License** and then click the Close button.
2. Edit the *New Project Idea* note by completing the following steps:
   a. Double-click the *New Project Idea* note icon.
   b. With the insertion point positioned at the beginning of *New* in the note title, press Delete three times to remove the word *New* and then key **Marketing**.
   c. Click the Close button.
3. Delete the *Buy Birthday Present for Mom* note by completing the following steps:
   a. Click the *Buy Birthday present for Mom* note icon.
   b. Click the Delete button on the Standard toolbar.
4. Print the notes in *Table Style* by completing the following steps:
   a. Click View, point to Current View, and then click Notes List.
   b. Click the Print button on the Standard toolbar.
   c. With *Table Style* selected in the Print style section of the Print dialog box, click OK.
5. Click View, point to Current View, and then click Icons.

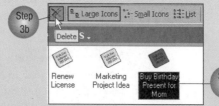

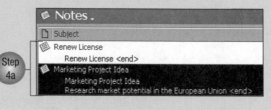

Placing a Note on the Desktop

Since notes are often used as a receptacle for storing reminders, placing a reminder note on the desktop ensures that you will see the prompt. To do this with the Notes folder active, minimize any other open applications that might be active in the background, and then resize the Outlook window until you can see a portion of the desktop. Drag a note icon from the Outlook Information Viewer and drop it on the desktop. The note is copied to the desktop as a separate file with the extension .msg. The two notes are not linked so that any changes made to one of the copies will not be reflected in the other. Figure 4.11 shows a copied note from the Outlook window to the desktop.

FIGURE

4.11 *Note Placed on Desktop*

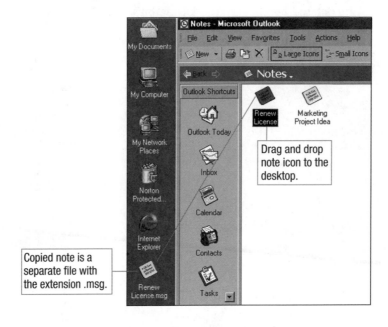

To move a note from the *Notes* folder to the desktop, hold down the Shift key while dragging the icon from the Information Viewer. The note will be placed on the desktop and removed from the *Notes* folder in Outlook.

When the reminder note on the desktop is no longer required, click the note icon on the desktop and then press the Delete key. Click <u>Y</u>es in the Confirm File Delete dialog box.

Assigning a Category to a Note

Notes can be organized by assigning them to categories and then changing to the By Category view. Assigning categories to notes is one way of organizing the folder since notes are typically used for unstructured text. If you use notes often, the Information Viewer can quickly become filled with several notes that are not related in an obvious manner, making locating a specific note more difficult. By default, notes are not sorted by the note title when viewed as icons.

Available categories for notes are the same as for any other Outlook item. Assigning categories to a note is accomplished in a similar manner as for any other Outlook item. A note can be assigned a category while creating it by clicking the note icon at the top left of the Note window and then clicking Categories at the drop-down menu that appears.

OUTLOOK

exercise 12

1. With Outlook open and the *Notes* folder active in Icons view, create a new note using the shortcut menu and assign a category by completing the following steps:
   a. Right-click in any unused area of the Information Viewer and then click New Note at the shortcut menu.
   b. With the insertion point positioned in the Note window, key **Call Kelly for help with Marketing Project**.
   c. Click the note icon at the top left of the Note window.
   d. Click Categories from the drop-down menu.
   e. Click *Ideas* in the Available categories list box and then click OK.
   f. Click the Close button.
2. Right-click the *Renew License* note icon and then click Categories at the shortcut menu. Click *Personal* in the Available categories list box and then click OK.
3. Click the *Marketing Project Idea* note, click Edit, and then click Categories. Click *Ideas* in the Available categories list box and then click OK.
4. Change the current view to By Category, expand the two category lists, and then print the notes by completing the following steps:
   a. Click View, point to Current View, and then click By Category.
   b. Click the expand button (plus symbol) next to *Categories : Ideas*.
   c. Click the expand button next to *Categories : Personal*.
   d. Click the Print button. With *Table Style* selected in the Print style section of the Print dialog box, click OK.
5. Click View, point to Current View, and then click Icons.

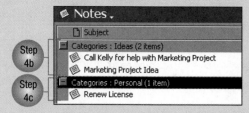

Changing Note Options

Open the Notes Options dialog box shown in figure 4.12 to change the color of the note, the size, or the font for the note text. Click Tools, Options, and then click the Note Options button in the Options dialog box.

FIGURE

4.12 *Notes Options Dialog Box*

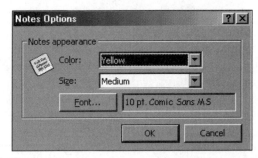

By default, notes are yellow in color, medium-sized, with text set in 10-point Comic Sans MS. The color of an individual note can be changed to make it stand out from the others in addition to changing the color of all new notes in the Notes Options dialog box. Using different colors is another way of organizing notes in the Notes folder.

Changing the Note View

In Icons view, the Standard toolbar contains buttons for changing the view from Large Icons to Small Icons and List. The Current View menu offers additional options for changing the view to Notes List, Last Seven Days, By Category, and By Color. As seen in exercise 11, Notes List view displays the notes one below the other with the entire note text visible, the date the note was created, and the category it has been assigned. The notes are arranged in the order they were created with the most recent at the top of the list.

exercise 13

CHANGING THE COLOR OF NOTES AND THE VIEW

1. With Outlook open and the *Notes* folder active in Icons view, change the color of all new notes and then create a new note by completing the following steps:
    a. Click Tools, Options, and then click Note Options in the Options dialog box.
    b. Click the down-pointing triangle next to Color and then click *Green* in the drop-down list.
    c. Click OK to close the Notes Options dialog box.
    d. Click OK to close the Options dialog box.
    e. Click File, point to New, and then click Note.
    f. With the insertion point positioned in a green Note window, key **Arrange meeting with Seth about anti-virus research.**
    g. Click the Close button. Notice the new note created is the color green while existing notes stayed yellow.

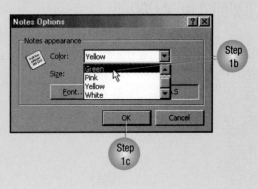

2. Right-click the *Renew License* note, point to Color at the shortcut menu, and then click *Blue*.

3. Change the current view to By Color, expand the three color lists, and then print the notes by completing the following steps:

   a. Click <u>V</u>iew, point to Current <u>V</u>iew, and then click By Color.
   b. Click the expand button next to *Color : Blue*.
   c. Click the expand button next to *Color : Green*.
   d. Click the expand button next to *Color : Yellow*.
   e. Click the Print button. With *Table Style* selected in the Print st<u>y</u>le section of the Print dialog box, click OK.

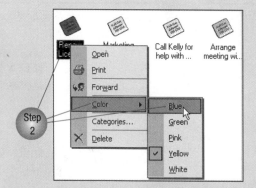

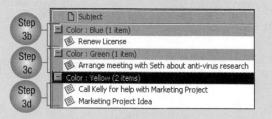

4. Click <u>V</u>iew, point to Current <u>V</u>iew, and then click Icons.

5. Change the color of all new notes back to the default color of yellow by completing the following steps:

   a. Click <u>T</u>ools, <u>O</u>ptions, and then click <u>N</u>ote Options in the Options dialog box.
   b. Click the down-pointing triangle next to Co<u>l</u>or and then click *Yellow* in the drop-down list.
   c. Click OK to close the Notes Options dialog box.
   d. Click OK to close the Options dialog box.

Creating Journal Entries

The *Journal* folder is a place where you can keep track of events or items that you want to remember such as what was said during a telephone conversation, the date a contract was signed, or the time spent working on a document for a client.

The ability to see at a glance your daily activities in one location can be an invaluable tool if you are required to reconstruct your day for any reason. Besides work that is completed using the computer, a journal entry could be created for time spent on noncomputer-related activities. For example, if part of your day is spent filing paper documents, you could create an entry to record the time you started filing and the duration of the task.

To open the journal, click My Shortcuts on the Outlook bar and then click the *Journal* icon. If the Microsoft Outlook message box shown in figure 4.13 displays asking if you want to turn the journal on, click <u>Y</u>es. Clicking the <u>P</u>lease do not show me this dialog again check box before responding <u>Y</u>es or <u>N</u>o will prevent the dialog box from reappearing each time you click the *Journal* icon.

4.13 *Activate Journal Dialog Box*

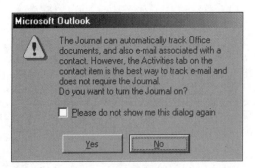

The Information Viewer displays journal entries in a timeline with eight days displayed in the default Week view as shown in figure 4.14. Entries stored in the *Journal* will appear below the date for which they are associated and are categorized by the type of entry. For example, e-mail messages are grouped separately from tasks.

FIGURE

4.14 *Journal Weekly View*

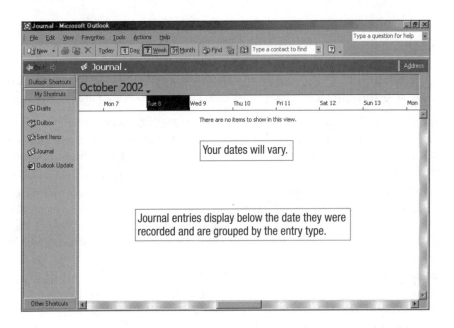

OUTLOOK

Automatically Recording Journal Entries

Outlook can automatically track e-mail messages; meeting requests, cancellations, and responses; and task requests and responses for individual contacts by activating the items in the Journal Options dialog box. In addition to Outlook items, the journal can automatically record documents that have been worked on in Word, Excel, PowerPoint, or Access.

Open the Journal Options dialog box shown in figure 4.15 to specify the Outlook items for contacts that you would like to automatically record and the types of Office documents that you want to track. Clicking an application such as Microsoft Access in the Also record files from list box means that each time you work in a database in Access, an entry will be recorded in the Journal with the date and time that you worked on the file and the path name to the database. The *Journal* will display an icon for the file that can be used as a shortcut to open the database. The action that is performed when you double-click a journal entry is also specified in *Journal* Options.

FIGURE

4.15 *Journal Options Dialog Box*

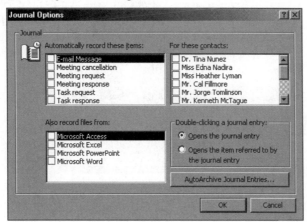

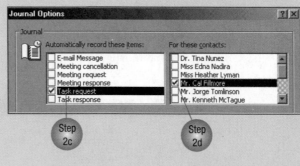

exercise 14

AUTOMATICALLY RECORDING JOURNAL ENTRIES FOR A CONTACT

1. With Outlook open, click My Shortcuts at the bottom of the Outlook bar and then click the *Journal* icon. Click Yes if the dialog box shown in figure 4.13 displays.
2. Turn on automatic recording of task requests for a contact by completing the following steps:
   a. Click Tools and then click Options.
   b. Click the Journal Options button in the Options dialog box.
   c. Click the Task request check box in the Automatically record these items list box.
   d. Click the check box for Mr. Cal Fillmore in the For these contacts list box.

e. Click OK to close the Journal Options dialog box.

f. Click OK to close the Options dialog box.

3. Create a task request to Mr. Cal Fillmore, view, and then print the associated journal entry that was automatically created by completing these steps:

a. Click the Outlook Shortcuts button at the top of the Outlook bar.

b. Click the *Tasks* icon on the Outlook bar.

c. Click the down-pointing triangle on the New Task button on the Standard toolbar and then click Task Request at the drop-down menu.

d. Click the To button in the Task window.

e. Click the down-pointing triangle next to the Show Names from the list box and then click *Contacts* in the drop-down list.

f. Double-click *Cal Fillmore* in the Name list box to add the name to the To list box and then click OK.

g. Click in the Subject text box and then key **Discuss co-op advertising budget for next year**.

h. Click the down-pointing triangle next to Priority and then click *High* in the drop-down list.

i. Click in the editing window and then key the following text:
Give me a call at your convenience to discuss how we can help with your advertising needs for next year. I have money budgeted for your company in our co-op advertising budget.

j. Click Send. *(Note: Since the e-mail addresses used for contacts in this book are fictitious, you will receive an undeliverable message in your* Inbox *from the mail server.)*

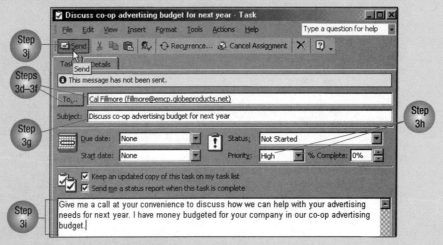

k. Click the My Shortcuts button at the bottom of the Outlook bar and then click the *Journal* icon.

l. Click the expand button (plus symbol) next to *Entry Type : Task request*. The journal entry created as a result of sending the task request to Cal Fillmore is displayed below the current date.

m. Double-click the journal entry to view the contents of the Journal Entry window.

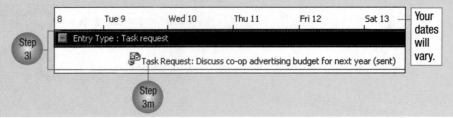

n. Double-click the shortcut to the Task Request in the editing window.
o. Click the Close button on the Task Request Title bar.
p. Click the Print button on the Journal Entry toolbar.
q. Click the Close button on the Journal Entry Title bar.

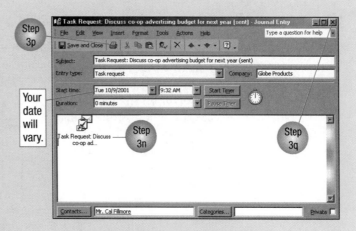

Step 3p

Your date will vary.

Step 3n

Step 3q

Tracking Office Documents in the Journal

Any document created in Word, Excel, Access, or PowerPoint can be automatically logged in the journal. Open the Journal Options dialog box to turn on automatic journaling of an application. Every file you open in the application, including the date, time, and how long the file was active is logged. If you work in an office that bills clients based on time spent on files, this feature is a valuable tool for documenting activities. The journal creates a link to the document so that you can open the document directly within the *Journal* folder. This may be advantageous if you work on several files during the course of a day that are stored in various folders on your system.

Depending on your needs, automatic journaling of files can create numerous journal entries that may or may not be needed. If you only occasionally need to log a document, manually recording the file in the journal would be preferable. To do this, open both Outlook and the My Computer or Windows Explorer window *(whichever method you prefer for viewing files on your computer)*, resize the windows so that they are both visible on the desktop, navigate to the location of the file in My Computer or Windows Explorer, and then drag the icon for the file to the *Journal* icon on the Outlook bar.

exercise 15

MANUALLY RECORDING A WORD DOCUMENT IN THE JOURNAL

(Note: To complete this exercise, you must have copied the student data files for this chapter to your data disk and the disk should be in the drive.)
1. With Outlook open and the *Journal* folder active in <u>W</u>eek view, manually create a journal entry to record a Word document by completing the following steps:
   a. Resize the Outlook window to approximately half the width of the desktop. If necessary move the window so that Outlook is positioned at the right side.
   b. If necessary, minimize any other open applications besides Outlook to the Taskbar.
   c. Double-click the *My Computer* icon on the desktop.
   d. Double-click the *3½ Floppy (A:)* icon in the My Computer window. *(Note: Navigate to a different drive and/or folder if your data files are stored in a location other than the floppy disk.)*

e. Resize the My Computer window to fit within the left side of the desktop. Both windows should now be visible.

f. Position the mouse pointer on the icon for the Word document *Co-opAdvertising.doc*, hold down the left mouse button, drag the file to the *Journal* icon on the Outlook bar and then release the mouse. A Journal Entry window will open in Outlook.

g. Click the Close button on the 3½ Floppy (A:) window Title bar. The Journal Entry window will move to the foreground. *(Note: If your computer is set to cascade the My Computer windows, click the Close button on the My Computer window Title bar so that Outlook is the only application left open.)*

h. Click the down-pointing triangle to the right of the Duration text box and then click *30 minutes* in the drop-down list.

i. Click the Save and Close button on the Journal Entry toolbar.

j. Maximize the Outlook window.

k. Click the expand button next to *Entry Type : Document*.

2. Change the current view for the journal and print the entries in table format by completing the following steps:

a. Click View, point to Current View, and then click Entry List.

b. Right-click the *Categories* column heading and then click Remove This Column at the shortcut menu.

c. Click the Print button on the Standard toolbar.

d. With *Table Style* selected in the Print style section of the Print dialog box, click OK.

e. Click View, point to Current View, and then click By Type.

Recording Other Activities in the Journal

Journal

Activities such as telephone discussions, conversations, or other noncomputer-related activities can be recorded through manual journal entries by opening the Journal Entry window.

To create a journal entry to record other activities, do one of the following actions:

- Click File, point to New, and then click Journal Entry.
- Click Actions and then click New Journal Entry.
- Click the New Journal Entry button on the Standard toolbar.
- Double-click in any unused space within the *Journal* folder.

A Journal Entry window opens which is similar in structure to an appointment window as shown in figure 4.16. By default, Entry type is *Phone Call* and the current day and time display next to Start time. A Start Timer button is

included which will track the amount of time spent on the journal entry. The elapsed time will be displayed in the Duration text box after the timer is started and then the Pause Timer button is clicked. The timer is useful if you need to track or bill clients for time spent on consultations during telephone calls. You could open the Journal Entry window, key the client's name and/or discussion topic in the Subject text box, and then click Start Timer when the telephone call is engaged. Key any notes about the discussion, such as the comments made during the telephone call, in the editing window at the bottom of the window.

FIGURE

4.16 *Journal Entry Window*

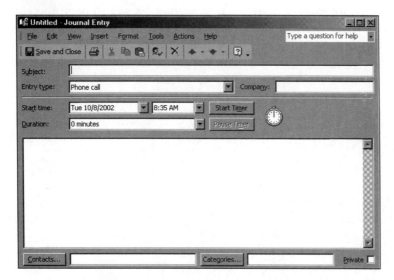

exercise 16

CREATING A JOURNAL ENTRY FOR A TELEPHONE CALL

1. With Outlook open and the *Journal* folder active in By Type view, create a journal entry to record a telephone discussion by completing the following steps:
   a. Click the New Journal Entry button on the Standard toolbar.
   b. With the insertion point positioned in the Subject text box, key **Consultant for marketing project.**
   c. Click in the editing window and then key the following text:
   Spoke with Tory O'Shea from O'Shea Market Research Associates. They can provide consulting services for us on the European project at an

   hourly rate of $75.00, billed monthly. Another service that is available is access to demographic profiles by region. These can be customized to our needs and are charged by individual report. Tory said a report usually costs $300-$500.

d. Click the <u>S</u>ave and Close button on the Journal Entry toolbar.
e. A new heading is added to the weekly timeline view for *Entry Type : Phone Call*.
f. Click the expand button next to *Entry Type : Phone Call*. The journal entry appears below the current date with a telephone icon and the subject text.
g. Click <u>V</u>iew, point to Current <u>V</u>iew, and then click Entry List.
h. Click the Print button on the Standard toolbar.
i. With *Table Style* selected in the Print style section of the Print dialog box, click OK.
j. Click <u>V</u>iew, point to Current <u>V</u>iew, and then click By Type.

Modifying a Journal Entry

Double-click a journal entry in the Information Viewer to open the entry in the Journal Entry window where you can make changes to the details. For example, an entry can be modified to change the time spent on the item, assign a contact name or category to the activity, or key update notes within the editing window.

exercise 17

1. With Outlook open and the *Journal* folder active in By Type view, modify the journal entry for the task request to Cal Fillmore by completing the following steps:
   a. If necessary, click the expand button next to *Entry Type : Task request*.
   b. Double-click the entry for the *Task Request: Discuss co-op advertising budget for next year (sent)*.
   c. Click the down-pointing triangle next to Entry type and then click *Task response* in the drop-down list.
   d. Click in the editing window beside the *Task Request* icon to position an insertion point, press Enter twice to move down the editing window below the icon, and then key the following text:
      Cal is prepared to start a new ad campaign soon but needs to wait for approval from the corporate office.
   e. Click the Print button on the Journal Entry toolbar.
   f. Click <u>S</u>ave and Close. Notice the editing of the entry has caused a new heading to appear.

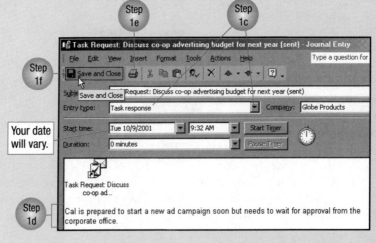

OUTLOOK

g. Click the expand button next to *Entry Type : Task response.*

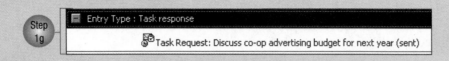

In chapter 3, exercise 15 you viewed e-mail messages sent to a contact on the Activities tab in the Contact window. Using the *Contacts* folder to view Outlook items by contact is preferable to the *Journal* since all of the items for the selected contact are shown in one place. Open the Contact window and then click the Activities tab. Outlook searches the Outlook folders and will list items that have been assigned to the contact's name.

CHAPTER summary

➤ Add jobs in your to-do list as tasks in the *Tasks* window or the TaskPad in the *Calendar* window.

➤ New tasks are added by clicking the mouse over the text *Click here to add a new Task*, keying a short description of the job, entering a due date if necessary, and then pressing Enter.

➤ Tasks can also be created by opening the Task window, keying a description of the task in the Subject text box, changing other fields as required, and then clicking the <u>S</u>ave and Close button.

➤ Double-click a task entry to open the Task window and make changes to the task details such as changing the <u>D</u>ue date, Sta<u>r</u>t date, Status:, Priorit<u>y</u>, or the % Comp<u>l</u>ete.

➤ When a task is finished, you can either delete the task from the Task table, or change the task status to *Completed*.

➤ A task that you perform on a regular basis can be set up as a recurring task. Recurring tasks appear one at a time in the task list—when you mark the existing occurrence of the task completed, Outlook automatically generates the next occurrence in the task list.

➤ You can assign a task to someone else by e-mailing the individual a task request.

➤ The task recipient can choose to accept the task, decline the task, or assign the task to someone else.

➤ When you accept a task request, you become the owner of the task. The owner is the only person who can make changes to the task details.

➤ By default, the originator of the task request is notified whenever the owner updates the task information or marks the task complete.

➤ The Current Ⅴiew menu provides several options to create and view task lists including creating a filtered list of only those tasks that have been assigned to others or displaying all tasks grouped by the task owner's name which can then be expanded and collapsed as required.

➤ Open the View Summary dialog box to change sort and/or filter settings to create a customized task list.

➤ You can e-mail comments about a task to other users, or report the status of the task to the task originator by opening the Task window, clicking Actions on the Menu bar, and then clicking Send Status Report.

➤ A copy of a task can be sent via e-mail to another user by opening the Task window, clicking Actions on the Menu bar, and then clickng Forward.

➤ Change the color that overdue and completed tasks are displayed or deselect the default options for tracking assigned tasks and setting reminders in the Task Options dialog box.

➤ Items in the *Notes* folder contain small amounts of unstructured text. Notes are generally created to be reminders or placeholders to store thoughts or ideas.

➤ The content of a note can be edited by double-clicking the note icon to open the Note window.

➤ Delete a note by clicking the note icon and then pressing the Delete key or clicking the Delete button on the Standard toolbar.

➤ A note can be copied or moved to the desktop to place a reminder in a prominent location.

➤ Assigning categories to notes is one way of organizing the folder since the Information Viewer can quickly become filled with several notes that are not related in an obvious manner.

➤ The color of an individual note can be changed to make it stand out from the others in addition to changing the color of all new notes in the Notes Options dialog box.

➤ The Current Ⅴiew menu provides options for changing the *Notes* folder from the default Icons view to Notes List, Last Seven Days, By Category, and By Color.

➤ The *Journal* folder is used to record entries for items that you want to remember such as what was said during a telephone conversation or the time spent working on a document for a client.

➤ Open the Journal Options dialog box to automatically track e-mail messages; meeting requests, cancellations, and responses; and task requests and responses for individual contacts.

➤ In addition to Outlook activities, documents created in Word, Excel, Access, or PowerPoint can be automatically or manually logged in the journal.

➤ To manually create an entry in the journal for a document, drag the file icon for the document from its source location to the *Journal* icon on the Outlook bar.

➤ Open a journal entry window to record noncomputer-related activities such as telephone calls, conversations, or time spent on miscellaneous activities.

➤ Double-click a journal entry to open the Journal Entry window where you can make changes to the details such as changing the type of entry or keying additional notes about the activity.

COMMANDS review

Command	Mouse/Keyboard	
Add task	Click File, New, Task; or click Actions, New Task	
Assign task	Click File, New, Task Request; or click Actions, New Task Request	
Assign categories	Click Edit, Categories	
Change current view	Click View, Current View	
Create a note	Click File, New, Note; or click Actions, New Note	
Create a journal entry	Click File, New, Journal Entry; or click Actions, New Journal Entry	
Delete task, note, or journal entry	Click Edit, Delete	
Send task status report	Click Actions, Send Status Report	
Send task information	Click Actions, Forward	
Task, Note, or Journal Options	Click Tools, Options	

CONCEPTS check

Completion: On a blank sheet of paper, indicate the correct term or command for each item.

1. Tasks can be created in the *Tasks* folder or in this folder.
2. Click this button in the Task window to set up a task that occurs on a regular basis.
3. When you assign a new task to someone else, he or she is notified of the task through this communication.
4. When an individual receives a task request, he or she responds by selecting Accept, Decline, or this.
5. Change to this view to create a list of only those tasks that have been assigned to someone else.
6. By default, overdue tasks are displayed in this color.
7. A task that is finished can either be deleted from the folder or retained in the folder with this status.
8. A note that has been created as a reminder to do something can be copied here to place it in a more prominent location.

9. One way of organizing notes is to group them by these.
10. An individual note can be changed to a different color or all new notes can be changed to a different color in this dialog box.
11. This view displays the notes one below the other with the entire note text visible along with the date and category.
12. Journal entries can be automatically created for Outlook items that are related to these individuals.
13. A journal entry for a document can be created using the mouse by completing this action with a window open for the file list and Outlook open at the same time.
14. This is the default Entry type when you open a new Journal Entry window.
15. By default, journal entries are displayed in a weekly timeline and grouped by this characteristic.

SKILLS check

Assessment 1

1. With Outlook open, display the *Calendar* folder and then add the following tasks in the TaskPad.
   Prepare anti-virus research presentation
   Prepare anti-virus executive summary
   Develop implementation schedule and cost projection
2. Delete the task with the subject *Start budget preparation for next year.*
3. Mark the task with the subject *Assemble research on anti-virus software* completed.
4. Display the *Tasks* folder and then create the following recurring task:
   a. Key **Monitor budget against actual spending** as the Subject.
   b. The task will recur monthly on the first Friday of the month.
   c. Assign a high-priority status to the task.
   d. Assign the task to the *Business* and *Goals/Objectives* categories.
5. Change the current view to Detailed List.
6. Print the tasks in *Table Style*.

Assessment 2

1. With Outlook open and the Tasks folder active in Detailed List view, create a task request as follows:

Task Recipient	Student from your Personal Address Book
Subject	**Anti-virus presentation**
Due Date	**two weeks from today**
Priority	High
Notes	

   Prepare a 10-minute presentation in PowerPoint on the importance of protecting a computer from viruses and worms. Include in the presentation recommendations for safe computer usage.
2. With the Task Request window open, print the task in Memo Style.
3. Send the task request.

Assessment 3

(Note: In order to complete this assessment, you must have received the task request in assessment 2 from another student.)

1. With Outlook open and the *Tasks* folder active in Detailed List view, display the *Inbox*.
2. Open the *Task Request: Anti-virus presentation* message and then respond to the request as follows:
   a. Decline the task request and then key the following response to the task originator:
      Please accept my regrets, but I cannot complete this task for you as I have just learned I have been transferred to another division.
   b. Print the response message.
   c. Send the response message to the originator.
3. Display the *Tasks* folder.

Assessment 4

1. With Outlook open and the *Tasks* folder active in Detailed List view, double-click the entry in the Task table with the subject *Prepare month-end sales reports*.
2. Click the Assign Task button on the Task window toolbar to delegate this task to someone else.
3. Click the To button and then add the name of the student you added to your Personal Address Book as the task recipient.
4. Send the task request.

Assessment 5

(Note: In order to complete this assessment, you must have completed exercise 6 where you accepted the task request to research anti-virus software.)

1. With Outlook open and the *Tasks* folder active in Detailed List view, double-click the entry in the Task table with the subject *Research anti-virus software*. Be sure to open the task that was assigned to you by another student and that you accepted.
2. Update the task as follows:
   a. Change the % Complete to 100%.
   b. Delete the text in the editing window.
3. With the Task window open, print the task in *Memo Style*.
4. Save and Close the Task window.

Assessment 6

1. With Outlook open and the *Tasks* folder active in Detailed List view, change the current view to Assignment.
2. Print the task list in *Table Style*.
3. Change the current view to By Person Responsible.
4. Expand the tasks below each owner's name and then print the task list in *Table Style*.
5. Change the current view to Simple List.

Assessment 7

1. With Outlook open and the *Tasks* folder active in Simple List view, change to the *Notes* folder.

2. Create the following two notes:
   Order two cases of photocopy paper
   Find out when next performance evaluation is due
3. Change the current view to Notes List.
4. Print the notes in *Table Style*.

Assessment 8

1. With Outlook open and the *Notes* folder active in Notes List view, change the current view to Icons.
2. Change the color of the following individual notes:
   Find out when next performance evaluation is due   *Blue*
   Order two cases of photocopy paper   *Green*
3. Change the current view to By Color and then expand the notes below each color heading.
4. Print the notes in *Table Style*.
5. Change the current view to Icons.

Assessment 9

(Note: To complete this assessment, you must have copied the student data files for this chapter to your data disk and the disk should be in the drive.)

1. With Outlook open and the *Notes* folder active in Icons view, display the *Journal* folder.
2. Open the Journal Options dialog box and then activate the following options:
   a. *Meeting request* in the Automatically record these <u>i</u>tems list box.
   b. *Mrs. Carla McWilliams* in the <u>F</u>or these contacts list box.
   c. *Microsoft Excel* in the A<u>l</u>so record files from list box.
3. Start Microsoft Excel, open the file named CoopAdvertisingBudget.xls, and then make the following changes to the cells indicated:
   C3   change from 1,500,000   to   1,775,000
   C5   change from 2,750,000   to   2,225,000
4. Save the worksheet using the same name (CoopAdvertisingBudget.xls).
5. Print the worksheet and then exit Microsoft Excel.
6. With Outlook open and the *Journal* folder active, display the *Calendar* folder.
7. Create and <u>S</u>end a new meeting request as follows:
   To   Mrs. Carla McWilliams (add her name to the <u>R</u>equired list box in the Select Attendees and Resources dialog box)
   Subject   **Sales promotion plan**
   Location   **Executive conference room**
   Start time: **Next Friday, 10:00 AM**
   Duration   *1 hour*
8. Display the *Journal* folder.
9. Change the current view to Entry List and then print the journal entries in *Table Style*.
10. Change the current view to By Type.

Assessment 10

1. With Outlook open and the *Journal* folder active in By Type view, open the Journal Options dialog box and then remove automatic recording of the following options:
   a. *Meeting request* and *Task request* in the Automatically record these <u>i</u>tems list box.
   b. *Mr. Cal Fillmore* and *Mrs. Carla McWilliams* in the <u>F</u>or these contacts list box.
   c. *Microsoft Excel* in the A<u>l</u>so record files from list box.

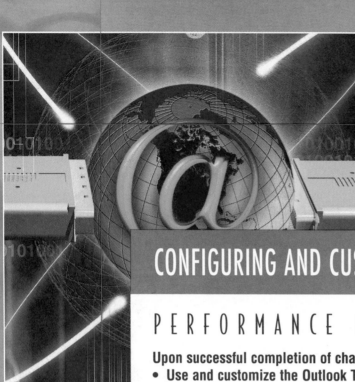

CONFIGURING AND CUSTOMIZING OUTLOOK

PERFORMANCE OBJECTIVES

Upon successful completion of chapter 5, you will be able to:
- Use and customize the Outlook Today page
- Change the folder that Outlook displays on startup
- Customize the Outlook bar
- Add, move, and remove options on menus
- Add, move, and remove buttons on toolbars
- Customize an Outlook view and restore a view to its original settings
- Create and use a custom form
- Specify advanced mail options
- Apply color to message headers for quick identification
- Specify Microsoft Word as the e-mail editor and viewer
- Set security and encryption options
- Create and configure a dial-up connection
- Create an offline folders file for remote use
- Specify folders for offline use and synchronize offline folders
- Switch from working online to working offline
- Download messages for remote use
- Create and use a personal folders file

(Note: There are no student data files to copy for this chapter however you will need a blank formatted disk for exercise 22 and assessment 8.)

A multitude of options are available for configuring Outlook to operate in the way that best suits your preferences. Outlook menus, toolbars, views, and forms can be customized to complement your working environment.

Setting up a dial-up connection, remote mail, and offline folders allow you to work with Outlook when you are away from the computer that you normally use. Synchronizing Outlook folders ensures that changes made to either folder while working offline or online are updated so that both files are identical.

The file where Outlook saves information is referred to as a *personal information store (pst)*. Additional pst files can be created as a method of organizing data or as a way to back up data in folders on the central server.

Using and Customizing Outlook Today

The Outlook Today page provides a glimpse of your current day by displaying a list of appointments, tasks, and the number of e-mail messages that you have received or not sent. You can instruct Outlook to display Outlook Today as the starting page whenever you open the program. The layout of the Outlook Today page and the content that is displayed can be customized to suit your needs.

Click the *Outlook Today* icon on the Outlook bar to display the Outlook Today page shown in figure 5.1. By default, five days of appointments, meetings, and events from the Calendar are displayed in the first column. Active tasks are displayed in the second column in descending order by due date with overdue tasks in red. The third column provides the number of messages that are currently not read in the *Inbox*, as well as any messages that may be saved in *Drafts* or the *Outbox*.

FIGURE

5.1 **Outlook Today Page**

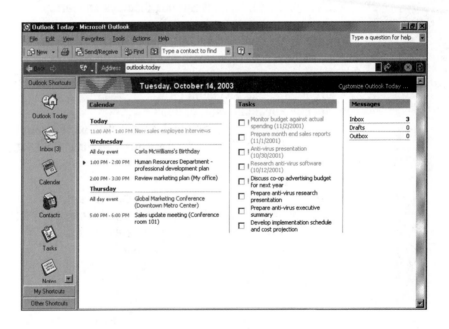

Each entry on the page is a link to the individual window or folder so that the user can click an appointment, task, or folder name and view the details directly from Outlook Today.

OUTLOOK

1. With Outlook open, click the *Outlook Today* icon on the Outlook bar.
2. View folders and update tasks from the Outlook Today page by completing the following steps:

    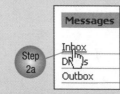

    a. Click the *Inbox* folder name in the Messages section. Notice *Inbox* appears underlined and the pointer changes to a hand with the index finger pointing upward as in a hyperlink when pointing at the word *Inbox*.

    b. With the *Inbox* folder active, click the <u>B</u>ack button to the left of the Folder banner.

    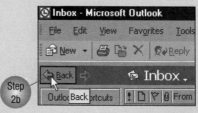

    c. Click over the task text *Prepare anti-virus executive summary*.

    d. With the Task window open, change the % Comp<u>l</u>ete to 25% and then click <u>S</u>ave and Close.

    e. Click the Completed check box next to the task *Prepare anti-virus research presentation*.

3. Customize the appearance of Outlook Today and set it as the page that is displayed whenever Outlook is started by completing the following steps:

    a. Click C<u>u</u>stomize Outlook Today located at the right side of the Outlook Today banner.

    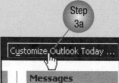

    b. Click the When starting, go directly to Outlook Today check box in the Startup section of the Customize Outlook Today window.

    c. Click the down-pointing triangle next to Show this number of days in my calendar in the Calendar section, and then click *2* in the drop-down list.

    d. Click the down-pointing triangle next to Show Outlook Today in this style in the Styles section, and then click *Winter* in the drop-down list.

    e. Click the Print button on the Standard toolbar and then click OK in the Print dialog box.

    f. Click Save Changes at the right side of the Customize Outlook Today banner. The Outlook Today page with the new settings appears in the Information Viewer.

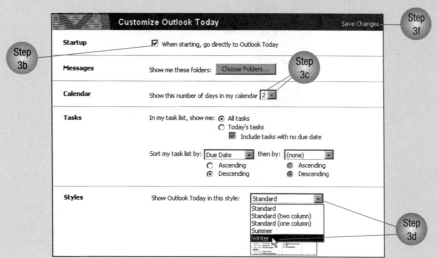

4. Click File and then Exit to close Microsoft Outlook. In the next step you will reopen Outlook to verify that Outlook Today is the default page shown.

5. Click *Start*, point to *Programs*, and then click *Microsoft Outlook*, or click the Launch Microsoft Outlook button on the Quick Launch toolbar. If necessary, enter your user name and password to connect to the server. The customized Outlook Today page appears in the Outlook window. Click the Print button on the Standard toolbar and then click OK in the Print dialog box.

6. Restore Outlook Today to the default settings by completing the following steps:
   a. Click Customize Outlook Today at the bottom of the Messages section.
   b. Click the When starting, go directly to Outlook Today check box in the Startup section of the Customize Outlook Today window to deselect it.
   c. Click the down-pointing triangle next to Show this number of days in my calendar in the Calendar section, and then click *5* in the drop-down list.
   d. Click the down-pointing triangle next to Show Outlook Today in this style in the Styles section, and then click *Standard* in the drop-down list.
   e. Click Save Changes at the right side of the Customize Outlook Today banner.

Specifying the Startup Folder

By default, *Inbox* is the active folder that is displayed when Outlook is started, or, as seen in the previous topic, Outlook Today can be set as the starting page. Open the Advanced Options dialog box shown in figure 5.2 to change the startup folder to any of the other Outlook folders. For example, you may prefer to have the *Calendar* folder automatically displayed whenever Outlook is started so that you can immediately see the day's appointments, meetings, and events.

FIGURE

5.2 *Advanced Options Dialog Box*

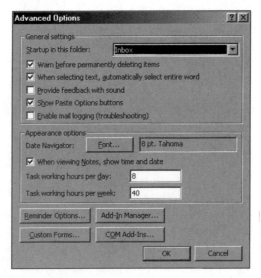

To open the Advanced Options dialog box, click Tools, Options, click the Other tab in the Options dialog box, and then click Advanced Options.

OUTLOOK

1. With Outlook open, and the Outlook Today page displayed, change the startup folder to the *Calendar* by completing the following steps:
   a. Click Tools and then click Options.
   b. Click the Other tab in the Options dialog box.
   c. Click the Advanced Options button in the General section of the Options dialog box with the Other tab selected.
   d. Click the down-pointing triangle next to Startup in this folder and then click *Calendar* in the drop-down list.
   e. Click OK to close the Advanced Options dialog box.
   f. Click OK to close the Options dialog box.

2. Click File and then Exit to close Microsoft Outlook. In the next step you will restart Outlook to verify that the *Calendar* folder is displayed when Outlook is opened.

3. Click *Start*, point to *Programs*, and then click *Microsoft Outlook*, or click the Launch Microsoft Outlook button on the Quick Launch toolbar. If necessary, enter your user name and password to connect to the server. The *Calendar* is displayed when Outlook is opened.

4. Change the startup folder back to the *Inbox* by completing the following steps:
   a. Click Tools, click Options, and then click the Other tab in the Options dialog box.
   b. Click the Advanced Options button in the Options dialog box.
   c. Click the down-pointing triangle next to Startup in this folder and then click *Inbox* in the drop-down list.
   d. Click OK to close the Advanced Options dialog box and then click OK to close the Options dialog box.

Advanced Options   **? X**

General settings

Startup in this folder: | Inbox |

Inbox
Calendar
Contacts
Tasks

☑ Warn before permanently
☑ When selecting text, aut
☐ Provide feedback with so

Step 1d

Customizing the Outlook Bar

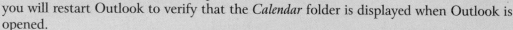

Three groups of icons exist on the Outlook bar: Outlook Shortcuts, My Shortcuts, and Other Shortcuts. The Outlook bar displays either large icons or small icons. Large icons is the default setting for Outlook Shortcuts and Other Shortcuts. Icons in the My Shortcuts group are displayed as small icons. Right-click in any blank area of the Outlook bar to display the shortcut menu shown in figure 5.3 to make changes to the Outlook bar.

5.3 *Outlook Bar Shortcut Menu*

To free up more space in the Information Viewer, you may choose to hide the Outlook bar while viewing a folder with a large amount of information. Hide the Outlook bar by clicking Hide Outlook Bar at the shortcut menu displayed in figure 5.3, or click View and then click Outlook Bar to remove the check mark on the option. Redisplay the Outlook bar after hiding it by clicking View on the Menu bar and then clicking Outlook Bar.

Icons can be moved on the Outlook bar by dragging and dropping the icon to the desired location. To move an icon from its current location on Outlook Shortcuts, My Shortcuts, or Other Shortcuts to any of the other groups, drag the icon to the desired group name. The Outlook bar will change to the target group where you can drop the icon in the location where you would like it to be relocated.

exercise 3

HIDING, REDISPLAYING, AND CUSTOMIZING THE OUTLOOK BAR

1. With Outlook open and the *Calendar* folder displayed, hide and then redisplay the Outlook bar by completing the following steps:
   a. Position the mouse pointer in any blank area of the Outlook bar and then right-click.
   b. Click Hide Outlook Bar at the shortcut menu. Notice the viewing area is increased.
   c. Click *Calendar* on the Folder banner and then click *Contacts* in the Folder List.
   d. Click View, point to Current View, and then click Address Cards. *(Note: Skip this step if your Contacts folder is already displayed in Address Cards view.)* Notice that without the Outlook bar, more contact records can be displayed in the Information Viewer.

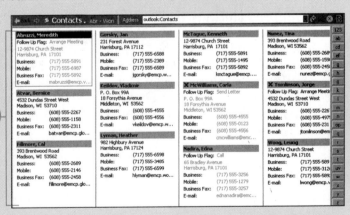

Step 1d

e. Click <u>V</u>iew and then click <u>O</u>utlook Bar to redisplay the Outlook bar.

2. Customize the appearance of the Outlook bar by changing to small icons and increasing the width of the bar by completing the following steps:

   a. Right-click in any blank area of the Outlook bar and then click S<u>m</u>all Icons at the shortcut menu.

   b. Position the mouse pointer on the right border of the Outlook bar until the pointer changes to a double vertical line with a left- and right-pointing arrow, hold down the left mouse button, drag right approximately 0.25 inch, and then release the left mouse button.

3. Move the *Sent Items* icon from the My Shortcuts group to the Outlook Shortcuts group below *Inbox* by completing the following steps:

   a. Click My Shortcuts at the bottom of the Outlook bar.

   b. Position the mouse pointer over the *Sent Items* icon, hold down the left mouse button, drag to Outlook Shortcuts at the top of the Outlook bar *(the Outlook bar will change to display the Outlook Shortcuts)*, drag just below the *Inbox* icon and above the *Calendar* icon *(a black line will appear indicating the position where the icon will be placed)*, and then release the left mouse button. *(Note: If you do not have a Sent Items icon on My Shortcuts, select another icon to move.)*

4. Restore the Outlook bar to the default settings by completing the following steps:

   a. With Outlook Shortcuts displayed, right-click in any blank area of the Outlook bar and then click Large Icons at the shortcut menu.

   b. Drag the right border of the Outlook bar left approximately 0.25 inch to decrease the width of the Outlook bar.

   c. Position the mouse pointer over the *Sent Items* icon, hold down the left mouse button, drag to My Shortcuts at the bottom of the Outlook bar, drag just above the *Journal* icon, and then release the left mouse button.

5. Click Outlook Shortcuts at the top of the Outlook bar and then click the *Tasks* icon.

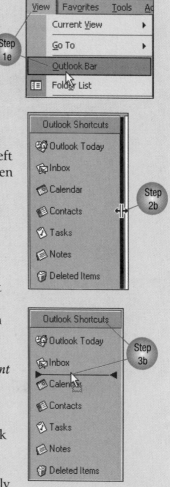

Customizing Menus

In chapter 1 you learned about Outlook's adaptive menus and toolbars that personalize the environment you are working within. After working with Outlook for a while you will get a feel for the options that you use frequently, those you use less frequently, and those that you do not use at all. For those options or commands that you do not use at all, you may choose to remove them from the menus or toolbars altogether. If an option or command that you use frequently is at the bottom of the menu, you could move it closer to the top to make it more easily accessible.

To customize menus in Outlook, open the Customize dialog box by clicking Tools and then Customize, and then perform the following actions for adding, removing, or moving a menu item.

- *Add a menu item.* Click the Commands tab in the Customize dialog box. Click the name of the category that the option is found within in the Categories list box. Drag the option from the Commands list box to the target menu, and while still holding down the left mouse button, drag the pointer to the location where you want the option to appear on the drop-down menu, and then release the mouse. Close the Customize dialog box. Figure 5.4 shows the Address Book being added to the View menu.
- *Move a menu item.* With the Customize dialog box open, click the menu that contains the option that you want to move. Drag the item from its current location on the drop-down menu to the desired location, and then close the Customize dialog box. Figure 5.5 shows Options being repositioned on the Tools menu.
- *Remove a menu item.* With the Customize dialog box open, click the menu that contains the option that you want to remove, drag the item from the drop-down menu into the Customize dialog box, and then close the Customize dialog box.

FIGURE

5.4 *Adding Address Book to the View Menu*

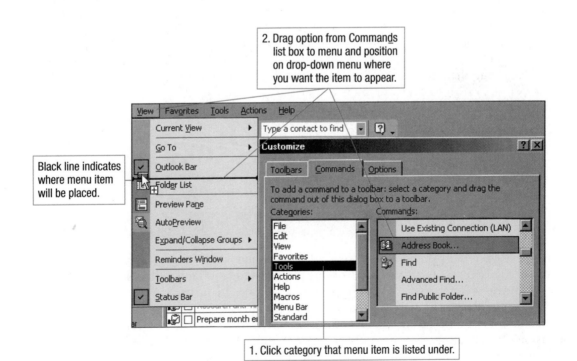

2. Drag option from Commands list box to menu and position on drop-down menu where you want the item to appear.

Black line indicates where menu item will be placed.

1. Click category that menu item is listed under.

5.5 Moving Options on the Tools Menu

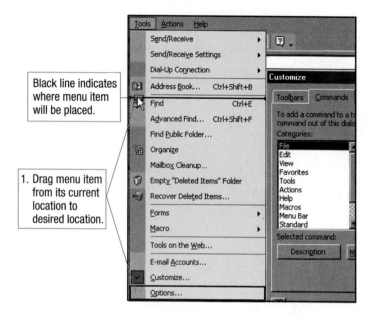

Black line indicates where menu item will be placed.

1. Drag menu item from its current location to desired location.

exercise 4

ADDING, MOVING, AND REMOVING ITEMS FROM MENUS

1. With Outlook open and the *Tasks* folder active, add the Address Book to the View menu by completing the following steps:
   a. Click Tools and then click Customize.
   b. Click the Commands tab in the Customize dialog box.
   c. Click *Tools* in the Categories list box.
   d. Scroll down the Commands list box until you see Address Book. Position the mouse pointer on *Address Book* in the Commands list box, drag to View on the Menu bar *(the View drop-down menu appears)*, drag between Outlook bar and Folder List on the View menu, and then release the mouse.
   e. Click the Close button in the Customize dialog box.

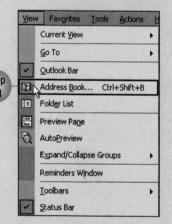

Step 1d

2. Move Options from the bottom of the Tools menu closer to the top by completing the following steps:
   a. Click Tools and then click Customize.
   b. With the Customize dialog box open, click Tools on the Menu bar.

c. Position the mouse pointer on <u>O</u>ptions, hold down the left mouse button, drag near the top of the <u>T</u>ools menu between Dial-Up Co<u>n</u>nection and Address <u>B</u>ook, and then release the mouse.

d. Click the Close button in the Customize dialog box.

3. Remove Address <u>B</u>ook from the <u>V</u>iew menu by completing the following steps:

a. Click <u>T</u>ools and then click <u>C</u>ustomize.

b. With the Customize dialog box open, click <u>V</u>iew on the Menu bar.

c. Position the mouse pointer on Address <u>B</u>ook, hold down the left mouse button, drag Address <u>B</u>ook to the Customize dialog box, and then release the mouse. An icon of a command button and a close button is attached to the pointer as you drag the mouse.

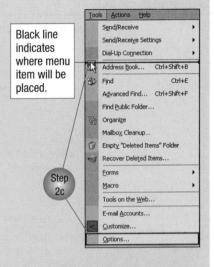

Black line indicates where menu item will be placed.

Step 2c

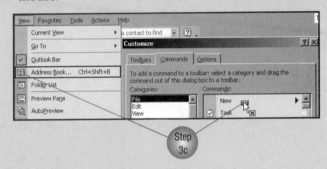

Step 3c

d. Click the Close button in the Customize dialog box.

4. Move <u>O</u>ptions back to the bottom of the <u>T</u>ools menu by completing steps similar to those in steps 2a–2d.

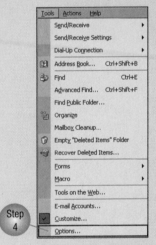

Step 4

Adding and Removing Buttons from Toolbars

Toolbar Options

With the default setting of Standard and Formatting toolbars occupying the same row, you may find that you are clicking the Toolbar Options button often to locate features that are not visible. Although toolbars are adaptive and a button moves to a visible location after it has been clicked from the Toolbar Options button, your preference may be to move the button to the toolbar in a more prominent location.

If a button on the Standard or Formatting toolbars is never used by you, consider removing it to allow room for other buttons that you do use. Additional buttons can be added to the toolbar for one-click access to frequently used commands. For example, you may want to add the Go to button to a toolbar to provide faster access to the feature rather than using the menus.

Click the Toolbar Options button on the toolbar that you want to customize, point to <u>A</u>dd or Remove buttons, point to the toolbar that you want to customize, and then select or deselect options from the cascading side menu. Figure 5.6 illustrates the <u>A</u>dd or Remove buttons Standard menu from a new message window.

OUTLOOK

5.6 *Add or Remove Buttons Menu for Standard Toolbar in Message Window*

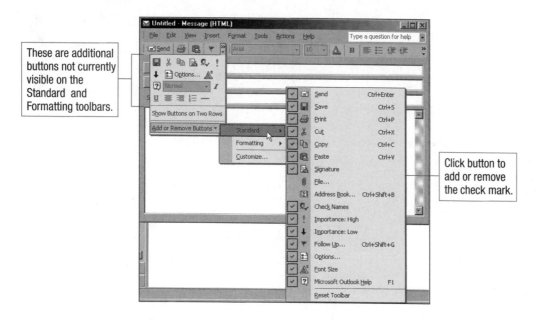

These are additional buttons not currently visible on the Standard and Formatting toolbars.

Click button to add or remove the check mark.

Options with a check mark beside them are active on the current menu. Click a checked option to deselect it and remove it from the toolbar. The Reset Toolbar option at the bottom of each Toolbar Options menu is used to restore the toolbar to its original settings. To add a button to a toolbar that is not found on the menu, click Customize from the Add or Remove Buttons menu. The same Customize dialog box that was used to add, move, and remove options on menus is displayed. Follow a procedure similar to that used to add, move, and remove options on menus to customize the toolbar.

The Show Buttons on Two Rows option on the Toolbar Options drop-down menu will split the Standard and Formatting toolbars to two rows in the window. This will provide you with a full row of Standard toolbar buttons and a full row of Formatting toolbar buttons. Click this option if you use toolbars often and don't mind giving up the space within the window that the extra row will occupy.

exercise **5**

ADDING, MOVING, AND REMOVING BUTTONS ON TOOLBARS

1. With Outlook open and the *Tasks* folder active, add the Print Preview button to the Standard toolbar by completing the following steps:
   a. Click the Toolbar Options button at the end of the Standard toolbar.
   b. Point to Add or Remove Buttons and then click Customize.
   c. If necessary, click the Commands tab in the Customize dialog box.
   d. With *File* already selected in the Categories list box, scroll down the Commands list box until you see *Print Preview*.

e. Position the mouse pointer on *Print Preview* in the Comman<u>d</u>s list box, drag to the Standard toolbar between the <u>N</u>ew and Print buttons, and then release the mouse.

f. Click the Close button in the Customize dialog box.

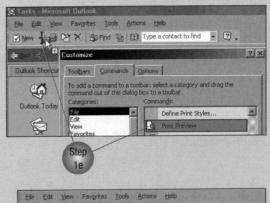

Step 1e

2. Move the Address Book button next to the Print button by completing the following steps:

a. Click the Toolbar Options button at the end of the Standard toolbar.

b. Point to <u>A</u>dd or Remove Buttons and then click <u>C</u>ustomize.

c. Position the mouse pointer on the Address <u>B</u>ook button on the Standard toolbar, hold down the left mouse button, drag to position the button between the Print and Move to Folder buttons, and then release the mouse.

Step 2c

d. Click the Close button in the Customize dialog box.

3. Remove the Organize button from the Standard toolbar by completing the following steps:

a. Click the Toolbar Options button at the end of the Standard toolbar.

b. Point to <u>A</u>dd or Remove Buttons and then point to Standard.

c. Click Organi<u>z</u>e to deselect it.

d. Click in the Information Viewer outside the menu to remove it.

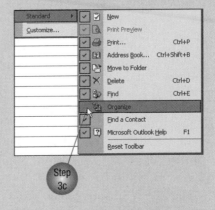

Step 3c

4. Restore the toolbar to the original settings by completing the following steps:

a. Click the Toolbar Options button at the end of the Standard toolbar.

b. Point to <u>A</u>dd or Remove Buttons and then point to Standard.

c. Click <u>R</u>eset Toolbar.

d. Click OK at the message *Are you sure you want to reset the changes made to the 'Standard' toolbar?*

e. Click in the Information Viewer outside the menu to remove it.

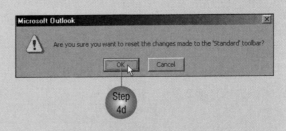

Step 4d

Customizing a View

In previous chapters you learned how to customize the current view by sorting, grouping, and filtering, and how to add and remove columns from the current view using the shortcut menu. In this topic, you will learn how to customize the current view using Fields and Other Settings in the View Summary dialog box.

To change a predefined view in any Outlook folder, display the view that you want to change, click View, point to Current View, and then click Customize Current View to open the View Summary dialog box. Click the Fields button in the View Summary dialog box to open the Show Fields dialog box. Figure 5.7 illustrates the Show Fields dialog box for the Active Tasks view in *Tasks*. The fields displayed in the list boxes will be dependent on the view that is active when the dialog box is opened.

FIGURE

5.7 *Show Fields Dialog Box for Active Tasks View*

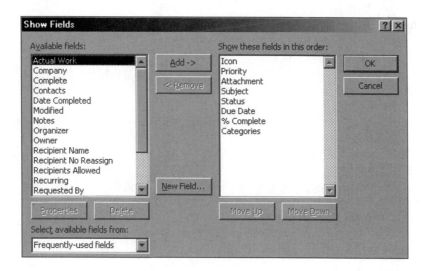

The Show these fields in this order list box displays the current view's fields in the order that they are presented in the Information Viewer. Click a field name and then click Remove to delete the column from the current view. Add a new column to the current view by scrolling in the Available fields list box, clicking the desired field name, and then clicking Add. To move a column, drag the field name in the list box to the desired location. Click OK when all changes have been made.

1. With Outlook open and the *Tasks* folder active, click <u>V</u>iew, point to Current <u>V</u>iew, and then click Active Tasks.
2. Customize the Active Tasks view by adding, deleting, and moving columns by completing the following steps:
   a. Click <u>V</u>iew, point to Current <u>V</u>iew, and then click <u>C</u>ustomize Current View.
   b. Click <u>F</u>ields in the View Summary dialog box.
   c. Click *Owner* in the A<u>v</u>ailable fields list box and then click <u>A</u>dd.
   d. Click *Attachment* in the Sh<u>o</u>w these fields in this order list box and then click <u>R</u>emove.
   e. Click *Categories* in the Sh<u>o</u>w these fields in this order list box and then click <u>R</u>emove.
   f. Position the mouse pointer over *Owner* in the Sh<u>o</u>w these fields in this order list box, hold down the left mouse button, drag until the dashed red line is positioned between Subject and Status, and then release the mouse. *(Note: You can also move a selected field using the Move <u>U</u>p and Move <u>D</u>own buttons.)*

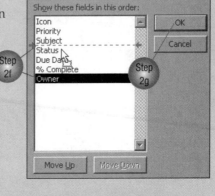

   g. Click OK to close the Show Fields dialog box.
   h. Click OK to close the View Summary dialog box.
3. Adjust column widths as necessary so that all data is visible within the columns.
4. Change the font of the column headings and data by completing the following steps:
   a. Click <u>V</u>iew, point to Current <u>V</u>iew, and then click <u>C</u>ustomize Current View.
   b. Click <u>O</u>ther Settings in the View Summary dialog box.
   c. Click <u>F</u>ont in the Column headings section.

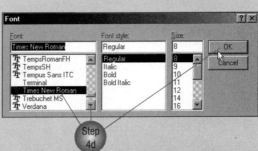

   d. Scroll down the <u>F</u>ont list box, click *Times New Roman*, and then click OK.
   e. Click <u>F</u>ont in the Rows section.
   f. Scroll up the <u>F</u>ont list box, click *Arial*, and then click OK.
   g. Click OK to close the Other Settings dialog box.
   h. Click OK to close the View Summary dialog box.

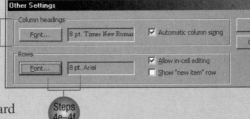

5. Click the Print button on the Standard toolbar. With *Table Style* selected in the Print style section of the Print dialog box, click OK. *(Note: The printout will correctly show the layout of the columns in the current view; however, font changes are for display purposes only. To change fonts for printing purposes, display the Page Setup dialog box and then click the Format tab.)*

To restore a predefined view that has been customized back to its original settings, activate the view, click <u>V</u>iew, point to Current <u>V</u>iew, and then click <u>D</u>efine Views. The Define Views for *"Folder Name"* dialog box opens with *<Current view settings>* in the View Name list box. Click R<u>e</u>set and then click OK at the message box that asks if you are sure you want to reset the view back to its original settings.

Changes made to fonts in the current view are retained despite restoring the columns to their original settings. Restore fonts by changing fonts back to the original fonts used in the Other Settings dialog box.

exercise 7

RESTORING THE CUSTOMIZED VIEW TO THE ORIGINAL SETTINGS

1. With Outlook open and the *Tasks* folder active in Active Tasks view, restore the view back to the original settings by completing the following steps:
   a. Click <u>V</u>iew, point to Current <u>V</u>iew, and then click <u>D</u>efine Views.
   b. With *<Current view settings>* selected in the View Name list box in the Define Views for "Tasks" dialog box, click R<u>e</u>set.
   c. Click OK at the message box asking *Are you sure you want to reset the view "Active Tasks" to its original settings?*
   d. Click Close at the bottom of the Define Views for "Tasks" dialog box.
2. Restore the fonts for the Active Tasks view back to the original settings by completing the following steps:
   a. Click <u>V</u>iew, point to Current <u>V</u>iew, and then click <u>C</u>ustomize Current View.
   b. Click <u>O</u>ther Settings in the View Summary dialog box.
   c. Click <u>F</u>ont in the Column headings section, scroll up the <u>F</u>ont list box, click *Tahoma*, and then click OK.
   d. Click <u>F</u>ont in the Rows section, scroll down the <u>F</u>ont list box, click *Tahoma*, and then click OK.
   e. Click OK to close the Other Settings dialog box and then click OK to close the View Summary dialog box.
   f. Adjust column widths as necessary so that all data is visible within the columns.

Steps
1–2

🗅	!	🔋	Subject	Status	Due Date ▲	% Complete	Categories
☑			Develop implementation schedule and cost projection	Not Started	None	0%	
☑			Prepare anti-virus executive summary	In Progress	None	25%	
🗐	!		**Discuss co-op advertising budget for next year**	**Not Started**	**None**	**0%**	
🗐	!		Research anti-virus software	Not Started	Fri 10/12/2001	0%	
🗐	!		Anti-virus presentation	Not Started	Tue 10/30/2001	0%	
🗐	!		Prepare month end sales reports	Not Started	Thu 11/1/2001	0%	
🗐	!		Monitor budget against actual spending	Not Started	Fri 11/2/2001	0%	Business, Go...

3. Click the Print button on the Standard toolbar. With *Table Style* selected in the Print style section of the Print dialog box, click OK.
4. Click <u>V</u>iew, point to Current <u>V</u>iew, and then click Simple List.

Creating Forms

When you create an e-mail message, schedule an appointment, add a contact record, or add a task, you are using one of Outlook's built-in forms in the Standard Forms Library. Every item that is created in Outlook is based on a form. Forms are used to standardize the way that data is entered. Some of Outlook's standard forms may not coincide with the work flows in your organization. For example, the contact form may contain fields that you will never use and may be missing fields for items that you would like to store. In some cases, a form may be required for which there is no existing form in the Standard Forms Library. An example might be creating a form for employees to use to submit equipment maintenance requests by e-mail. Rather than using the standard e-mail message, you may want to include fields for the department name, the equipment identification number, the contact person, and so on.

You can create a new form by designing it from scratch, or create a new form based upon an existing form to which fields are added and deleted as required. Publish the form to a forms library to make a custom form that you have created available to other users.

To create a form based upon an existing form, click Tools, point to Forms, and then click Design a Form. The Design Form dialog box shown in figure 5.8 opens. By default, forms in the *Standard Forms Library* are displayed in the Design Form list box. Notice the names of the forms in the Standard Forms Library are the names of the items you have been creating in previous chapters when working in the various Outlook folders. Click the form that you want to use as the base for creating the new form, and then click Open, or double-click the form name. The selected form is opened in a Design window where you can add, move, resize, and delete fields, add explanatory text to users, and insert a company logo or other graphic. Figure 5.9 illustrates the Design window for the Contact form. The tabs labeled (P.2), (P.3), to (P.6) are blank tabs where you can create your own fields grouped by logical units.

FIGURE

5.8 *Design Form Dialog Box*

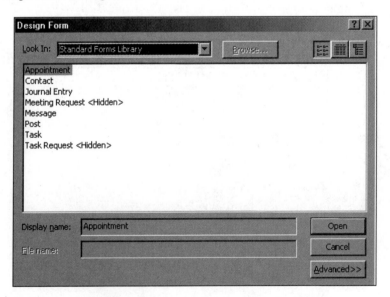

5.9 *Contact Form Design Window*

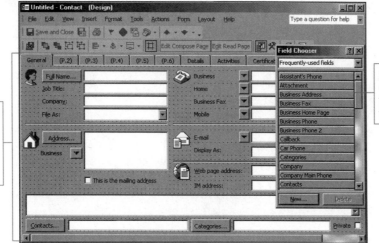

In Design view, each element on the form can be edited, moved, resized, or deleted.

Field Chooser dialog box used to add new fields to the form.

Each element of the form is a separate object that can be modified by editing labels, resizing text boxes, or moving fields to a different order. The dotted grid in the background is used to assist with positioning objects so that they align correctly with other objects beside, above, or below. A feature called *Snap to Grid* is turned on by default in the Design window. This means that when an object is moved, it will automatically be pulled to the closest grid points, or dots.

To edit an object, position the mouse pointer over the item that you want to modify and then click the left mouse button. Eight white boxes, called *sizing handles*, display within a shaded border surrounding the graphic, label, or text box indicating the object is selected. A selected object can be moved, resized, deleted, or edited. In exercise 8, you will customize a contact form that will involve practicing all of these actions in addition to adding new fields to a form.

exercise 8

CREATING A CUSTOM CONTACT FORM

1. With Outlook open and the *Tasks* folder active in Simple List view, click *Contacts* on the Outlook bar. *(Note: It is not necessary to be in the folder for which you are creating a form—you have changed to* Contacts *simply to refresh your memory on the type of data that is stored in a contact record.)*

2. Open a contact form in a Design window by completing the following steps:

   a. Click *Tools*, point to *Forms*, and then click *Design a Form*.

   b. With *Standard Forms Library* selected in the *Look In* list box in the Design Form dialog box, click *Contact* in the forms list box and then click *Open*.

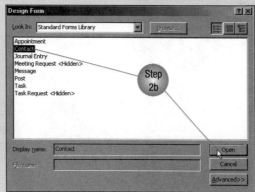

3. Remove objects in the contact form by completing the following steps:
   a. Maximize the Design window to facilitate editing.
   b. Click the icon of the world with the white page in the foreground next to <u>W</u>eb page address. Eight white sizing handles display in a shaded border around the image.

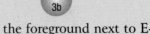

Step
3b

   c. Press the Delete key. The icon is deleted from the form. In the next steps, you will select multiple objects and then delete them in one operation.
   d. Click the icon of the open envelope with the white page in the foreground next to E-mail.
   e. Hold down the Shift key and then click *E-mail*. E-mail and Display As are referred to as a *group* and are both selected in addition to the icon.
   f. Hold down the Shift key and then click the white text box next to Display As. All objects from the first group to the white text box are selected.
   g. Hold down the Shift key and then click the white text box next to IM Address. All objects from the first group to the white text box are selected.

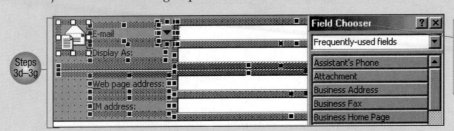

Steps
3d–3g

If necessary, drag the Title bar of the Field Chooser dialog box to move it out of the way.

   h. Click <u>E</u>dit and then click Cu<u>t</u>, or press the Delete key. The selected objects are deleted.
   i. Complete steps similar to those in steps 3d–3h to remove fields in the Design window until the form displays as shown. *(Note: Holding down Ctrl while clicking an object on a form allows you to select multiple objects that are not adjacent.)*

Step
3i

4. Move objects in the contact form by completing the following steps:
   a. Click *Business Fax*.
   b. Hold down the Shift key and then click the white text box next to Business Fax to select both objects.
   c. Position the mouse pointer on the shaded border of either of the selected objects until the pointer changes to the four-headed arrow,

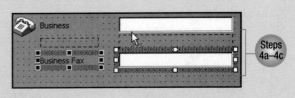

Steps
4a–4c

   hold down the left mouse button, drag the objects closer to Business as shown, and then release the mouse. Both objects move simultaneously. As you drag, a dashed border outlining the objects moves with the mouse so that you can see how the objects will be repositioned.

OUTLOOK

5. Add, move, and resize objects to the form by completing the following steps:

   a. Position the mouse pointer on Car Phone in the Field Chooser dialog box. *(Note: If the Field Chooser dialog box is not visible, click the Field Chooser button* [🔲] *on the Form Design toolbar.)*

   b. Hold down the left mouse button, drag the pointer to a blank area in the form window below the white text box next to Business Fax, and then release the mouse. The field title and an adjacent white text box are dropped onto the form with both objects selected.

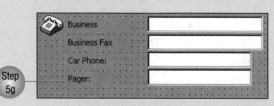

Step
5b

   c. With the Car Phone objects selected, position the mouse pointer on the shaded border of either of the selected objects until the pointer changes to the four-headed arrow, hold down the left mouse button, drag the selected objects to align them below Business Fax as shown, and then release the mouse.

Step
5c

   d. Click in the form window outside the selected objects to deselect them.

   e. Click the white text box beside Car Phone and then move the text box until it is aligned below the Business Fax white text box above it by dragging its border. *(Note: Click the Snap to Grid button on the Form Design toolbar* [🔲] *if you have difficulty aligning objects. When Snap to Grid is turned on, objects jump to the closest grid points [dots] on the form when you release the mouse.)*

   f. Scroll down the Field Chooser dialog box until *Pager* is visible.

   g. Add the *Pager* field to the form and align it below Car Phone by completing steps similar to those in steps 5a–5e.

Step
5g

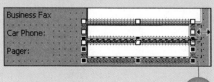

   h. Click the white text box beside Car Phone, hold down Shift, and then click the white text box next to Pager to select both objects.

   i. Drag the right middle sizing handle of either selected object to the right until the Car Phone and Pager text boxes are the same width as the text boxes above them.

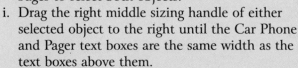

Steps
5h–5i

   j. Click in the form window outside the selected objects to deselect them.

   k. Scroll up the Field Chooser dialog box, add the *Assistant's Phone* field to the form, and then move it below Pager. Resize the text box to make it the same width as the text boxes above it.

6. Save the form to the Personal Forms Library by completing the following steps:

   a. Click <u>T</u>ools, point to <u>F</u>orms, and then click Publish <u>F</u>orm.

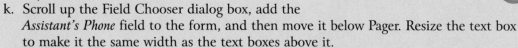

b. Click the down-pointing triangle next to Look In, if necessary scroll up the list box, and then click *Personal Forms Library*.

c. Click in the Display name text box and then key **Vendor Sales Rep**.

d. Click Publish.

7. Click File and then Close, or click the Close button on the Design window Title bar. Click No when prompted to save changes.

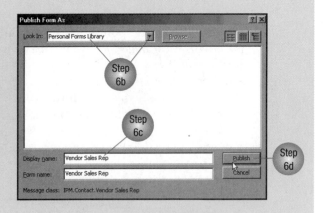

Forms Libraries

Three libraries are available in which to save forms that you have created: Standard Forms Library, Personal Forms Library, and Outlook Folders. In exercise 8, you saved the Vendor Sales Rep form to the Personal Forms Library which is accessible only to you. Forms saved in Outlook Folders can be made accessible to other users by placing the form within a public folder on the server.

If you are connected to a Microsoft Exchange Server you will also have access to an Organizational Forms Library which allows custom forms to be available to all users connected to the Exchange Server.

Using Custom Forms

Once a custom form has been published, it can be used to enter new data into the Outlook folder for which it was created. Activate the required folder on the Outlook bar and then open the Choose Form dialog box. Change from the Standard Forms Library to the library that contains the custom form, choose the form name in the list box, and then open it. In exercise 9 you will add a new record to *Contacts* using the Vendor Sales Rep form created in exercise 8.

exercise 9

USING A CUSTOM FORM

1. With Outlook open and the *Contacts* folder active, add a new record to the current view using the Vendor Sales Rep form by completing the following steps:

a. Click Tools, point to Forms, and then click Choose Form, or click File, point to New, and then click Choose Form.

b. Click the down-pointing triangle next to Look In and then click *Personal Forms Library*.

c. Double-click *Vendor Sales Rep* in the forms list box.

d. With the insertion point positioned in the Full Name text box, key **Erin Malec**, and then press Tab.

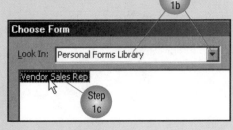

OUTLOOK

e. Key **Sales Representative** in the Job title text box and then press Tab.

f. Key **Malec Enterprises** in the Company text box.

g. Click in the Address text box and then key the following text:

   1801 Gardenview Lane
   Madison, WI 53710

h. Key the following telephone numbers in the appropriate text boxes:

Business	**608 555 2496**
Business Fax	**608 555 3248**
Car Phone	**608 555 3214**
Pager	**608 555 1457**
Assistant's Phone	**608 555 1347**

i. Click the Print button on the Contact window toolbar.

j. Click Save and Close.

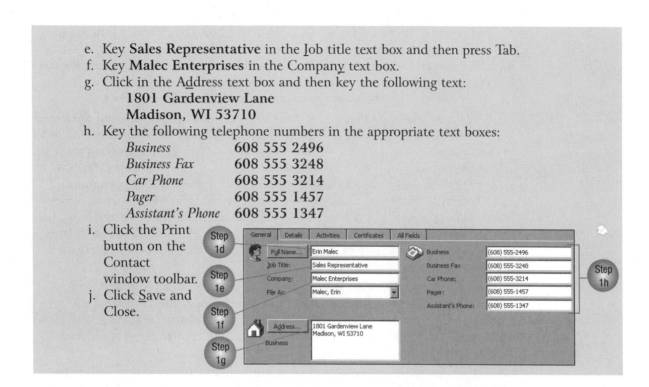

Setting Advanced E-Mail Options

In chapter 1 you learned how to change the mail format to HTML, specify how Outlook processes mail that is sent and received, and control the actions that are performed with respect to the handling of mail. In this chapter, you will explore the Advanced E-mail Options dialog box shown in figure 5.10 in more detail.

FIGURE

5.10 *Advanced E-mail Options Dialog Box*

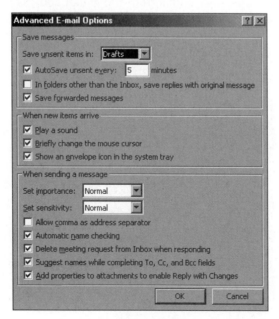

To open the Advanced E-mail Options dialog box, click Tools, Options, and then click E-mail Options in the E-mail section of the Options dialog box. Click Advanced E-mail Options in the Message handling section of the E-mail Options dialog box. The Advanced E-mail Options dialog box is divided into three sections: *Save messages*, *When new items arrive*, and *When sending a message*.

By default, messages that you are working on but have not yet sent are stored in the *Drafts* folder. Click the down-pointing triangle next to Save unsent items in to choose *Inbox*, *Sent Mail*, or *Outbox*. Choose the time interval for saving messages as you are working on them in the AutoSave unsent every [] minutes text box. Selecting the In folders other than the Inbox, save replies with original message check box will ensure that a copy of each reply is stored in the *Sent Items* folder. For example, if you reply to a message while the active folder is not the *Inbox*, the reply is saved in the folder that is open at the time of the reply. You can instruct Outlook not to save a copy of each message that you forward on to others by deselecting the Save forwarded messages check box.

By default, when a new mail message is received, a chime is played, the mouse pointer briefly changes to an icon of an envelope, and an envelope is displayed in the system tray at the right side of the Taskbar. Deselect any of these check boxes in the When new items arrive section to change the way Outlook notifies you of incoming mail.

You can set the importance and sensitivity options for all new messages to settings other than Normal in the When sending a message section. If you want Outlook to separate multiple addresses with a comma in addition to the semicolon, click the Allow comma as address separator check box. The Automatic name checking feature looks for matching names as you key text in address text boxes. If an exact match is found, the name is underlined. If a red wavy line appears under the name, right-click the name to see a list of names that Outlook has found that match what you have keyed. Outlook automatically deletes meeting requests once you have responded to them. If you prefer to keep a copy of the meeting request message, deselect the Delete meeting request from Inbox when responding check box. The Suggest names while completing To, Cc, and Bcc fields check box means that as you start to key a name in an address text box, Outlook will offer suggestions from the global address list. The Add properties to attachments to enable Reply with Changes check box allows you to make changes to attached documents that have been sent with messages and then reply back to the original sender.

exercise 10

SETTING ADVANCED E-MAIL OPTIONS

1. With Outlook open and the *Contacts* folder active, click *Inbox* on the Outlook bar.
2. Instruct Outlook not to save copies of forwarded messages, not to show an envelope in the system tray when a new message arrives, and not to delete meeting requests after you have responded by completing the following steps:
   a. Click Tools and then Options.
   b. Click E-mail Options in the Options dialog box.
   c. Click Advanced E-mail Options in the E-mail Options dialog box.

OUTLOOK

d. Click Save forwarded messages in the Save messages section to deselect it. *(Note: Skip this step if Save forwarded messages is already deselected.)*

e. Click Show an envelope icon in the system tray in the When new items arrive section to deselect it. *(Note: Skip this step if Show an envelope icon in the system tray is already deselected.)*

f. Click Delete meeting request from Inbox when responding in the When sending a message section to deselect it. *(Note: Skip this step if Delete meeting request from Inbox when responding is already deselected.)*

g. Click OK to close the Advanced E-mail Options dialog box.

h. Click OK to close the E-mail Options dialog box.

i. Click OK to close the Options dialog box.

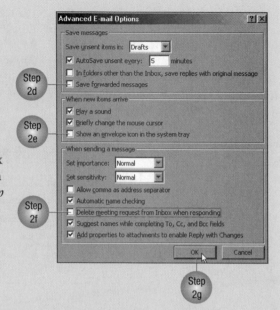

3. Create and send a message to yourself and then forward the message to another student to test the new options by completing the following steps:

a. With *Inbox* the active folder, click the New Mail Message button on the Standard toolbar.

b. With the insertion point positioned in the To... text box, key your own e-mail address.

c. Click in the Subject text box and then key **Advanced E-mail Options**.

d. Click in the message editing window and then key the following text:
This message is to test the changes to the advanced e-mail options so that an envelope does not appear in the system tray when a new mail message arrives.

e. Click Send.

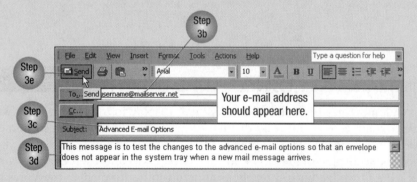

f. In a few seconds, the message should appear in your *Inbox. (Note: If the message does not appear within a few seconds, display the* Outbox, *click the message header, and then click the Send/Receive button on the Standard toolbar.)*

g. Double-click the message header to open it and then click the Forward button.

h. Click the To... button, change to the Personal Address Book in the Select Names dialog box, and then double-click the name of the student you added to the Personal Address Book in chapter 1.

i. Click in the message editing window and then key the following text:
This message is to test the changes to the advanced e-mail options so that Outlook does not save copies of messages I have forwarded.

j. Click Send.

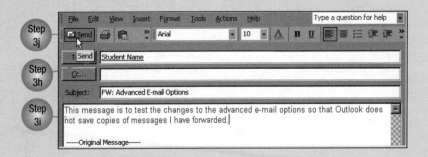

k. Change the active folder to *Sent Items*. Notice that Outlook has not retained a copy of the forwarded message—only the original message that you sent to yourself.

l. Change the active folder back to *Inbox*.

4. Restore the options back to the original default settings by completing the following steps:

a. Click Tools, Options, E-mail Options, and then click Advanced E-mail Options in the E-mail Options dialog box.

b. Click Save forwarded messages in the Save messages section to select it.

c. Click Show an envelope icon in the system tray in the When new items arrive section to select it.

d. Click Delete meeting request from Inbox when responding in the When sending a message section to select it.

e. Click OK three times.

Applying Color to Messages

Organize

Having messages from selected individuals display in a different color will allow you to manage your *Inbox* by distinguishing those that might need immediate attention. For example, you might choose to have all messages where your boss is the sender display in green. To do this, click Tools and then click Organize, or click the Organize button on the Standard toolbar to display the Ways to Organize Inbox pane. Click Using Colors and then change the settings as required in the Color messages section.

Figure 5.11 shows the Ways to Organize Inbox pane with Using Colors selected. Messages can be colored based on the individual that the message is *from* or the individual the message is *sent to*. By default, the name of the sender in the message that is currently selected in the *Inbox* is automatically inserted in the name text box. Click an existing message in the folder from the individual, or key the name of the individual in the text box next to Color messages *from* or *sent to*.

Click the down-pointing triangle next to the color list box (displays *Red* by default) and then choose a color from the drop-down list. Click Apply Color and then close the Ways to Organize Inbox pane by clicking <u>T</u>ools, Organi<u>z</u>e, or clicking the Organize button on the Standard toolbar.

The option to change the color for messages sent only to you will help you to distinguish between messages where you are the only recipient and messages where you are part of a distribution list of recipients.

F I G U R E

5.11 ***Ways to Organize Inbox Pane with Using Colors Selected***

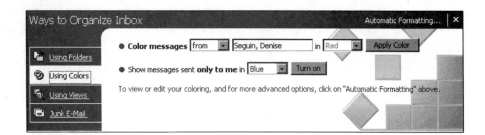

exercise 11

APPLYING COLOR TO MESSAGES

1. With Outlook open and the Inbox folder active, click <u>T</u>ools and then click Organi<u>z</u>e, or click the Organize button on the Standard toolbar to open the Ways to Organize Inbox pane.
2. Have the color teal applied to any message received from you by completing the following steps:
   a. Click Using Colors in the Ways to Organize Inbox pane.
   b. Key your name in the format *Lastname, Firstname* in the text box next to Color messages from.
   c. Click the down-pointing triangle next to the color list box (currently displays *Red*), and then click *Teal* in the drop-down list.
   d. Click Apply Color. The message *Done!* Appears next to the Apply Color button.
   e. Click <u>T</u>ools and then click Organi<u>z</u>e, or click the Organize button on the Standard toolbar to close the Ways to Organize Inbox pane.

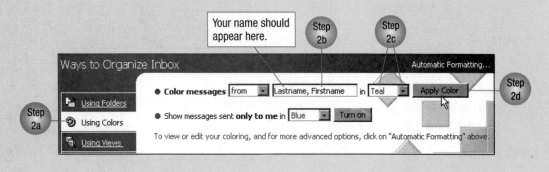

Configuring and Customizing Outlook

3. Any existing messages in the *Inbox* folder that have your name as the sender should now appear in teal. For example, the message header for the message that you sent yourself in exercise 10, step 3 should now be shown in teal if you have not already deleted it. Create and then send a message to yourself to test the color application by completing the following steps:

a. With *Inbox* the active folder, click the New Mail Message button on the Standard toolbar.

b. With the insertion point positioned in the To... text box, key your own e-mail address.

c. Click in the Subject text box and then key **Apply Color to Messages**.

d. Click in the message editing window and then key the following text: **This message is to test the change to the Ways to Organize Inbox pane where any messages that have my name as the sender should be shown in Teal.**

e. Click Send.

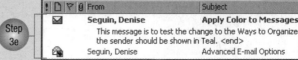

When coloring to messages is turned on for a selected individual in the Ways to Organize Inbox pane, Outlook creates a message rule. A message rule is an action that you want Outlook to perform based upon a condition. In this case, the action is the application of the color teal to a message header based upon the condition that the sender is you.

To turn off the message rule for the color application, click Automatic Formatting in the Ways to Organize Inbox pane, click *Mail received from Lastname, Firstname* in the Rules for this view list box, click Delete, and then click OK.

exercise 12

DELETING THE MESSAGE RULE TO APPLY COLOR

1. With Outlook open and the *Inbox* folder active, click Tools and then click Organize, or click the Organize button on the Standard toolbar to open the Ways to Organize Inbox pane.

2. Delete the message rule created in exercise 11 by completing the following steps:

a. Click Using Colors in the Ways to Organize Inbox pane.

b. Click Automatic Formatting at the top right of the Ways to Organize Inbox pane (next to the Close button.)

c. Click *Mail received from Lastname, Firstname* (where your name is substituted for *Lastname, Firstname*) in the Rules for this view list box.

d. Click Delete.

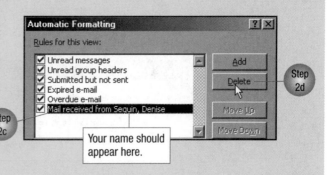

e. Click OK.

f. Click Tools and then click Organi<u>z</u>e, or click the Organize button on the Standard toolbar to close the Ways to Organize Inbox pane.

Using Word as the Mail Editor and Viewer

On an initial installation of Outlook, Microsoft Word is the default application in which to create, edit, and view messages. Word is set as the default editor in order to take advantage of Word's capabilities such as automatic spelling and grammar checking, tables, themes, and autoformatting to name a few. Changing to Outlook as the mail editor will speed up the process initially when you start using Outlook, since Outlook must start Word if it is not already running when Word is the editor.

Display the Options dialog box with the Mail Format tab selected to choose whether to use Word as the e-mail editor or Outlook. If Word is turned off as the e-mail editor, you can still use Word for viewing messages that you receive. This will ensure that all formatting in the message is retained. If you receive a lot of messages that contain text formatting and/or graphics, you might want to consider leaving Word as the mail viewer.

When Word is the mail editor, the message window shown in figure 5.12 appears when you start a new message. Notice the Menu bar and toolbars are the same as Word's Menu bar and toolbars since you are using Microsoft Word inside of Outlook.

FIGURE

5.12 *Message Window with Microsoft Word as the Mail Editor*

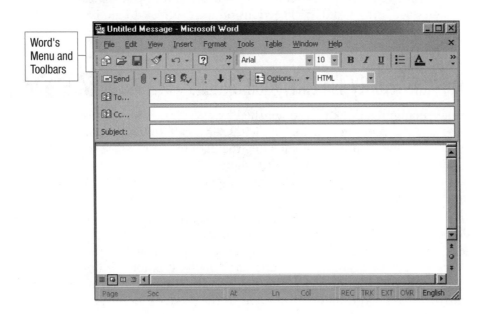

1. With Outlook open and the *Inbox* folder active, check the current setting for e-mail editing and viewing on the computer you are using by completing the following steps:
   a. Click Tools and then click Options.
   b. Click the Mail Format tab in the Options dialog box.
   c. Look in the Message format section for the options Use Microsoft Word to edit e-mail messages, and Use Microsoft Word to read Rich Text e-mail messages. If one or both options has a check mark in the check box, then Word is the editor and/or viewer. If the boxes are empty, then Outlook is the editor and/or viewer.
   d. Click OK to close the Options dialog box.

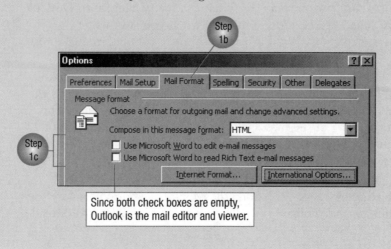

Since both check boxes are empty, Outlook is the mail editor and viewer.

If Microsoft Word is not currently the mail editor and you want to compose just one message using Word, click Actions on the Outlook Menu bar, point to New Mail Message Using, and then click Microsoft Word.

Setting Mail Security and Encryption Options

Securing e-mail in Outlook is accomplished by encrypting information within a message that you send, or attaching a digital certificate to your message, or both. Encryption involves a process of encoding the data in the message so that it is unreadable to anyone but the person to whom it was sent. If the message is intercepted by an unauthorized person, the message looks garbled. A digital certificate authenticates to the recipient that the message was sent by you.

If you often are required to send data in e-mail messages that could be considered confidential, securing the mail with encryption and certificates is a prudent course of action. As messages are routed throughout the Internet and travel across network servers to the recipient's mailbox, potential for unauthorized access exists. Secure messages ensure privacy, and where necessary in business transactions, can provide authentication as to the sender's identity.

Digital IDs

Digital IDs are obtained from certification authorities usually for a small fee that is renewable each year. An example of one certification authority is VeriSign. Outlook provides a Get a Digital ID button in the Options dialog box with the Security tab selected. Clicking Get a Digital ID will connect you to a Microsoft Web site with links to certification authority Web sites where you can purchase and install a certificate. If you are connected to a Microsoft Exchange server, the system administrator can provide you with a digital certificate for sending messages across the Exchange network. Certificates can be copied from one computer to another by importing and exporting so that you do not have to purchase multiple certificates if you own more than one system and also so that you can retain a backup of the certificate on a floppy disk.

A digital certificate fixes your identity using two keys: a private key and a public key. To exchange encrypted or digitally signed messages with another user on the Internet, you must first send your certificate to the recipient and the recipient must in turn send you his or her certificate.

The easiest way to do this is to send the recipient a message to which you have attached your certificate, and the recipient returns a message to you with his or her certificate attached. When you receive the message with the certificate attached, add the individual to the *Contacts* folder and automatically import the digital certificate by opening the message, right-clicking the name of the sender, and then clicking Add to Contacts at the shortcut menu. The digital ID will be stored with the contact and can be viewed by clicking the Certificates tab in the Contact window for the individual.

The private key in the digital certificate remains stored on the digital certificate owner's computer. Messages sent that have a digital certificate attached contain a public key. This dual private key/public key encryption method works to secure mail by scrambling the message with the intended recipient's public key. Once it is encrypted, the message can be decrypted only with the recipient's private key which would be stored only on the recipient's computer.

Configuring Outlook's Security Options

Click Tools, Options, and then click the Security tab in the Options dialog box to display the dialog box shown in figure 5.13. Click Encrypt contents and attachments for outgoing messages and/or Add digital signature to outgoing messages check boxes in the Secure e-mail section to turn on these features for all new messages. The Send clear text signed message when sending signed messages option allows a recipient whose e-mail system does not support the digital signatures to read the message without verification. Choose Request secure receipt for all S/MIME signed messages if you want to receive a message, similar to a read receipt, when your signature is verified by the recipient.

5.13 *Options Dialog Box with Security Tab Selected*

To encrypt or attach a digital signature to an individual message, click <u>V</u>iew on the message window Menu bar and then click Options, or click the O<u>p</u>tions button on the message window toolbar to open the Message Options dialog box. Click Securi<u>t</u>y Settings in the Security section of the Message Options dialog box to open the Security Properties dialog box shown in figure 5.14. Click <u>E</u>ncrypt message contents and attachments to encrypt the message, and/or click Add <u>d</u>igital signature to this message and then click OK.

Options

5.14 *Security Properties Dialog Box*

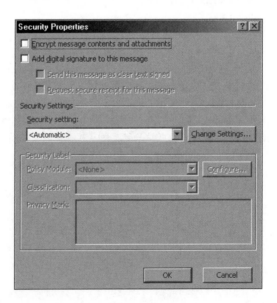

OUTLOOK

1. With Outlook open and the *Inbox* folder active, check the current setting for e-mail security by completing the following steps:
   a. Click Tools and then ciick Options.
   b. Click the Security tab in the Options dialog box.
   c. Look in the Secure e-mail section for the Encrypt contents and attachments for outgoing messages and Add digital signature to outgoing messages options. If both check boxes are empty, mail messages are not encrypted or digitally signed. Clicking the check boxes will make encryption and digital signatures the default setting for all new mail messages.
   d. Click OK to close the Options dialog box.
2. Turn on encryption of an individual message by completing the following steps:
   a. With *Inbox* the active folder, click the New Mail Message button on the Standard toolbar.
   b. With the insertion point positioned in the To text box, key your own e-mail address.
   c. Click in the Subject text box and then key **Mail Security**.
   d. Click in the message editing window and then key the following text:
      This is a test of how to encrypt an individual message.
   e. Click View and then click Options, or click the Options button on the message window toolbar.
   f. Click Security Settings in the Message Options dialog box.
   g. Click Encrypt message contents and attachments in the Security Properties dialog box.
   h. Click OK to close the Security Properties dialog box.
   i. Click Close to close the Message Options dialog box.
   j. Click Send. Outlook looks for valid digital certificates and if none are present will display an Invalid Certificate message box.
   k. Click OK at the Invalid Certificate message box stating that Microsoft Outlook could not sign or encrypt the message.
   l. Close the message window. Click No when prompted to save changes.

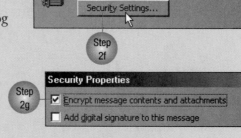

Security Zones

Restricting actions that messages received in HTML can perform is significant since HTML messages can potentially contain embedded scripts that could harm your system by infecting it with a virus or surreptitiously obtaining information from your system.

Security zones in Outlook are the same zones as defined in Microsoft's Internet Explorer. By default, Outlook applies the Restricted sites security zone setting to all incoming HTML messages. This setting prevents most of the activities that could harm your computer. To change the security zone or modify the settings of the current zone, click the Zone Settings button in the Secure content section of the Options dialog box with the Security tab selected. The Security dialog box shown in figure 5.15 opens. Choose a Web content zone or click <u>C</u>ustom Level to modify the settings of the current zone.

5.15 *Security Dialog Box*

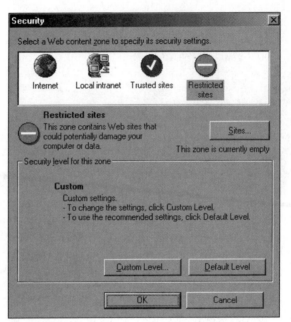

exercise 15

MODIFYING THE SECURITY ZONE

1. With Outlook open and the *Inbox* folder active, check the current security zone setting and modify the security level for the current zone by completing the following steps:
   a. Click <u>T</u>ools and then click <u>O</u>ptions.
   b. Click the Security tab in the Options dialog box.
   c. Click Zo<u>n</u>e Settings in the Secure content section.
   d. Click OK at the Microsoft Outlook message box warning you that you are about to change security settings that will affect the way scripts and active content can run in Microsoft Internet Explorer, Outlook, Outlook Express, and any other programs that use Security Zones.

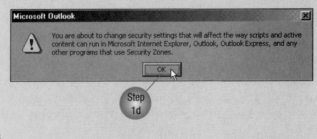

Step 1d

   e. With Restricted sites selected as the current Web content zone, click <u>C</u>ustom Level.

f. Scroll down the Settings list box in the Security Settings dialog box, review the current settings as you are scrolling, and then click Automatic logon with current username and password in the User Authentication Logon section.

g. Click OK.

h. Click Yes at the Warning message asking if you are sure you want to change the security settings for this zone.

i. Click OK to close the Security dialog box.

j. Click OK to close the Options dialog box.

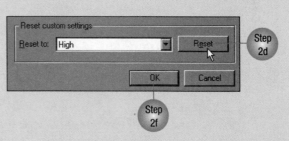

2. Restore the zone settings for the Restricted sites security zone by completing the following steps:

a. Click Tools, Options, and then click the Security tab in the Options dialog box.

b. Click Zone Settings in the Secure content section and then click OK at the Microsoft Outlook message box.

c. With Restricted sites selected as the current Web content zone, click Custom Level.

d. Click Reset in the Reset custom settings section of the Security Settings dialog box.

e. Click Yes at the Warning message asking if you are sure you want to change the security settings for this zone.

f. Click OK to close the Security Settings dialog box.

g. Click OK to close the Security dialog box and then click OK to close the Options dialog box.

Creating a Dial-Up Connection

Dial up networking allows you to connect to a network server from a remote location via a modem and download messages, schedule appointments, or create tasks as if you were using Outlook on your usual desktop computer. A modem is a device that allows digitized information from the computer to be converted into analog signals that can travel over telephone lines. This process is called *mo*dulation. The computer at the receiving end also must have a modem which then translates the analog signals back into digital data—referred to as *dem*odulation.

To create a dial-up connection, you need to have established an account with an ISP or the system administrator of your network. At a minimum, he or she will provide you with the following information that you will need to configure the dial-up connection:

• Telephone number of the server that you will be connecting to remotely.
• User name for the account when connecting to the network.
• Password for your user name.

Outlook uses the same Make New Connection Wizard that is used by Windows to create a new dial-up connection. The Make New Connection Wizard for Windows ME or Windows 98 involves three dialog boxes where you key a user-friendly name for the connection such as the name of your workplace or ISP, select the modem you are using, and then key the telephone number of the computer to which you want to connect. An icon is created which when double-clicked will dial the remote computer. Once the connection is established, a dialog box appears where you key your user name and password.

In exercise 16 you will create a dial-up connection using the Make New Connection Wizard in Windows ME or Windows 98. If you are using Windows 2000, proceed to exercise 17.

exercise 16

CREATING A DIAL-UP CONNECTION USING WINDOWS ME OR WINDOWS 98

(Note: Check with your instructor before proceeding to complete this exercise. You will need the telephone number of the remote computer to which you are connecting, and a valid user name and password once the connection is established. If necessary, you can key fictitious data in the Make New Connection dialog boxes to practice the steps.)

1. With Outlook open and the *Inbox* folder active, click <u>F</u>ile and then E<u>x</u>it to close Outlook.
2. Create a new dial-up connection using Windows ME or Windows 98 by completing the following steps:

   a. Click *Start*, point to *Settings*, and then click *Dial-Up Networking* if you are using Windows ME. If you are using Windows 98, double-click the *My Computer* icon on the desktop and then double-click *Dial-Up Networking* in the My Computer window. *(Note: If Dial-Up Networking does not exist, then the component was not installed when Windows was set up on the computer you are using. You will need to install it using Windows Setup and then reboot the system before proceeding.)*

   b. Double-click *Make New Connection* in the Dial-Up Networking window.

   c. With *My Connection* selected in the <u>T</u>ype a name for the computer you are dialing, key **My Remote Server**. *(Note: Normally you would key the name of the ISP or workplace that is providing the host you are connecting to.)*

   d. The Select a <u>d</u>evice list box should default to the modem that is installed on the computer you are using. If necessary, click the down-pointing triangle next to the Select a <u>d</u>evice list box and then select another modem.

   e. Click <u>N</u>ext.

OUTLOOK

f. In the second Make New Connection dialog box, the Area code and Country or region code should default to the correct location. If necessary, change these settings for your area code and country/region.

g. Click in the Telephone number text box, key the telephone number of the computer to which you are connecting, and then click Next.

h. At the last Make New Connection dialog box, click Finish.

i. A new icon is added in the Dial-Up Networking window with the name My Remote Server. Click the Close button on the Dial-Up Networking Title bar. If you are using Windows 98, click the Close button on the My Computer Title bar.

3. Connect to a remote computer using a dial-up connection by completing the following steps:

a. Click *Start*, point to *Settings*, and then click *Dial-Up Networking*.

b. Double-click *My Remote Server* in the Dial-Up Networking window. The Connect To dialog box opens.

c. Key your user name for your account on the remote computer in the User name text box.

d. Key your password for the account on the remote computer in the Password text box. *(Note: Click the Save password check box if you want Windows to remember the password so that you don't have to key it each time you dial up.)*

e. Click Connect. In a few seconds you will be connected to the remote computer. A progress box displays messages on the screen as the computer dials and then verifies your user name and password. When you have successfully established a connection, the progress box disappears and a dial-up networking icon appears in the system tray on the Taskbar next to the current time.

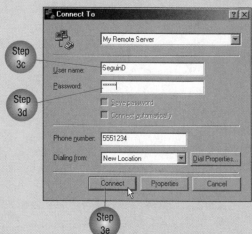

f. Close the Dial-Up Networking window.

4. Start Outlook. If necessary, key your user name and password at the Enter Password dialog box. At this point, you can work with Outlook remotely. In a later exercise you will learn how to download message headers only and mark selected messages to be downloaded. Downloading only those messages that you need to reply to will speed up the time spent on the remote connection.

5. Disconnect from the remote computer by completing the following steps:
   a. Double-click the dial-up networking icon in the system tray on the Taskbar next to the current time. The Connected to My Remote Server dialog box opens.
   b. Click Disconnect.

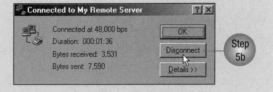

Step 5b

exercise 17

(Note: Skip this exercise if you completed exercise 16. Check with your instructor before proceeding to complete this exercise. You will need the telephone number of the remote computer to which you are connecting, and a valid user name and password once the connection is established. If necessary, you can key fictitious data in the Network Connection Wizard dialog boxes to practice the steps.)

1. With Outlook open and the *Inbox* folder active, click File and then Exit to close Outlook.
2. Create a new dial-up connection using Windows 2000 by completing the following steps:
   a. Click *Start*, point to *Settings*, point to Network and Dial-up Connections, and then click *Make New Connection*.
   b. The Network Connection Wizard opens with a Welcome message describing what the wizard can do. Click Next.
   c. With Dial-up to private network selected in the second Network Connection Wizard dialog box, click Next. *(Note: If you are creating a dial-up connection to an ISP, click Dial-up to the Internet instead. The remaining screens will vary slightly. Your ISP will have provided you with instructions.)*
   d. With the insertion point positioned in the Phone number text box, key the telephone number of the computer to which you are connecting, and then click Next.

Step 2b

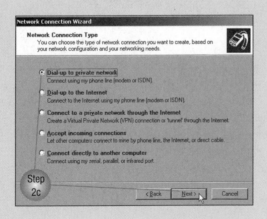

Step 2c

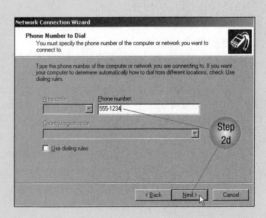

Step 2d

e. Click <u>O</u>nly for myself in the Create this connection section and then click <u>N</u>ext.
f. With *Dial-up Connection* selected in the <u>T</u>ype the name you want to use for this connection text box, key **My Remote Server**, and then click Finish.
g. Click Cancel in the Connect My Remote Server dialog box. You will be connecting in step 3.

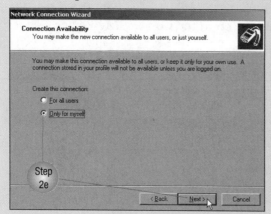

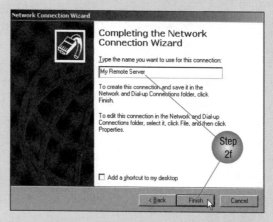

3. Connect to a remote computer using a dial-up connection by completing the following steps:

a. Click *Start*, point to *Settings*, point to *Network and Dial-up Connections*, and then click *My Remote Server*. The Connect My Remote Server dialog box opens.

b. Key your user name for your account on the remote computer in the <u>U</u>ser name text box.

c. Key your password for the account on the remote computer in the <u>P</u>assword text box. *(Note: Click the <u>S</u>ave password check box if you want Windows to remember the password so that you don't have to key it each time you dial up.)*

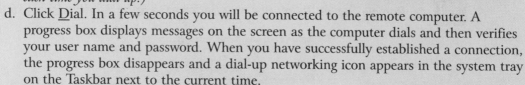

d. Click <u>D</u>ial. In a few seconds you will be connected to the remote computer. A progress box displays messages on the screen as the computer dials and then verifies your user name and password. When you have successfully established a connection, the progress box disappears and a dial-up networking icon appears in the system tray on the Taskbar next to the current time.

4. Start Outlook. If necessary, key your user name and password at the Enter Password dialog box. At this point, you can work with Outlook remotely. In a later exercise you will learn how to download message headers only and mark selected messages to be downloaded. Downloading only those messages that you need to reply to will speed up the time spent on the remote connection.

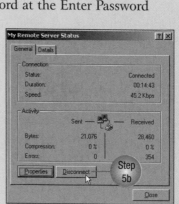

5. Disconnect from the remote computer by completing the following steps:

a. Double-click the dial-up networking icon in the system tray on the Taskbar next to the current time. The My Remote Server Status dialog box opens.

b. Click <u>D</u>isconnect.

Open the Properties dialog box for the Dial-up connection to change options related to networking, security, or dialing settings. Figure 5.16 shows the Properties dialog box for the My Remote Server dial-up connection for Windows ME. Right-click the Dial-up connection icon and then click P<u>r</u>operties at the shortcut menu to open the Properties dialog box. Figure 5.17 shows the dialog box for the My Remote Server dial-up connection in Windows 2000. Click *Start*, point to *Settings*, point to *Network and Dial-up Connections*, and then click *My Remote Server*. Click the Pr<u>o</u>perties button in the Connect My Remote Server dialog box.

FIGURE

5.16 *My Remote Server Dialog Box with Dialing Tab Selected (Windows ME)*

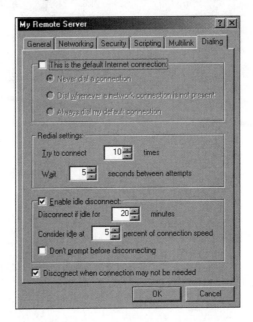

FIGURE

5.17 *My Remote Server Dialog Box with Options Tab Selected (Windows 2000)*

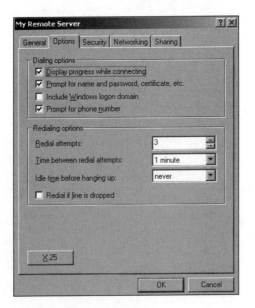

Creating an Offline Folders File

Offline folders allow you to work with your data in Outlook while you are not connected to the network server. When you later connect to the server, the offline folders are synchronized with the folder on the Microsoft Exchange Server so that information in both places is identical. An offline folders file ends with the file extension *.ost*.

Remote mail allows you to download only the message headers when you are away from your normal place of work instead of the complete content associated with each message. This speeds up the download time and gives you the opportunity to choose for which messages you want to download the entire content. Since remote mail involves dialing up to the mail server and connection speeds can sometimes be slow or unstable, downloading only those critical messages will save time.

This section discusses how to configure remote mail and create offline folders for users that are connected to a Microsoft Exchange Server. Users who are running Outlook connected to a non-Microsoft Exchange server generally have messages downloaded to a file on the local computer when they establish a connection, therefore, access to the mail content is immediately available.

To use remote mail, Outlook looks for offline folders; therefore, the first step in the process of configuring remote mail is to create an offline folders file. In exercise 18, you will create a new offline folders file to be stored on the local hard drive. If the computer you are using is already configured for remote mail with an offline file, skip exercise 18.

exercise 18

	CREATING AN OFFLINE FOLDERS FILE

(Note: If you are not connected to a Microsoft Exchange Server, you will not be able to complete this exercise. Since Outlook files become very large in size, storing on a floppy disk is not feasible. Exercise 18 assumes the offline folder will be created in the My Documents *folder on drive C. Check with your instructor for alternate instructions if you will be creating the offline folder in a different location.)*

1. With Outlook open and the *Inbox* folder active, create a new offline folders file for working with remote mail by completing the following steps:
   a. Click <u>T</u>ools and then click E-mail <u>A</u>ccounts.
   b. If necessary, click <u>V</u>iew or change existing e-mail accounts in the E-mail section of the E-mail Accounts dialog box, and then click <u>N</u>ext.
   c. If necessary, click *Microsoft Exchange Server* in the Name list box below Outlook processes e-mail for these accounts in the following order, and then click <u>C</u>hange.
   d. Click <u>M</u>ore Settings at the bottom right of the Exchanger Server Settings section.

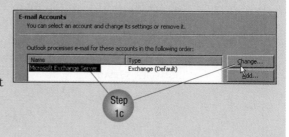

e. Click the Advanced tab in the Microsoft Exchange Server dialog box.

f. Click Offline *F*older File Settings.

g. Key **C:\My Documents\Outlook.ost** in the *F*ile text box in the Offline Folder File Settings dialog box and then click OK. *(Note: The default path and file name that appears in the *F*ile text box is normally used as the offline file name and location.)*

h. Click *Y*es at the Microsoft Outlook Offline Folders message box saying the file could not be found and asking if you would like to create it.

i. Click OK to close the Microsoft Exchange Server dialog box.

j. Click *N*ext in the E-mail Accounts dialog box with the Exchanger Server Settings displayed.

k. Click Finish in the E-mail Accounts dialog box with the E-mail Accounts displayed.

l. Exit Outlook.

2. Restart Outlook to see the prompt for working offline by completing the following steps:

a. Start Outlook. Notice a dialog box appears with buttons to *C*onnect, *W*ork Offline, or Cancel.

b. At the Microsoft Exchange Server login dialog box, click *C*onnect.

c. If necessary, key your user name and password in the Enter Password dialog box.

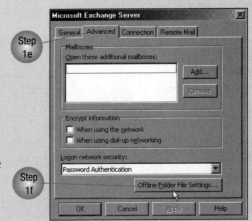

Step 1e

Step 1f

Step 1g

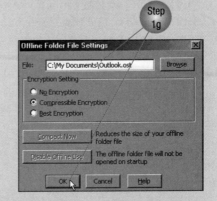

Step 2b

Working Offline

Prior to being able to work in an offline folder, with Outlook connected to the network server, specify the folders that you want available offline, and then synchronize the offline folders with the folders in your mailbox on the Exchange server. Once the offline folders file is synchronized, you can switch back and forth between working online and offline by clicking *F*ile, Wor*k* Offline, or restarting Outlook and choosing to *C*onnect or *W*ork Offline. A check mark next to Wor*k* Offline on the *F*ile menu means you are not currently connected to the network server.

OUTLOOK

Specifying Folders for Offline Use

By default, *Calendar, Contacts, Deleted Items, Inbox, Outbox, Sent Items, Tasks, Journal, Notes,* and *Drafts* are automatically made available offline. Deselect the folders that you do not need if you only work with certain items when offline. To do this, click Tools, point to Send/Receive Settings, and then click Define Send/Receive Groups. In the Send/Receive Groups dialog box, click *All Accounts* or click the name of the individual account that you want to specify for offline folders, and then click Edit. Select and deselect folders in the Check folders to include in send/receive folder list, click OK, and then click Close.

To specify an individual folder that is the active folder for offline use, click Tools, point to Send/Receive Settings, and then click Make This Folder Available Offline. Complete the same steps to deselect a folder from the offline folders settings to remove it from the next synchronization activity.

Synchronizing Folders

Offline folders can be synchronized manually or automatically. To manually synchronize the folders click the Send/Receive button on the Standard toolbar or click Tools, point to Send/Receive, and then click Send and Receive All. To synchronize the active folder only, click This Folder on the Send/Receive menu. Outlook displays the Outlook Send/Receive Progress dialog box shown in figure 5.18 during the synchronization process. Depending on the amount of data in the folders, synchronization can take a few moments.

Send/Receive

F I G U R E

5.18 *Outlook Send/Receive Progress Dialog Box*

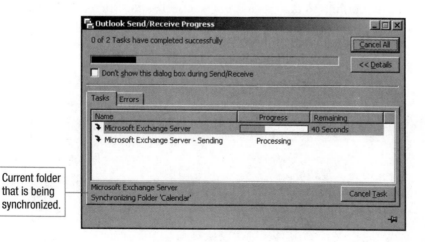

Automatic Synchronization

To configure Outlook to automatically synchronize folders at specific time intervals, display the Send/Receive Groups dialog box by clicking Tools, pointing to Send/Receive Settings, and then clicking Define Send/Receive Groups. Click the account for which you want to specify automatic synchronization (default setting is *All Accounts*) and then choose the settings you require in the When Outlook is Online and When Outlook is Offline sections as shown in figure 5.19.

FIGURE

5.19 *Outlook Send/Receive Groups Dialog Box*

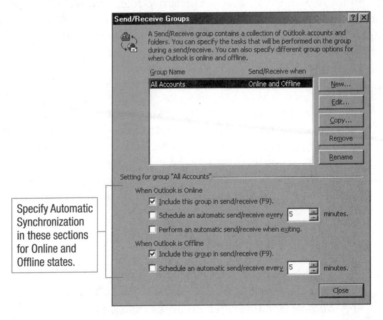

Specify Automatic Synchronization in these sections for Online and Offline states.

In exercise 19, you will specify the folders that you want to use offline, synchronize the offline folder created in exercise 18, and then switch between working online to working offline. If the computer you are using already has offline folders specified and you want to retain the current settings, skip exercise 19.

exercise 19

SPECIFYING FOLDERS FOR OFFLINE USE, SYNCHRONIZING FOLDERS, & SWITCHING TO OFFLINE STATUS

(Note: If you are not connected to a Microsoft Exchange Server, you will not be able to complete this exercise.)

1. With Outlook open and the *Inbox* folder active, specify the folders that you want to use offline by completing the following steps:

   a. Click Tools, point to Send/Receive Settings, and then click Define Send/Receive Groups.

   b. With *All Accounts* selected in the Group Name list box in the Send/Receive Groups dialog box, click Edit.

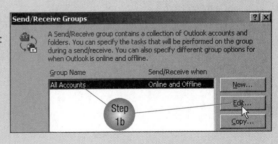

OUTLOOK

c. With *Microsoft Exchange Server* selected in the Accounts bar of the Send/Receive Settings - All Accounts dialog box, specify the *Calendar, Contacts*, and *Inbox* folders to be made available offline by completing the following steps:

   1) Click *Deleted Items* to deselect the folder. If the folder is already deselected, skip this step.
   2) Click *Outbox* to deselect the folder. If the folder is already deselected, skip this step.
   3) Click *Sent Items* to deselect the folder. If the folder is already deselected, skip this step.
   4) Click *Tasks* to deselect the folder. If the folder is already deselected, skip this step.
   5) Deselect any other folders that may be selected so that *Calendar, Contacts*, and *Inbox* are the only remaining selected folders in the folder list.
   6) Click OK.

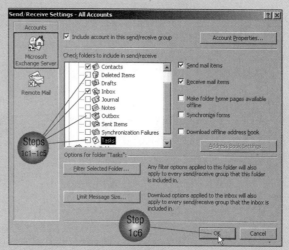
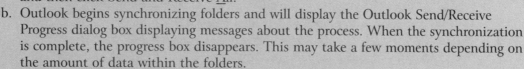

d. Click C<u>l</u>ose in the Send/Receive Groups dialog box.

2. Synchronize the offline folders with the folders on the Exchange server by completing the following steps:

   a. Click <u>T</u>ools, point to S<u>e</u>nd/Receive, and then click Send and Receive <u>A</u>ll.

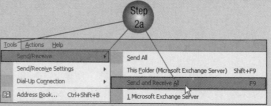

   b. Outlook begins synchronizing folders and will display the Outlook Send/Receive Progress dialog box displaying messages about the process. When the synchronization is complete, the progress box disappears. This may take a few moments depending on the amount of data within the folders.

3. Switch to working offline by completing the following steps:

   a. Click <u>F</u>ile.
   b. Click Wor<u>k</u> Offline. You are now working in an offline state. If new messages are received at the server, you will not see them appear in the *Inbox* until you return to online status.

4. Exit Outlook.

Downloading Messages for Remote Use

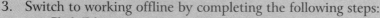

When Outlook is set up for remote mail with offline folders, you can download message headers only from the mail server for review. Once the message headers are downloaded, you can then selectively mark for which messages you want to download the actual content. When you are away from your normal place of work, dial up to the network server, download the message headers, and then disconnect to save time and perhaps long-distance charges for the connection. Once you have reviewed the headers and marked the messages to download, dial up to the server again, and download the message content.

To download message headers, click Tools, point to Send/Receive, point to Work With Headers, and then click Download Headers. To mark a message for downloading, click the message header, click Tools, point to Send/Receive, point to Work With Headers, point to Mark/Unmark Messages, and then click Mark to Download Message(s). To mark in one operation, use Shift or Ctrl to select multiple messages prior to accessing the menu.

Once all messages are selected for downloading, click Tools, point to Send/Receive, point to Work With Headers, and then click Process Marked Headers.

exercise 20

CREATING AND SENDING MESSAGES FOR PRACTICE WITH REMOTE MAIL

(Note: In this exercise you are sending two messages to yourself so that you will have new mail in the Inbox when you complete exercise 21 on remote mail. If you are not connected to a Microsoft Exchange Server, skip this exercise.)

1. Start Outlook. Click Connect at the Microsoft Exchange Server dialog box and then key your user name and password to connect to the server.
2. With Outlook open and the *Inbox* folder active, create and send two messages to yourself to provide new messages in the *Inbox* by completing the following steps:
   a. Click the New Mail Message button.
   b. Key your e-mail address in the To... text box.
   c. Key **Ch 05, Ex 20 Practice** in the Subject text box.
   d. Key **This message is for learning how to use remote mail** in the message editing window.
   e. Click Send.
   f. Click the New Mail Message button.
   g. Key your e-mail address in the To... text box.
   h. Key **Ch 05, Ex 20 Practice 2** in the Subject text box.
   i. Key **This message is for learning how to use remote mail** in the message editing window.
   j. Click Send.
3. Exit Outlook.

exercise 21

DOWNLOADING MESSAGE HEADERS, MARKING MESSAGES, AND PROCESSING MARKED HEADERS

(Note: If you are not connected to a Microsoft Exchange Server, you will not be able to complete this exercise.)

1. Start Outlook. Click Work Offline at the Microsoft Exchange Server dialog box. Since you are now working in the offline folders file, notice the messages sent to yourself in exercise 20 are not displayed in the *Inbox*.
2. Download message headers from the mail server by completing the following steps:
   a. Click Tools, point to Send/Receive, point to Work With Headers, and then click Download Headers.

OUTLOOK

b. Key your user name and password in the Enter Password dialog box. Outlook will connect to the mail server and download the message headers. *(Note: If you were working in Outlook at a remote location, you would also be required to use the dial-up connection to dial up to the server.)*

3. Mark a message to download the message content by completing the following steps:

   a. Click the message header for the message with the subject *Ch 05, Ex 20 Practice*.

   b. Click <u>T</u>ools, point to S<u>e</u>nd/Receive, point to Work With <u>H</u>eaders, point to Mark/Unmark M<u>e</u>ssages, and then click Mar<u>k</u> to Download Message(s). A down-pointing blue arrow appears on the page icon in the *Header Status* column.

New column for Header status added to view.

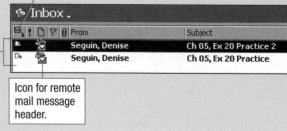

Step 2b

Icon for remote mail message header.

Step 3b

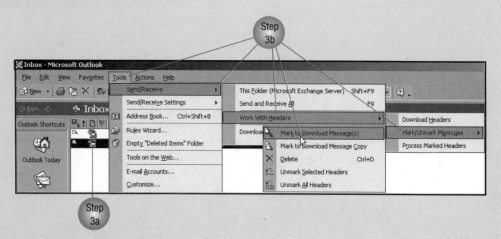

Step 3a

4. Download the message content for the marked message by completing the following steps:

   a. Click <u>T</u>ools, point to S<u>e</u>nd/Receive, point to Work With <u>H</u>eaders, and then click P<u>r</u>ocess Marked Headers.

   b. The message content for the marked message is downloaded and the icon in the Header Status column disappears since the offline folder is now in synchronization with the Exchange folder for the message. The header icon remains on the message with the subject *Ch 05, Ex 20 Practice 2* since we did not download the message.

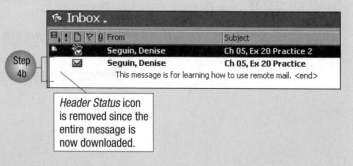

Step 4b

Header Status icon is removed since the entire message is now downloaded.

5. Exit Outlook.

Creating a Personal Folders File

All of the data in the Outlook folders is stored in a single file that is referred to as a *personal information store* and has the file name extension *.pst*. The default name for the personal information store is *Outlook.pst*. Outlook users who are connected using a Microsoft Exchange Server have all of their data stored on the central Exchange server in a file referred to as *private store*.

Creating multiple personal folders is one method of organizing your Outlook data. For example, you may be working on a project in which you send and receive several e-mail messages. Creating a personal folders file for the project and moving the messages to the folder will keep all of the information in one place. When you need to look up a message related to the project you will not have to sift through other messages that are not related. Organizing data using personal folders is very similar to how you would create folders on your hard disk to organize data in other programs.

If you are using Outlook connected to an Exchange server, you may want to create a personal folders file to move or copy messages from the centralized file to a pst file stored on your computer's hard drive. This ensures that you will have access to the messages whether you are connected to the server or not.

Complete the following steps to create a personal folders file.

1. Click File, point to New, and then click Outlook Data File. The New Outlook Data File dialog box shown in figure 5.20 opens.
2. With *Personal Folders File (.pst)* selected in the Types of storage list box, click OK. The Create or Open Outlook Data File dialog box opens.
3. Browse to the location where you would like the pst file stored, key a name for the pst file in the File name text box, and then click OK. The Create Microsoft Personal Folders dialog box appears.
4. Key in the Name text box a unique name to describe the personal folders file. For example, key the name of the project for which you are creating the separate pst file.
5. If you want to password protect the pst file as a security precaution, key the password in the Password and Verify Password text boxes.
6. Click OK. Outlook creates the new pst file and automatically makes it the active folder.

FIGURE

5.20 *New Outlook Data File Dialog Box*

OUTLOOK

Once the personal folders file is created you can move or copy Outlook items to it by creating new folders within the pst file, and then dragging and dropping with the Folder List open.

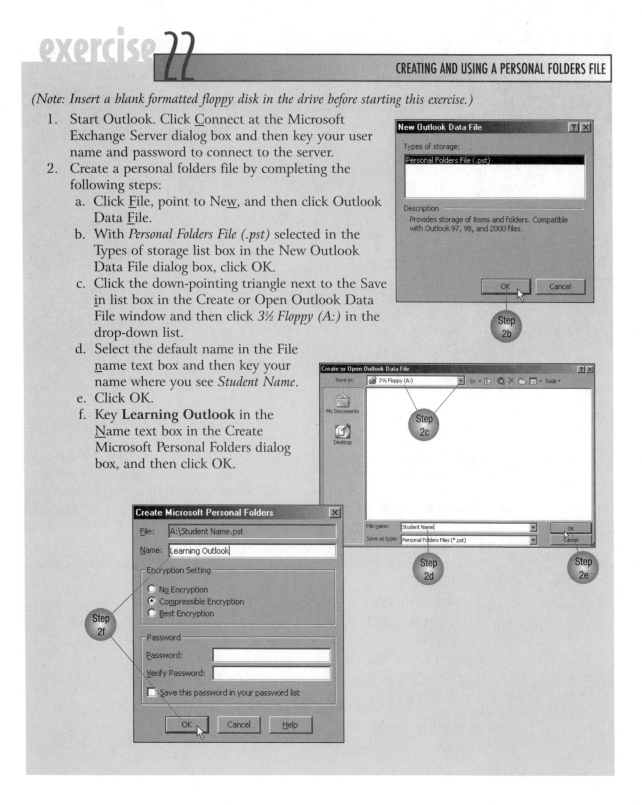

exercise 22

(Note: Insert a blank formatted floppy disk in the drive before starting this exercise.)

1. Start Outlook. Click Connect at the Microsoft Exchange Server dialog box and then key your user name and password to connect to the server.
2. Create a personal folders file by completing the following steps:
   a. Click File, point to New, and then click Outlook Data File.
   b. With *Personal Folders File (.pst)* selected in the Types of storage list box in the New Outlook Data File dialog box, click OK.
   c. Click the down-pointing triangle next to the Save in list box in the Create or Open Outlook Data File window and then click *3½ Floppy (A:)* in the drop-down list.
   d. Select the default name in the File name text box and then key your name where you see *Student Name*.
   e. Click OK.
   f. Key **Learning Outlook** in the Name text box in the Create Microsoft Personal Folders dialog box, and then click OK.

3. With *Learning Outlook* the active folder, create a new folder for storing e-mail messages and then move messages to the new folder by completing the following steps:
   a. Right-click Learning Outlook on the Folder banner.
   b. Click <u>N</u>ew Folder at the shortcut menu.
   c. With the insertion point positioned in the <u>N</u>ame text box in the Create New Folder dialog box, key **Exercise 22**, and then click OK.
   d. Click <u>N</u>o if prompted to create a shortcut to the folder on the Outlook bar. The Folder List pane opens.
   e. Click *Inbox* in the Folder List.
   f. Position the mouse pointer over the message with the subject *Ch 05, Ex 20 Practice*, hold down the left mouse button, drag to the folder named *Exercise 22* in the Folder List and then release the mouse. *(Note: If you do not have the specified message in your* Inbox, *select another message to move.)*

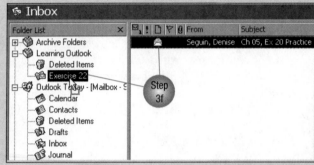

   g. Click *Exercise 22* in the Folder List to display the folder contents in the Information Viewer.
   h. Click *Inbox* in the Folder List.
   i. Click the Close button on the Folder List pane, or click <u>V</u>iew, Fold<u>e</u>r List to remove the pane.

After working in Outlook for a while, pst files become very large. When you delete items in Outlook, the file size does not decrease. Backing up a pst file to a removable device is often not possible due to the large file size. Outlook includes a compact feature that you should run periodically to keep the size of the pst file as small as possible. Complete the following steps to compact a pst file:

1. Click <u>F</u>ile and then click Data <u>F</u>ile Management.
2. Click the name of the file that you want to compact in the Outlook Data Files list box.
3. Click <u>S</u>ettings.
4. Click <u>C</u>ompact Now in the Personal Folders dialog box. A message displays telling you the file is being compacted.
5. Click OK to close the Personal Folders dialog box.
6. Click <u>C</u>lose to close the Outlook Data Files dialog box.

Depending on the amount of data in the selected file, compacting can take a few moments to complete.

OUTLOOK

CHAPTER summary

➤ Outlook Today provides a glimpse of your current day by displaying a list of appointments, tasks, and the number of e-mail messages that you have received or not sent.

➤ Outlook Today can be set as the starting page whenever you load Outlook and the appearance and content can be customized.

➤ Any Outlook folder can be set as the starting page in the Advanced dialog box which is found on the Other tab of the Options dialog box.

➤ Three groups of icons exist on the Outlook bar that can be displayed as large icons or small icons: Outlook Shortcuts, My Shortcuts, and Other Shortcuts.

➤ Hide the Outlook bar by clicking View, Outlook Bar, or by right-clicking on the Outlook bar and then selecting Hide Outlook Bar.

➤ Icons can be moved on the Outlook bar by dragging and dropping them to a different location.

➤ Click Tools and then Customize to add, move, or delete options on the Menu bar.

➤ Items are added to menus by clicking the Commands tab in the Customize dialog box, choosing a category, and then dragging the option to the desired location on the Menu bar.

➤ Move items on menus by dragging them from their current location to the desired location with the Customize dialog box open.

➤ Remove items from menus by dragging the menu option into the Customize dialog box.

➤ Customize a toolbar by clicking Toolbar Options, pointing to Add or Remove buttons, pointing to the toolbar that you want to customize, and then selecting or deselecting options from the cascading side menu.

➤ To add a button that is not found on the menu to a toolbar, click Customize from the Add or Remove buttons menu to open the Customize dialog box. Click the Commands tab, select the category, and then drag the required option from the Customize dialog box to the toolbar.

➤ Move a button on the toolbar by dragging it to the desired location with the Customize dialog box open.

➤ The active view in any Outlook folder can be customized by clicking View, pointing to Current View, and clicking Customize Current View. Click the Fields button in the View Summary dialog box to open the Show Fields dialog box where you can add, remove, or move fields.

➤ To restore a customized active view back to its original settings, click View, point to Current View, and then click Define Views. Click Reset and then click OK.

➤ Every item in Outlook is based on a form. Forms are used to standardize the way that data is entered.

➤ To create a form based upon an existing form, click Tools, point to Forms, and then click Design a Form. Click the form in the Standard Forms Library that you want to use as the base for the new form, and then click Open.

- Each element of the form is a separate object that can be modified by editing labels, resizing text boxes, or moving fields to a different order.

- Three libraries are available in which to save forms that you have created: Standard Forms Library, Personal Forms Library, and Outlook Folders.

- Open a custom form from the Choose Form dialog box. Change from the Standard Forms Library to the library that contains the custom form, and then double-click the form name.

- Open the Advanced E-mail Options dialog box to modify the default settings by clicking Tools, Options, E-mail Options, and then clicking Advanced E-mail Options. The Advanced E-mail Options dialog box is divided into three sections: Save messages, When new items arrive, and When sending a message.

- Click Tools and then click Organize to display the Ways to Organize Inbox pane from which you can choose Using Colors to instruct Outlook to apply a different color to the message header for messages received from or sent to selected individuals.

- Outlook creates a message rule when coloring to messages is turned on for a selected individual. A message rule is an action that you want Outlook to perform based upon a condition.

- By default, Microsoft Word is the application that is used to create, edit, and view messages in order to take advantage of Word features such as automatic spelling and grammar checking, tables, themes, and autoformatting.

- Display the Options dialog box with the Mail Format tab selected to choose whether to use Word as the e-mail editor or Outlook.

- Securing e-mail in Outlook is accomplished by encrypting information within a message that you send and/or attaching a digital certificate to your message.

- Digital IDs are obtained from certification authorities usually for a small fee that is renewable each year.

- A digital certificate fixes your identity using two keys: a private key and a public key.

- Prior to exchanging encrypted or digitally signed messages, both you and the mail recipient must have swapped certificates.

- Set Outlook's security options in the Options dialog box with the Security tab selected.

- By default, Outlook applies the Restricted sites security zone setting to all incoming HTML messages. Open the Security dialog box to change the security zone or modify the settings of the current zone. Click the Zone Settings button in the Options dialog box with the Security tab selected.

- Dial-up networking is used to connect to a network server from a remote location and use Outlook as if you were at your normal desktop computer.

- The Make New Connection Wizard that is used to create a new dial-up connection involves three dialog boxes where you key a user-friendly name for the connection, select the modem you are using, and then key the telephone number of the computer to which you want to connect.

- Open the Properties dialog box for the dial-up connection to change options related to networking, security, or dialing settings.

- Offline folders are used to work with Outlook data while not connected to the network server.

- The offline folders are synchronized with the folder on the Exchange server the next time a connection is made to the server so that information in both places is identical.

➤ An offline folders file ends with the file extension *.ost.*

➤ The offline folders must be synchronized with the folders on the Exchange server prior to being able to work offline.

➤ Switch between working online and offline by clicking File, Work Offline, or restarting Outlook and choosing Connect or Work Offline.

➤ Click Tools, Send/Receive Settings, Define Send/Receive Groups and then edit the account to select and deselect folders that you want to be made available offline.

➤ Click the Send/Receive button on the toolbar to manually synchronize folders, or click Tools, Send/Receive, and then Send and Receive All.

➤ Set a time interval to automatically synchronize folders by clicking Tools, Send/Receive Settings, Define Send/Receive Groups, and then choosing the settings you require in the When Outlook is Online and When Outlook is Offline sections.

➤ Click Tools, Send/Receive, Work With Headers, and then click Download Headers to download message headers only from the mail server.

➤ Mark the active message header for which you want to download message content by clicking Tools, Send/Receive, Work With Headers, Mark/Unmark Messages, and then clicking Mark to Download Message(s).

➤ Click Tools, Send/Receive, Work With Headers, and then Process Marked Headers once all messages are marked and you are ready to download message content.

➤ Data in Outlook folders is stored in a single file referred to as a personal information store with a default name of Outlook.pst.

➤ Create multiple personal folders to organize groups of related data in different folders.

➤ Once a new personal folders file is created you can move or copy Outlook items to it by dragging and dropping with the Folder List open.

➤ Since pst files can become very large in size, Outlook includes a compact feature that you should run periodically to keep the size of the pst file as small as possible.

COMMANDS review

Command	Mouse/Keyboard
Advanced e-mail options	Click Tools, Options, E-mail Options, Advanced E-mail Options
Compact pst file	Click File, Data File Management
Create a custom form	Click Tools, Forms, Design a Form
Create an offline folder	Click Tools, E-mail Accounts
Create personal folders file	Click File, New, Outlook Data File
Customize a view	Click View, Current View, Customize Current View, Fields

Customize menus or toolbars	Click Tools, Customize
Download message content for marked messages	Click Tools, Send/Receive, Work With Headers, Process Marked Headers
Download message headers	Click Tools, Send/Receive, Work With Headers, Download Headers
Encrypt active message	Click View, Options
Hide Outlook bar	Click View, Outlook Bar
Mark message headers	Click Tools, Send/Receive, Work With Headers, Mark/Unmark Messages, Mark to Download Message(s)
Set security options	Click Tools, Options, Security
Set startup folder	Click Tools, Options, Other, Advanced Options
Set ways to Organize Inbox pane	Click Tools, Organize
Set Word as e-mail editor	Click Tools, Options, Mail Format
Specify offline folders	Click Tools, Send/Receive Settings, Define Send/Receive Groups
Synchronize folders	Click Tools, Send/Receive, Send and Receive All
Use a custom form	Click Tools, Forms, Choose Form
Work offline	Click File, Work Offline

CONCEPTS check

Completion: On a blank sheet of paper, indicate the correct term or command for each item.

1. Click this button on the Outlook Today banner to change the appearance of the Outlook Today page.
2. Display this dialog box to change the default folder that Outlook displays whenever Outlook is opened.
3. The Outlook bar consists of these three groups of icons.
4. Click this tab in the Customize dialog box to add a new menu item.
5. Click this button on the toolbar that you want to customize to turn on or off the display of individual buttons.

OUTLOOK

6. Click this button in the View Summary dialog box to open the Show Fields dialog box.
7. This forms library is stored on the computer you are using, making the form not accessible to other users.
8. Open this dialog box to create a new contact record using a custom design form.
9. Change the actions that Outlook performs when a new mail message is received in this dialog box.
10. Display this pane to define a message rule where a different color is applied to message headers for messages received from a specified individual.
11. Click this tab in the Options dialog box to set Microsoft Word as the e-mail editor and/or viewer.
12. A digital certificate is comprised of these two keys.
13. By default, Outlook applies this security zone setting to all incoming HTML messages.
14. Create a new dial-up connection using this wizard.
15. An offline folders file name ends with this extension.
16. Manually synchronize folders by clicking this button on the Standard toolbar.
17. Click this option on the Send/Receive Settings menu to specify the folders that you want made available offline.
18. Download message content for marked messages by clicking this menu sequence.
19. All data in Outlook folders is stored in a file name with a pst extension that is referred to as this.
20. A pst file can be reduced in size after items have been deleted by performing this operation.

SKILLS check

Assessment 1

1. With Outlook open, click the Outlook Today page on the Outlook bar and then customize the appearance of Outlook Today as follows:
   a. Make Outlook Today the startup page.
   b. Show one day in the calendar.
   c. Show Today's tasks only in the task list.
   d. Change to the Summer style.
2. Save the changes and then print the Outlook Today page.
3. Exit Outlook.
4. Restart Outlook to make sure Outlook Today is the starting page.
5. Restore Outlook Today to the default settings as follows:
   a. Remove Outlook Today as the startup page.
   b. Show five days in the calendar.
   c. Show all tasks in the task list.
   d. Change to the Standard style.
6. Save the changes and then print the Outlook Today page.
7. Display the *Inbox*.

Assessment 2

1. With Outlook open and the Inbox folder active, customize the Outlook bar as follows:
   a. Change the display of the Outlook Shortcuts group to Small Icons.
   b. Move *Drafts, Outbox,* and *Sent Items* to the bottom of the Outlook Shortcuts group.
   c. Increase the width of the Outlook bar by approximately 0.5 inch.
2. Print an image of the screen with the customized Outlook bar by completing the following steps:
   a. Press the Print Screen key on the keyboard. This will place a copy of the current screen image on the clipboard.
   b. Start Microsoft Word.
   c. At a blank document screen, key your first and last name at the top of the screen and then press Enter twice. *(Note: Check with your instructor to see if you should key any other identifying information, such as class or program number.)*
   d. Click the Paste button on the Standard toolbar, click Edit and then Paste, or press Ctrl + V to paste the contents of the clipboard.
   e. Click the Print button on the Standard toolbar.
   f. Exit Microsoft Word. Click No when prompted to save changes.
3. Restore the Outlook bar to the default settings as follows:
   a. Change the display of the Outlook Shortcuts group to Large Icons.
   b. Move *Drafts, Outbox,* and *Sent Items* back to the top of the My Shortcuts group.
   c. Decrease the width of the Outlook bar by approximately 0.5 inch.

Assessment 3

1. With Outlook open and the Inbox folder active, customize the Menu bar as follows:
   a. Add Go To as the first option on the Actions menu. *(Note: Go To is to remain in its current position on the View menu—this step is creating a menu option in an additional place.)*
   b. Move Reply on the Actions menu to the second position from the top.
   c. Delete Reply to All from the Actions menu.
2. With the Actions drop-down menu displayed, print an image of the customized menu by completing steps similar to those in Assessment 2, step 2.
3. Restore the Actions menu to its original settings as follows:
   a. Remove Go To from the menu.
   b. Move Reply below the gray line after Junk E-mail.
   c. Add Reply to All back to the menu below Reply.

Assessment 4

1. With Outlook open and the *Inbox* folder active, click the New Mail Message button on the Standard toolbar and then maximize the message window.
2. Customize the new message window Standard toolbar as follows:
   a. Remove the Importance: Low button from the toolbar.
   b. Move the Insert File button between the Save and Print buttons.
   c. Add a Properties button between the Options and the Font Size buttons.
3. Print an image of the customized toolbar in the message window by completing steps similar to those in Assessment 2, step 2.
4. Restore the toolbar to its original settings using the Reset Toolbar option.
5. Close the message window. Click No if prompted to save changes.

Assessment 5

1. With Outlook open and the *Inbox* folder active, click the *Contacts* icon on the Outlook bar.
2. Change the current view to By Company and then make sure all company group lists are expanded.
3. Customize the current view in the Show Fields dialog box as follows:
   a. Remove the following fields: *Icon, Attachment, Flag Status, Company, File As, Department, Business Fax, Home Phone,* and *Categories.*
   b. Add the E-mail address and position it between Job Title and Business Phone. (*Hint: E-mail addresses are in a separate category of fields.*)
4. Expand column widths so that all data within the columns and the column headings are visible.
5. Print the contacts in *Table Style.*
6. Reset the current view back to its original settings using the Define Views dialog box.
7. Change the current view to Address Cards.

Assessment 6

1. With Outlook open and the *Contacts* folder active, create a new form based on the Contact form in the Standard forms library.
2. Add, delete, and move objects on the form to match the form shown in figure 5.21.
3. Publish the form to the Personal Forms Library and name it Customers.
4. Using the Customers form, add the following record to Contacts:

Full Name	**Jose Gonsalez**
Job Title	**Purchasing Manager**
Company	**Gonsalez Industries**
Department	**Finance**
Address	**55 Queen Street**
	Madison, WI 53710
Business	**608 555 4985**
Business Fax	**608 555 4968**
Home	**608 555 1247**
Pager	**608 555 3495**

5. Change the current view to Detailed Address Cards.
6. Select the record for Jose Gonsalez and then print the selected record only in *Card Style.*
7. Change the current view to Address Cards.

FIGURE

5.21 *Assessment 6*

Assessment 7

1. With Outlook open and the *Contacts* folder active, display the *Inbox*.
2. Create and then send a new message as follows:

To	(Student from personal address book)
Subject	**Colored Message Headers**
Message	**This message is to test applying color to messages**

3. Display the *Sent Items* folder in the Information Viewer.
4. Add the *From* column heading to the current view by completing the following steps:
   a. Right-click any column heading and then click Field Chooser at the shortcut menu.
   b. Drag the *From* field to the column headings row and position it between *To* and *Subject*.
   c. Close the Field Chooser dialog box.
   d. Expand the width of the *From* column so that the recipient's names are visible.
5. Create a message rule using the Ways to Organize Sent Items pane that will apply the color fuchsia to messages sent to the student in your personal address book.
6. Print an image of the *Sent Items* folder contents by completing steps similar to those in Assessment 2, step 2.
7. Delete the message rule created in step 5.
8. Close the Ways to Organize Sent Items pane.
9. Display the *Inbox* folder.

Assessment 8

(Note: Make sure your student data disk is in the drive before completing this assessment.)

1. With Outlook open and the *Inbox* folder active, create a new personal folders file as follows:
   a. Save the new pst file on the floppy disk drive and name it Student Name, Ch 05 SA 08, substituting your name for Student Name.
   b. Key **Practicing Outlook** as the <u>N</u>ame and assign a password to the file.
2. With Practicing Outlook the default folder, create a new folder and name it *Assessment 8.*
3. With the Folder List pane open, click *Sent Items.*
4. Move all messages sent to the student you added to the personal address book from *Sent Items* to *Assessment 8.*
5. Display the *Assessment 8* folder in the Information Viewer.
6. Print an image of the *Assessment 8* folder contents by completing steps similar to those in Assessment 2, step 2.
7. Display *Sent Items* and then remove the *From* column heading from the current view by right-clicking the *From* column heading and then clicking <u>R</u>emove This Column at the shortcut menu.
8. Click *Inbox* and then close the Folder List pane.

Assessment 9

1. With Outlook open and the *Inbox* folder active, close the personal folders files created in this chapter by completing the following steps:
   a. Click <u>V</u>iew and then click Fol<u>d</u>er List.
   b. Right-click Learning Outlook in the Folder List pane and then click <u>C</u>lose "Learning Outlook" at the shortcut menu.
   c. Right-click Practicing Outlook in the Folder List pane and then click <u>C</u>lose "Practicing Outlook" at the shortcut menu.
2. Close the Folder List pane.

CHAPTER **6**

INTEGRATING AND MANAGING OUTLOOK COMPONENTS

PERFORMANCE OBJECTIVES

Upon successful completion of chapter 6, you will be able to:
- Assign categories to messages
- Assign a task and a note to a contact
- View Outlook activities tracked by contact
- Create an Office document from Outlook
- Send e-mail from Microsoft Excel
- Import a vCard and vCalendar file into Outlook
- Export contacts to an Access table
- Archive folders manually and automatically
- Assign a Web page as the folder home page
- Set permissions to share a folder
- Open another user's calendar
- Publish and obtain free/busy data for users on the Internet
- Create a private appointment
- Send and receive newsgroup messages
- Send and receive instant messages
- Schedule an online meeting using NetMeeting

Outlook Chapter 6

(Note: There are two student data files to copy for this chapter.)

Data is easily integrated between Outlook folders and between Outlook and other applications within the Microsoft Office suite. Like any other Outlook item, messages can be organized by categories. All Outlook items can be tracked and viewed by individual contact. Any Office document can be created within Outlook as well as importing and exporting of Outlook information to and from Outlook to the other applications in the Microsoft suite.

Sharing Outlook information with other users, marking items as private when folders are shared, and using alternative communication mediums such as newsgroups, instant messaging, and NetMeetings are also methods in which Outlook can be integrated with other components.

Assigning Categories to Messages

A message sent or received can be associated with a keyword in the category list and can then be grouped by the category using the Advanced Find dialog box. Assigning a category to a message is one of the methods that can be used for locating or managing messages in the mail folders. Right-click a message header and then click Categories at the shortcut menu, or click Edit, Categories to open the Categories dialog box. Choose from one or more of the predefined categories in the Available categories list box, or key your own category name in the Item(s) belong to these categories text box, and then click Add to List.

A category can be assigned to a message while the message window is open by displaying the Message Options dialog box. Key the category name in the Categories text box or click Categories to display the Categories dialog box.

To view a list of messages grouped by a specific category, display the Find bar, click the Options button, and then click Advanced Find, or click Tools, Advanced Find. Click the More Choices tab in the Advanced Find dialog box and then enter the category name in the Categories text box. When you click Find Now, the Advanced Find dialog box expands with the list of message headers in the search results list box at the bottom of the dialog box.

FIGURE

6.1 *Advanced Find Dialog Box with More Choices Tab Selected*

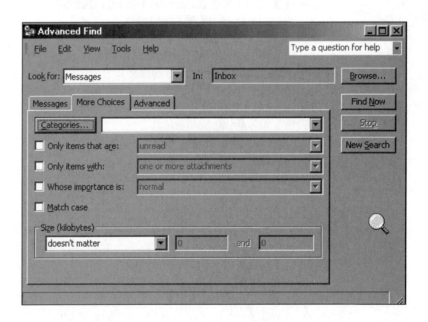

You can open, print, reply to, forward, delete, and move messages from the Advanced Find dialog box. Clicking New Search will clear the current settings and messages in the Advanced Find dialog box so that you can begin a new search.

OUTLOOK

ASSIGNING CATEGORIES TO A MESSAGE AND USING ADVANCED FIND

1. With Outlook open and *Inbox* the active folder, create and send a new message and assign it to multiple categories by completing the following steps:
   a. Click the New Mail Message button on the Standard toolbar.
   b. Click the To button, change to the *Personal Address Book* in the Select Names dialog box, and then add the student you added to the PAB in chapter 1 as the message recipient.
   c. Key **Managing Mail** in the Subject text box.
   d. Click in the message editing window and then key the following text:
      Outlook provides several methods for managing messages including assigning categories to messages, creating new folders and moving messages to folders, and creating multiple personal folders files.
   e. Click <u>V</u>iew on the message window Menu bar and then click Options, or click the Options button on the Standard toolbar.

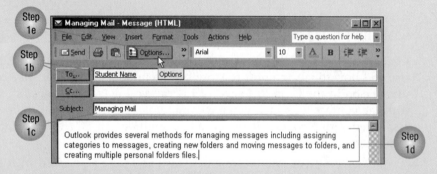

   f. Click the Categories button in the Message Options dialog box.
   g. Click *Ideas, Personal, Strategies* in the A<u>v</u>ailable categories list box and then click OK.
   h. Click the Close button in the Message Options dialog box.
   i. Click <u>S</u>end.
2. View a list of messages assigned to a category, open, and then print a message in the search results list by completing the following steps:
   a. Click <u>T</u>ools and then click A<u>d</u>vanced Find.
   b. Click the More Choices tab in the Advanced Find dialog box.
   c. Click in the <u>C</u>ategories text box and then key **Ideas**.
   d. Click <u>B</u>rowse. *(Note: By default, Outlook looks in the active folder only for messages that meet the criteria. Click Browse to add other folders to the search.)*

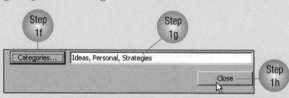

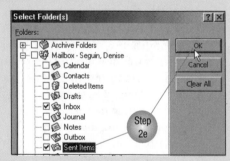

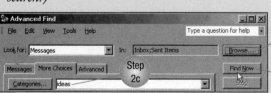

e. Click *Sent Items* in the Folders list box in the Select Folder(s) dialog box and then click OK.

f. Click Find Now.

g. Double-click the message header for the message sent in step 1 in the search results list box to open the message.

h. Click the Print button on the message window toolbar and then close the message window.

i. Click the Close button on the Advanced Find Title bar.

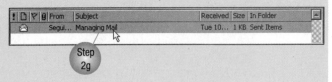

!	D	Y	0	From	Subject		Received	Size	In Folder	
				Segui...	Managing Mail		Tue 10...	1 KB	Sent Items	

Step
2g

Once your mail folders become filled with messages sent and received, using categories to easily locate related messages can be a time-saving technique.

Assigning Tasks and Notes to Contacts

In chapter 4 you learned how to create task requests to assign a task to someone else and how to create notes to store brief reminders. Tasks can also be assigned to a person in the *Contacts* folder, or instead you may want to associate a task with the contact for which you are completing the work. Likewise, a note can be associated with a contact if the note is a reminder for an activity related to a contact.

In exercise 2 you will create a new task and note associated with a contact and in exercise 3 you will view all activities in the Outlook folders for a contact in one window.

exercise 2

ASSIGNING A TASK AND NOTE TO A CONTACT

1. With Outlook open and the *Inbox* folder active, create a new task and associate it with a contact by completing the following steps:

   a. Click the down-pointing triangle on the New button on the toolbar and then click Task in the drop-down list. *(Note: Since Outlook data is closely integrated, you can create any Outlook item from any folder. In this exercise you are creating a task and a note without leaving the* Inbox *folder.)*

   b. With the insertion point positioned in the Subject text box, key **New Product Pricing Memo**.

   c. Change the Priority to *High*.

   d. Click Contacts.

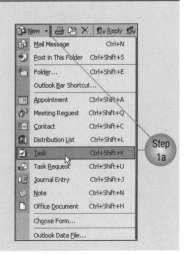

New ▾				X	Reply	
	Mail Message				Ctrl+N	
	Post in This Folder				Ctrl+Shift+S	
	Folder...				Ctrl+Shift+E	
	Outlook Bar Shortcut...					
	Appointment				Ctrl+Shift+A	
	Meeting Request				Ctrl+Shift+Q	
	Contact				Ctrl+Shift+C	
	Distribution List				Ctrl+Shift+L	
	Task				Ctrl+Shift+K	
	Task Request				Ctrl+Shift+U	
	Journal Entry				Ctrl+Shift+J	
	Note				Ctrl+Shift+N	
	Office Document				Ctrl+Shift+H	
	Choose Form...					
	Outlook Data File...					

Step
1a

OUTLOOK

e. With *Contacts* selected in the Look in list box in the Select Contacts dialog box, double-click *Atvar, Bernice* in the Items list box.

f. Click Save and Close in the Task window. The task is added to the task list and will also be tracked by the contact for which the task was associated.

2. Create a new note and associate it with a contact by completing the following steps:

a. Click the down-pointing triangle on the New button on the toolbar and then click Note in the drop-down list.

b. With the insertion point positioned in the Note window, key **Call Bernice about new product pricing**.

c. Click the note icon at the left edge of the Note Title bar.

d. Click Contacts in the drop-down menu.

e. Click in the Contacts text box in the Contacts for Note dialog box, key **Atvar, Bernice**, and then click Close.

f. Click the Close button on the Note Title bar. The note is added to the *Notes* folder and will also be tracked by the contact for which the note was associated.

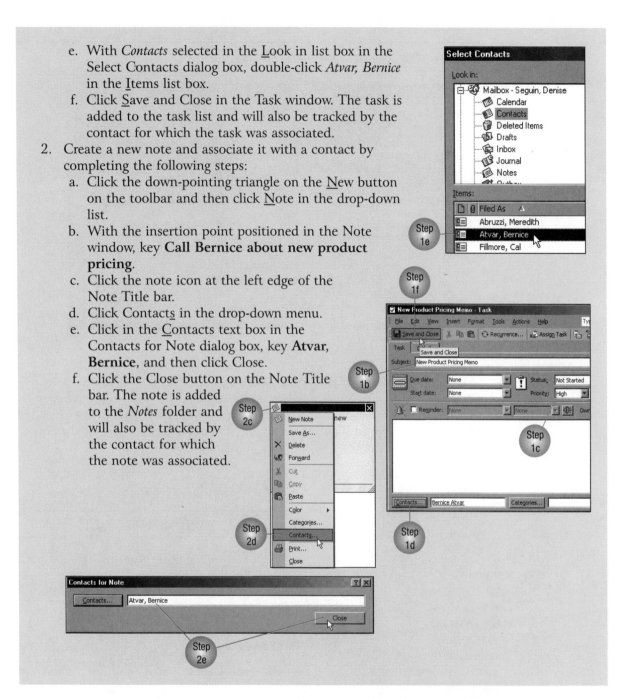

Tracking Activities for a Contact

The Activities tab in the Contact window shown in figure 6.2 displays all Outlook items that have been associated with the active contact. The Show list box defaults to *All Items*. Click the down-pointing triangle next to Show to choose to display only those items in *Contacts, E-mail, Journal, Notes,* or *Upcoming Tasks/Appointments*. Items are displayed in the list box in descending order by subject. Click the *Subject* column heading to sort the list in ascending order, or click the *In Folder* column heading to sort items by folders.

6.2 *Contact Window with Activities Tab Selected*

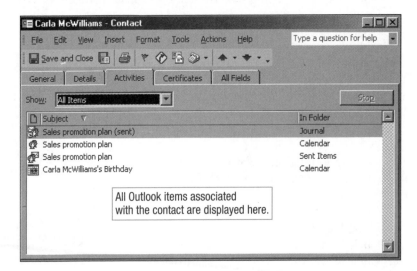

Managing contacts for which you have sent and received e-mail messages, scheduled appointments, created tasks, notes, or journal entries is much easier when all of the information for an individual contact is displayed in one place. Double-click any item in the Activities tab to open, view, edit, or print the entry details in its own window.

exercise 3

VIEWING ACTIVITIES TRACKED BY CONTACT

1. With Outlook open and the *Inbox* folder active, view all of the Outlook items that have been associated with Bernice Atvar by completing the following steps:
   a. Click *Contacts* on the Outlook bar.
   b. Double-click *Atvar, Bernice*.
   c. Click the Activities tab in the Contact window.

2. Open the task item from the Contact window, mark it as complete, and then print the task by completing the following steps:
   a. Double-click the item with the subject *New Product Pricing Memo* to open the task in the Task window.
   b. Change % Complete to 100.
   c. Click File and then Print.
   With *Memo Style* selected in the Print style section of the Print dialog box, click OK.
   d. Click Save and Close.

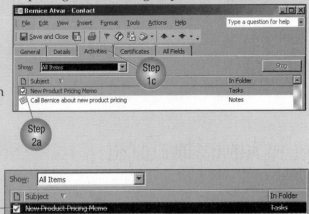

OUTLOOK

3. Open the note item from the Contact window, append additional text to the note, and then print the note by completing the following steps:
   a. Double-click the item with the subject *Call Bernice about new product pricing* to open the note in the Note window.
   b. With the insertion point positioned at the beginning of the note text, move the insertion point to the end of the existing text, press Enter twice and then key the following text:

      Bernice is away on vacation and will be back in the office two weeks from today
   c. Click the note icon at the left edge of the Note Title bar and then click Print at the drop-down menu. With *Memo Style* selected in the Print style section of the Print dialog box, click OK.
   d. Click the Close button on the Note Title bar.
   e. Click the Close button on the Contact window Title bar.
4. Click the *Tasks* icon on the Outlook bar and then view the entry added to the task list in exercise 2 and updated in this exercise.
5. Click the *Note* icon on the Outlook bar and then view the note added to the notes list in exercise 2 and updated in this exercise.
6. Click *Inbox* on the Outlook bar.

Creating an Office Document from Outlook

In chapter 3 you integrated the *Contacts* folder with Outlook by creating a letter for a selected contact using the Letter wizard in Microsoft Word. You also performed a mail merge in Microsoft Word using the contacts as the data source. A Word document, an Excel worksheet, or a PowerPoint presentation can be started from within any of the folders in Outlook.

Click File, point to New, and then click Office Document, or click the down-pointing triangle on the New button and then click Office Document in the drop-down menu. The New Office Document dialog box with the General tab selected opens as shown in figure 6.3. Double-click the icon for the application in which you want to work.

FIGURE

6.3 *New Office Document Dialog Box with General Tab Selected*

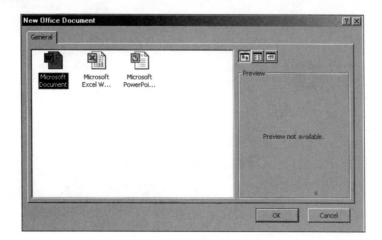

(Note: Insert the student data disk in the drive before starting this exercise.)

1. With Outlook open and the *Inbox* folder active, start Microsoft Excel and create a worksheet by completing the following steps:

    a. Click File, point to New, and then click Office Document.

    b. Double-click the *Microsoft Excel Worksheet* icon in the General tab of the New Office Document dialog box. Microsoft Excel opens and a blank worksheet screen appears.

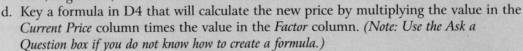

    c. Create the worksheet shown to the right. Use buttons on the Formatting toolbar to apply font, alignment, and color attributes to the cells.

    d. Key a formula in D4 that will calculate the new price by multiplying the value in the *Current Price* column times the value in the *Factor* column. *(Note: Use the Ask a Question box if you do not know how to create a formula.)*

    e. Copy the formula from D4 to the range D5:D7. *(Note: Use the Ask a Question box if you do not know how to copy cells.)*

    f. Format the cells in the range D4:D7 to two decimal places and then deselect the range. *(Note: Use the Decrease Decimal button on the Formatting toolbar.)*

    g. Click the Save button on the Standard toolbar.

    h. Click the down-pointing triangle next to the Save in list box and then click *3½ Floppy (A:)* in the drop-down list.

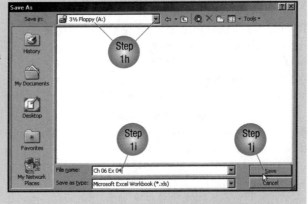

    i. Select the text in the File name text box and then key **Ch 06 Ex 04**.

    j. Click Save.

2. E-mail the worksheet, associate the worksheet with a contact, and print the worksheet by completing the following steps:

    a. Click the E-mail button [icon] on the Standard toolbar. An e-mail header pane opens above the worksheet with the worksheet file name automatically inserted in the Subject text box.

    b. Click the To button, change to the *Personal Address Book* in the Select Names dialog box, and then add the student you added to the PAB in chapter 1 as the message recipient.

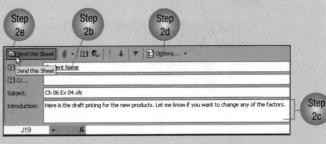

    c. Click in the Introduction text box and then key the following text:
    Here is the draft pricing for the new products. Let me know if you want to change any of the factors.

    d. Click the Options button, click in the Contacts text box in the Message Options dialog box, key **Atvar, Bernice**, and then click Close.

e. Click <u>S</u>end this Sheet.

3. Click <u>F</u>ile and then E<u>x</u>it to close Microsoft Excel. Click <u>N</u>o if prompted to save changes. You are returned to Microsoft Outlook since Excel was started from within Outlook.

4. View the updated list of activities that have been associated with Bernice Atvar by completing the following steps:

   a. With Outlook open and the *Inbox* folder active, click the *Contacts* icon on the Outlook bar.

   b. Double-click *Atvar, Bernice*.

   c. Click the Activities tab in the Contact window.

   d. Double-click the item with the subject *Ch 06 Ex 04.xls*. The

Step 4d

   message window opens for the message sent to the student in the PAB from Excel.

   e. Click the Print button on the message window toolbar.

   f. Close the message window.

   g. Close the Contact window.

5. Click *Inbox* on the Outlook bar.

In exercise 4, the Excel worksheet that was sent via e-mail was embedded in the message window below the introductory text. To send the worksheet as a file attachment, click <u>F</u>ile, point to Sen<u>d</u> To, and then click M<u>a</u>il Recipient (as Attachment). A message window opens with the Excel worksheet file name automatically inserted as a file attachment to the message.

Importing Information into Outlook

Outlook includes the Import and Export wizard which can be used to transfer data from other sources into Outlook, or to send data from Outlook to other applications. For example, you may want to import contacts from another user's personal folders file (pst) to include them in your contact list. The first dialog box in the Import and Export wizard shown in figure 6.4 is used to choose the action you want to perform and the source of the data if you choose to import.

FIGURE

6.4 *Import and Export Wizard*

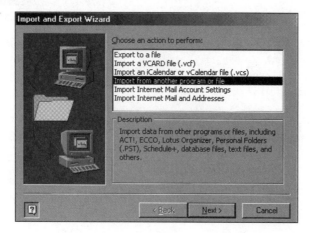

The remaining dialog boxes that appear and the actions required will vary depending on the type of import or export you are performing. Data can be imported to Outlook from the following sources:

- *Import a VCARD file (.vcf).* Contact information can be shared among users by means of vCards, which are often called virtual business cards. The vCard standard is widely used as a means of importing to an electronic address book. If you receive a vCard from someone as an e-mail attachment, you can often import it by simply double-clicking the file.

- *Import an iCalendar or vCalendar (.vcs).* Sharing calendar and scheduling information with other users can be done using the iCalendar (.ics) format or the vCalendar (.vcs) format. In either case, the recipient of the file can import scheduled appointments, meetings, or events into his or her calendar. As with a vCard, if you receive a vCalendar file as an e-mail attachment, you can often import it by double-clicking the file.

- *Import from another program or file.* Use this option in the Import and Export Wizard to import data into Outlook from other sources such as ACT!, ECCO, Lotus Organizer, Personal Folder Files (.pst), Schedule+, Access, Excel, or text-only files.

- *Import Internet Mail Account Settings.* When Outlook is installed on a computer that was previously used with another Internet e-mail system, use this option to import the e-mail account information to Outlook.

- *Import Internet Mail and Addresses.* In addition, to importing the non-Outlook e-mail account information, you can choose this option to also import stored messages and address books that were used in the old system. Outlook can recognize file formats for Eudora and Netscape.

exercise 5

IMPORTING A VCARD AND VCALENDAR FILE

(Note: Make sure the student data disk is in the drive before starting this exercise.)

1. With Outlook open and the *Inbox* folder active, import a vCard file to the *Contacts* folder by completing the following steps:
   a. Click File and then click Import and Export.
   b. Click *Import a VCARD file (.vcf)* in the Choose an action to perform list box in the first Import and Export Wizard dialog box, and then click Next.
   c. Click the down-pointing triangle next to the Look in list box in the VCARD File dialog box, and then click *3½ Floppy (A:)* in the drop-down list.
   d. Double-click *Jona Thorne.vcf* in the file list box. The contact information is added to the *Contacts* folder.

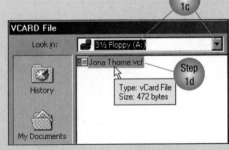

   e. Click *Contacts* on the Outlook bar.
   f. Click the *t* letter box to scroll right and select the contact record for *Thorne, Jona*.
   g. Double-click *Thorne, Jona*.
   h. Click File and then Print. With *Memo Style* selected in the Print style section of the Print dialog box, click OK.
   i. Close the Contact window.

OUTLOOK

2. With the *Contacts* folder active, import a vCalendar file to the *Calendar* folder by completing the following steps:

    a. Click <u>F</u>ile and then click Impor<u>t</u> and Export.

    b. Click *Import an iCalendar or vCalendar file (.vcs)* in the <u>C</u>hoose an action to perform list box in the first Import and Export Wizard dialog box, and then click <u>N</u>ext.

    c. Click the down-pointing triangle next to the Look <u>i</u>n list box in the Browse dialog box, and then click *3½ Floppy (A:)* in the drop-down list.

    d. Click the down-pointing triangle next to the Files of type list box and then click *vCalendar Format (*.vcs)* in the drop-down list.

    e. Double-click *Meeting with Jona Thorne.vcs* in the file list box. The appointment information is added to the *Calendar* folder.

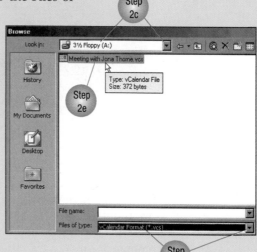

    f. Click *Calendar* on the Outlook bar.

    g. Press Ctrl + G to display the Go to Date dialog box.

    h. Key **10/15/2003** in the <u>D</u>ate text box and then press Enter.

    i. The appointment with Jona Thorne at 10:00 am is in the appointment area. Double-click the entry to open the Appointment window.

    j. Click <u>F</u>ile and then <u>P</u>rint. With *Memo Style* selected in the Print st<u>y</u>le section of the Print dialog box, click OK.

    k. Close the Appointment window.

3. Click *Inbox* on the Outlook bar.

Exporting Information from Outlook

Exporting data from the Outlook folders to another application is performed using the Import and Export wizard shown in the previous topic. When you select *Export to a file* in the <u>C</u>hoose an action to perform list box and then click <u>N</u>ext in the Import and Export wizard, the Export to a File dialog box shown in figure 6.5 appears.

FIGURE

6.5 *Export to a File Dialog Box*

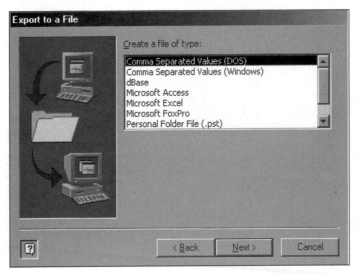

Data can be converted to file formats for use in dBase, Access, Excel, or FoxPro. In addition, information can be exported to a Personal Folder File (.pst), or a generic format for use in other applications where data is separated in the file by commas or tabs. In exercise 6 you will export the information in *Contacts* to Access and then open the table in Access to view how the data was transferred.

exercise 6

EXPORTING CONTACT DATA TO ACCESS

(Note: Make sure the student data disk is in the drive before starting this exercise.)

1. With Outlook open and the *Inbox* folder active, export the data in *Contacts* to a table in Microsoft Access by completing the following steps:
   a. Click File and then click Import and Export.
   b. Click *Export to a file* and then click Next.
   c. Click *Microsoft Access* in the Create a file of type list box in the Export to a File dialog box and then click Next. *(Note: Check with your instructor if a message appears asking if you want to install the translator now—the required program files may not be installed on the computer you are using.)*
   d. Click *Contacts* in the Select folder to export from list box and then click Next.

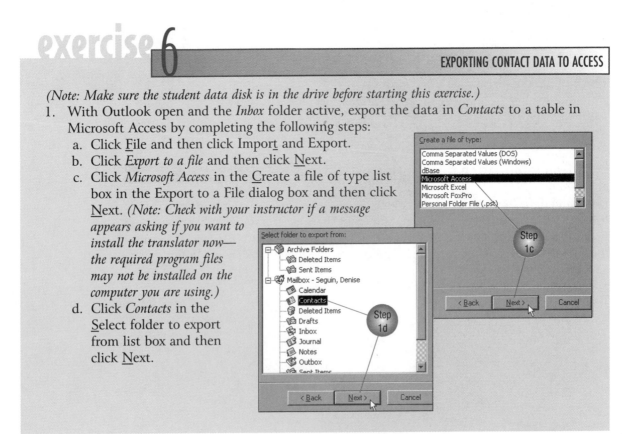

e. Key **A:\Contacts Ch 06 Ex 06** in the <u>S</u>ave exported file as text box and then click
    <u>N</u>ext.

f. Click Finish at the last Export to a File dialog box with the action *Export "Contacts"
    from folder: Contacts* selected in the actions list box. Notice the message below the
    actions list box states *This may take a few minutes and cannot be canceled*. A progress box
    displays as Outlook converts the data and
    saves it to disk.

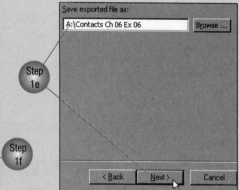

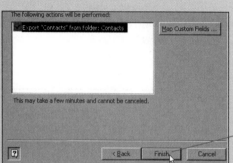

2. Open, view, and print the data exported from Outlook in Microsoft Access by completing
    the following steps:

    a. Click *Start*, point to <u>P</u>rograms, and then click *Microsoft Access*.

    b. Click the Open button on the Standard
        toolbar.

    c. Click the down-pointing triangle next to the
        Look <u>i</u>n list box in the Open dialog box and
        then click *3½ Floppy (A:)* in the
        drop-down list.

    d. Double-click *Contacts Ch 06 Ex 06.mdb*.

    e. With *Tables* selected on the Contacts window
        Objects bar, double-click *Contacts* in the
        Tables list.

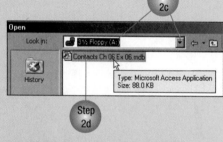

    f. Scroll right to view all of the columns and
        data in the table datasheet.

    g. Print the first page only of the datasheet by
        completing the following steps:

        1) Click <u>F</u>ile and then click <u>P</u>rint.

        2) Click Pages in the Print Range section of
            the Print dialog box.

        3) With the insertion point positioned in
            the <u>F</u>rom text box, key **1**, press Tab, and
            then key **1** in the <u>T</u>o text box.

        4) Click OK.

    h. Close the Contacts : Table window.

    i. Click <u>F</u>ile and then click E<u>x</u>it to close Microsoft Access.

Once the information resides in a table in Microsoft Access you can make changes to the table structure such as inserting, modifying, or deleting fields. Within Access, you can use the contact information to generate queries and create reports.

The last Export to a File dialog box in exercise 6 contained a button named Map Custom Fields. Click this button to choose the fields you want to export to Access as opposed to exporting all of the fields. Figure 6.6 shows the Map Custom Fields dialog box for the contacts exported in exercise 6. Dragging a field name from the To list box to the From list box removes the field from the export operation. Removing unnecessary fields will reduce the size of the exported database and result in a faster export operation.

FIGURE

6.6 **Map Custom Fields Dialog Box**

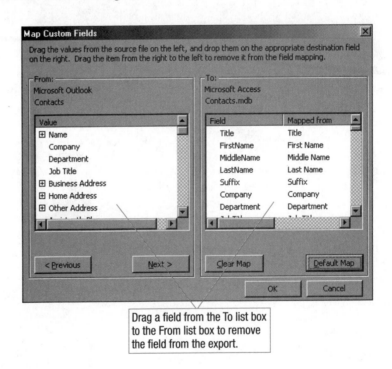

Drag a field from the To list box to the From list box to remove the field from the export.

Data in folders other than *Contacts* can be exported to other applications, such as Microsoft Excel, by following a similar procedure to that in exercise 6. Messages can be exported to a personal folders file which is one method that you can employ to back up important information. Archiving, which is another method of backing up data, is discussed in the next section. The difference between exporting and archiving message folders is that exporting makes a copy of the original data in the exported file, while archiving removes the messages from the current folder after copying them to the archive file.

Archiving Folders

If you receive on average 10 messages per day, that means your *Inbox* folder will have approximately 300 messages at the end of the month! Over time, your mail folders can grow quite large due to the number of messages stored in them. If you use e-mail for business communication, you should archive the messages instead of deleting them so that you maintain essential records. An *archive* is a file containing old messages that have been purged from the mail folder. The archived messages can be retrieved if necessary by opening the archive folder.

You can manually transfer old items to the archive file, or you can rely on the global *AutoArchive* feature to have Outlook do the transferring automatically. Items are considered for archiving when they reach a specified age. The default setting is for AutoArchive to run every 14 days and clean out items that are older than 6 months. If you prefer, you can set different options for each Outlook folder. AutoArchive can either delete the items or move old items to the storage file. The default setting is to move the old items to a file named *archive.pst*.

To change the default options for AutoArchive, display the Options dialog box, click the Other tab, and then click AutoArchive. In the AutoArchive dialog box shown in figure 6.7, choose the options that you want, and then click OK.

FIGURE

6.7 *AutoArchive Dialog Box*

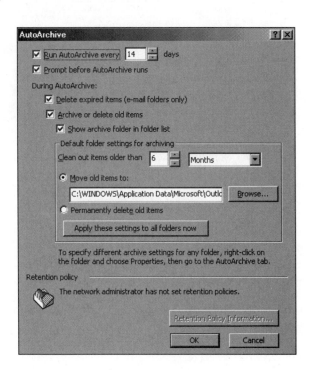

To set AutoArchive options for individual folders, right-click the folder name in the Folder List, click Properties, and then click the AutoArchive tab in the Properties dialog box. Choose one of the following three options: *Do not archive items in this folder, Archive items in this folder using the default settings,* or *Archive this folder using these settings.* When you click Archive this folder using these settings, the options shown in figure 6.8 become active. Choose the time period you want items archived in the Clean out items older than text boxes, choose the location to move the items to, or choose to delete the old items. Changes made to individual folder AutoArchive properties override the global settings in the Options dialog box.

FIGURE

6.8 *Inbox Properties Dialog Box with AutoArchive Tab Selected*

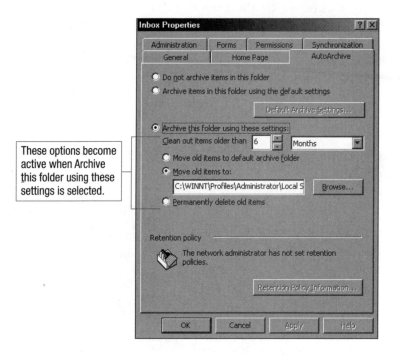

These options become active when Archive this folder using these settings is selected.

The AutoArchive process runs automatically whenever you start Outlook and by default, you will be prompted to click Yes if you want AutoArchive to proceed to clean out old items. The properties of each folder are checked by date, and old items are moved to your archive file. The default AutoArchive option for each Outlook folder is: *Calendar, 6 months, Tasks, 6 months, Journal, 6 months, Sent Items, 2 months,* and *Deleted Items, 2 months. Inbox, Notes, Drafts,* and *Outbox* do not have AutoArchive activated automatically. The *Contacts* folder does not have an AutoArchive tab in the Properties dialog box since contacts are not time-sensitive items.

Manually Archiving Items

To archive at your discretion, turn off AutoArchive by clearing the R̲un AutoArchive every [] days check box in the AutoArchive dialog box. When you are ready to start a manual archive, click F̲ile, and then click A̲rchive to open the Archive dialog box shown in figure 6.9. Click A̲rchive all folders according to their AutoArchive settings to start the archive process for all folders based on each folder's AutoArchive properties. To choose an individual folder to archive, click Ar̲chive this folder and all subfolders, and then click the folder name in the list box. Change the date in the Archive items o̲lder than text box, key an archive file name, or click B̲rowse to navigate to a drive and/or folder in the Archive f̲ile text box, and then click OK.

FIGURE

6.9 *Archive Dialog Box*

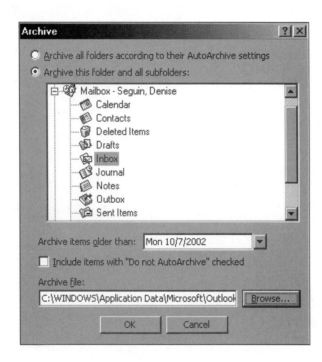

The Status bar displays the message *Archiving 'folder name'* as the archive process is running and you will notice the messages in the folder being removed.

(Note: Check with your instructor before completing the manual archive in step 3 of this exercise for a location that you have write access to on the network or hard drive as archive files are generally too large to store on a floppy disk. Alternatively, delete unnecessary messages in the Sent Items *folder before completing this exercise to reduce it to the smallest possible size.)*

1. With Outlook open and the *Inbox* folder active, check the global AutoArchive settings on the computer you are using by completing the following steps:
   a. Click Tools and then click Options.
   b. Click the Other tab in the Options dialog box.
   c. Click AutoArchive in the AutoArchive section of the Options dialog box with the Other tab selected.
   d. Review the settings in the AutoArchive dialog box and then click OK.
   e. Click OK to close the Options dialog box.

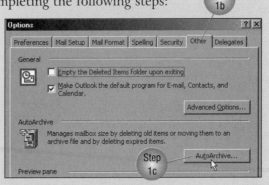
Step 1b

Step 1c

2. View and then change AutoArchive settings for the *Inbox* folder by completing the following steps:
   a. Right-click *Inbox* on the Folder banner.
   b. Click Properties at the shortcut menu.
   c. Click the AutoArchive tab in the Inbox Properties dialog box and then review the current settings for archiving the *Inbox* folder.
   d. Click Archive this folder using these settings. *(Note: Skip this step if Archive this folder is already active.)*
   e. Click the up- or down-pointing triangle next to the value in Clean out items older than until the number is *2*, and then click OK.

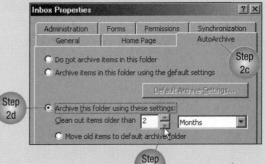
Step 2c

Step 2d

Step 2e

3. Manually archive the *Sent Items* folder by completing the following steps:
   a. Click File and then click Archive.
   b. If necessary, click Archive this folder and all subfolders.
   c. Click *Sent Items* in the Folder List.
   d. Click the down-pointing triangle next to Archive items older than and then click a date in the drop-down calendar that is two weeks prior to the current date.
   e. Delete the file name in the Archive file text box and then key **A:\Sent Items Archive**. *(Note: Key a different drive and/or folder if your instructor has advised that you have write access to a location other than the floppy disk.)*
   f. Click OK. Depending on the number of messages in *Sent Items*, archiving may take a few moments to complete.

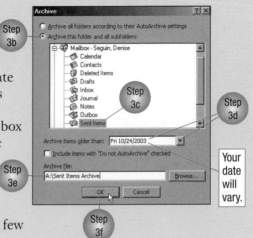
Step 3b

Step 3c

Step 3d

Your date will vary.

Step 3e

Step 3f

4. Restore the *Inbox* folder AutoArchive properties back to the default settings by completing the following steps:
   a. Right-click *Inbox* on the Folder banner.
   b. Click Properties at the shortcut menu.
   c. Click the AutoArchive tab in the Inbox Properties dialog box.
   d. Click Do not archive items in this folder and then click OK.

Mailbox Cleanup Tool

Click Tools and then click Mailbox Cleanup to open the Mailbox Cleanup dialog box shown in figure 6.10. From this dialog box you can view the current size of your mailbox and the individual folders, find old items, start an AutoArchive process, or view and empty the *Deleted Items* folder. The Mailbox Cleanup dialog box provides all of the folder management features in one location.

FIGURE

6.10 *Mailbox Cleanup Dialog Box*

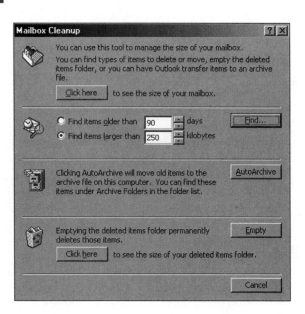

Restoring Archived Items

You can restore items from an archive by importing the archive file. Click File and then click Import and Export to start the Import and Export wizard. Choose *Import from another program or file* in the Choose an action to perform and *Personal Folder File (.pst)* in the Select file type to import from list boxes. When you import, you can select to move all of the archived items back into the folders from which they were archived, or you can choose to import the archived items into a new folder.

Another method that can be used to retrieve items in an archive file is to use the Open command on the File menu to open the archive file name. Click File, point to Open, and then click Outlook Data File. Browse to the location of the archive file and then double-click the file name. When you use this method, an archive folder is added to your folder list. Display the contents of the required archive folder, then open and view messages as required. You can also manually copy or move items to current folders if necessary. Right-click the archive folder name in the Folder banner and then click Close "Archive Folders" at the shortcut menu when finished.

Assigning a Web Page as a Folder Home Page

A Web page can be assigned as the home page for any Outlook folder. Clicking the folder icon on the Outlook bar causes the designated Web page to load in the Information Viewer. This feature is useful to access a company intranet site from within Outlook, saving the time and resources to load a separate Web browser application.

To assign a Web page to a folder, display the Properties dialog box and then click the Home Page tab. Key the URL for the Web page in the Address text box. Click the Show home page by default for this folder check box and then click OK.

exercise 8

ASSIGNING A DEFAULT FOLDER HOME PAGE

1. With Outlook open and the *Inbox* folder active, create a new folder to be used as a Web folder by completing the following steps:
   a. Right-click *Inbox* on the Folder banner and then click New Folder at the shortcut menu.
   b. Key **Web View Folder** in the Name text box in the Create New Folder dialog box.
   c. Click *Mailbox* or *Personal Folders* next to the *Outlook Today* icon in the Select where to place the folder list box. This will place the *Web View* folder at the same level in the folder hierarchy as *Inbox*.
   d. Click OK. Click No if prompted to add a shortcut to the folder on the Outlook bar.

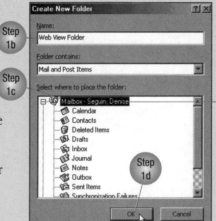

If you are connected to a server where all messages are automatically downloaded to the local computer, this will say *Personal Folders*.

2. Assign a Web page as the default folder home page for the folder created in step 1 by completing the following steps:
   a. With the Folder List pane open, click *Web View Folder* in the Folder List.
   b. Close the Folder List pane.
   c. Right-click *Web View Folder* in the Folder banner and then click Properties at the shortcut menu.

OUTLOOK

d. Click the Home Page tab in the Web View Folder Properties dialog box.

e. Key **www.emcp.com** in the Address text box.

f. Click the Show home page by default for this folder check box.

g. Click OK.

h. The home page for EMCParadigm, the publishers of this textbook, will display in the Information Viewer. *(Note: If you are not currently connected to the Internet, the Dial-Up Connection or other logon dialog box will display.)*

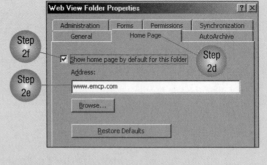

3. View Web pages in Outlook using the *Web View* folder by completing the following steps:

a. Click *Inbox* on the Outlook bar.

b. Click *Inbox* on the Folder banner and then click *Web View Folder* in the Folder List.

c. The Web page for EMCParadigm redisplays in the Information Viewer as it is the default home page set for the folder.

d. Click in the Address text box next to the Folder banner, key **www.microsoft.com**, and then press Enter.

e. Click a link on the Microsoft home page that interests you to display another page.

f. Click *Inbox* on the Outlook bar.

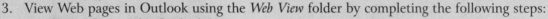

Assigning Permissions to Someone Else to Share a Folder

The items that you have been creating in the various Outlook folders are considered private and can be accessed only by yourself. However, if you are working in Outlook connected to a Microsoft Exchange Server, you can choose to share a folder with another user on the server. For example, sharing folders is useful if more than one person working together on a project wants access to the same items in a message, calendar, or tasks folder. One person can create a new folder in which items related to the project will be stored and then assign permission to the other user to access the folder. Various permission levels are available that define what types of activities the other person can perform in the folder as follows:

- *Owner.* Create, read, edit, and delete all items, and create subfolders.
- *Publishing Editor.* Create, read, edit, and delete all items and create subfolders. A publishing editor is not, however, an *owner*, and therefore cannot assign permissions to other users.
- *Editor.* Create, read, edit, and delete all items.
- *Publishing Author.* Create and read items and create subfolders, and edit and delete only items that the author has created.
- *Author.* Create and read items, and edit and delete only items that the author has created.
- *Contributor.* Create items only.
- *Reviewer.* Read items only.
- *Custom.* Perform a combination of activities defined by the folder owner.

(Note: If you are not connected to a Microsoft Exchange Server, you will not be able to complete this exercise. Check with your instructor before completing this exercise for instructions on to whom you should grant permission to your Calendar *folder.)*

1. With Outlook open and the *Inbox* folder active, assign permission for another user to access your Calendar folder by completing the following steps:
   a. Click *Calendar* on the Outlook bar.
   b. Right-click *Calendar* in the Folder banner and then click Properties at the shortcut menu.
   c. Click the Permissions tab in the Calendar Properties dialog box. *(Note: If the Permissions tab does not exist in the Calendar Properties dialog box, you are not currently connected to a Microsoft Exchange Server—you will not be able to complete the exercise.)*
   d. Click Add.
   e. Key the last name of the person to whom you want to grant permission to your *Calendar* folder in the Type Name or Select from List text box in the Add Users dialog box, or scroll down the list of users and then click the name in the Name list box.
   f. Click Add.
   g. Click OK to close the Add Users dialog box.
   h. Click the down-pointing triangle next to the Permission Level list box in the Permissions section and then click *Author* in the drop-down list.
   i. Click OK to close the Calendar Properties dialog box.
2. Click *Inbox* on the Outlook bar.

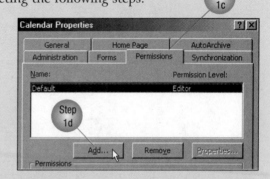

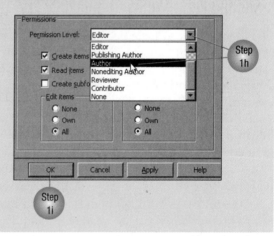

Assigning a Delegate to a Folder

A *delegate* is another user for which you have assigned permission rights to open your folder, create items in the folder, and *respond to items on your behalf*. The recipient of a message sent by your delegate will see both your name and the delegate's name in the message. Adding delegate permissions to a folder is useful for a manager who wants to provide the ability to an assistant to respond to messages or other requests on the manager's behalf while he or she is unavailable.

To assign delegate permissions, open the Options dialog box and click the Delegates tab. Click Add and then key the last name for the delegate or scroll down the Name list box and then click the delegate's name. Click Add and then click OK to close the Add Users dialog box. The Delegate Permissions dialog box shown in figure 6.11 opens where you can set the permissions for each folder.

The Delegates tab does not display in the Options dialog box if you are not connected to a Microsoft Exchange Server.

6.11 *Delegate Permissions Dialog Box*

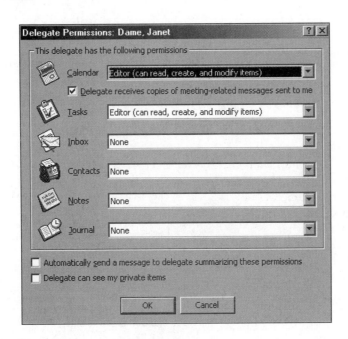

Opening Another User's Folder

When someone has added permission rights to you to access one of their folders, you can open his or her folder and use it as if it were one of your own folders dependent on the permission level the folder owner granted.

Click File, point to Open, and then click Other User's Folder. The Open Other User's Folder dialog box shown in figure 6.12 opens. Key the person's name in the Name text box with the last name followed by first name and separated by a comma and one space, or click Name to choose the folder owner in the Select Name dialog box. Click the down-pointing triangle next to Folder and then click the name of the folder for which you have access. Click OK and the folder opens in the Information Viewer. If you do not have the required permission to the requested folder, an error message displays.

6.12 *Open Other User's Folder Dialog Box*

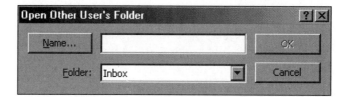

exercise 10

OPENING ANOTHER USER'S CALENDAR FOLDER

(Note: In order to complete this exercise you must have been assigned permission to another student's Calendar *folder in exercise 9.)*

1. With Outlook open and the *Inbox* folder active, open the *Calendar* folder of another user by completing the following steps:
   a. Click File, point to Open, and then click Other User's Folder.
   b. With the insertion point positioned in the Name text box, key the name of the student who assigned you permission rights to his or her *Calendar* folder in exercise 9 in the format lastname, firstname.
   c. Click the down-pointing triangle next to Folder and then click *Calendar* in the drop-down list.
   d. Click OK.
2. Close the *Calendar* folder for the other student.

Step 1b — Key name of student who assigned permissions to you to share his or her calendar as last name first followed by comma one space, and then first name.

Step 1d

Step 1c

Publishing and Obtaining Free/Busy Calendar Information for People on the Internet

Users connected to a Microsoft Exchange Server can see the times when other people are free or busy automatically when planning a meeting just by adding the individual to the attendee list. However, if you frequently communicate with people outside your company to set up meetings and so on, you can choose to publish your free/busy information to a shared location either on your company's Web server or by using the Microsoft Office Internet Free/Busy Service. The other users can then access your information through the Internet. Likewise, the other users need to publish their information for you to be able to view their free/busy data.

The Microsoft Office Internet Free/Busy Service is an application hosted by Microsoft Corporation. You can publish your free/busy blocks of time to a secure shared Web-based location. People who are not members of the service and/or who are not authorized by you to view your free/busy times will not have access to the information.

To join the Microsoft Office Free/Busy Service, complete the following steps:

1. Click Tools and then click Options.
2. Click Calendar Options in the Options dialog box.
3. Click Free/Busy Options in the Advanced section of the Calendar Options dialog box.
4. Click the Publish and search using Microsoft Office Internet Free/Busy Service check box in the Internet Free/Busy section of the Free/Busy Options dialog box shown in figure 6.13.
5. Click the Request free/busy information in meeting invitations check box. This will enable you to view the free/busy times for other members who have authorized you to view their information. For people whose free/busy times cannot be accessed, Outlook automatically adds information to the meeting request message inviting him or her to join the free/busy service.
6. Click Manage. You will be required to log on to Microsoft Passport. If you do not have a Passport account you will have to create one to join the Free/Busy service and make sure the account is set up to work with Outlook. Follow the on-screen directions to continue and when the account is successfully created and you have joined the service click OK to close the Free/Busy Options dialog box. *(Note: If the feature has not been installed on the computer you are using, you will be prompted to install the feature now. Click Yes.)*
7. Click OK to close the Calendar Options dialog box and then click OK to close the Options dialog box.

FIGURE

6.13 *Free/Busy Options Dialog Box*

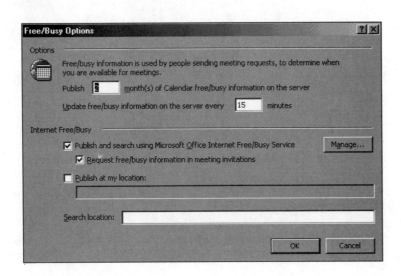

Change the number of months of free/busy information to publish and the time interval between updates in the Options section of the Free/Busy Options dialog box.

The Publish at my location check box is used to specify a location on another server such as your company's Web server for publishing free/busy information. Key the URL for the free/busy information in the Publish at my location text box and then key the server name in the Search location text box. Free/busy data is stored in a file with an extension of .vfb. The location address can be one that uses FTP or HTTP protocols.

exercise 11

CHANGING FREE/BUSY OPTIONS

1. With Outlook open and the *Inbox* folder active, change the free/busy options for publishing your *Calendar* information by completing the following steps:
   a. Click Tools and then click Options.
   b. Click Calendar Options in the Options dialog box.
   c. Click Free/Busy Options in the Advanced section of the Calendar Options dialog box.
   d. Key **3** in the Publish [] month(s) of Calendar free/busy information on the server text box in the Options section of the Free/Busy Options dialog box.
   e. Press Tab and then key **60** in the Update free/busy information on the server every [] minutes text box.

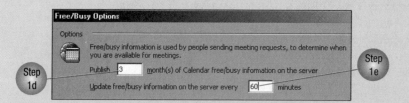

   f. Click the Publish and search using Microsoft Office Internet Free/Busy Service check box in the Internet Free/Busy section. *(Note: Skip this step if the check box is already selected.)*
   g. Click the Request free/busy information in meeting invitations. *(Note: Skip this step if the check box is already selected.)*
   h. Click OK to close the Free/Busy

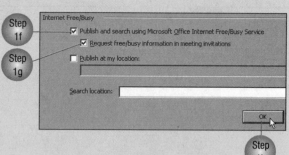

   Options dialog box. If the feature has not been installed on the computer you are using, you will be prompted to install it now. Check with your instructor if necessary. *(Note: Normally you would click Manage before clicking OK, proceed to set up your account on Microsoft Passport, and then join the Internet Free/Busy service. Since Web sites are often updated and any changes made by Microsoft could cause a change in how to proceed, these steps have been left out of this exercise.)*
   i. Click OK to close the Calendar Options dialog box and then click OK to close the Options dialog box.

OUTLOOK

2. Change the free/busy options back to the default settings by completing the following steps:
   a. Click Tools, Options, and then click Calendar Options.
   b. Click Free/Busy Options in the Calendar Options dialog box.
   c. Key **2** in the Publish [] month(s) of Calendar free/busy information on the server text box.
   d. Press Tab and then key **15** in the Update free/busy information on the server every [] minutes text box.
   e. Click OK three times.

Creating a Private Appointment

When another user has access to your *Calendar* folder either as a delegate or through permissions on the folder properties, he or she can view all of the appointments in your folder. If you are creating an appointment and do not want other users to see the appointment details, click the Private check box in the Appointment window. The appointment details will appear in your folder, but details will be hidden when others access the folder.

To mark an existing appointment private, right-click the appointment box in the Appointment area, and then click Private at the shortcut menu.

exercise 12

CREATING A PRIVATE APPOINTMENT

1. With Outlook open and the *Inbox* folder active, click *Calendar* on the Outlook bar.
2. Press Ctrl + G to open the Go To Date dialog box, key **10/15/2003** in the Date text box and then press Enter or click OK.
3. Create a new appointment and mark it as private by completing the following steps:
   a. Double-click next to *12 PM* in the Appointment area to open an Appointment window.
   b. With the insertion point positioned in the Subject text box, key **Doctor's appointment**.
   c. Change the End time to *1:00 PM*.
   d. Click the Private check box in the lower right corner of the Appointment window.
   e. Click Save and Close. The appointment appears in the Appointment area with an icon of a key indicating to you the appointment is private.

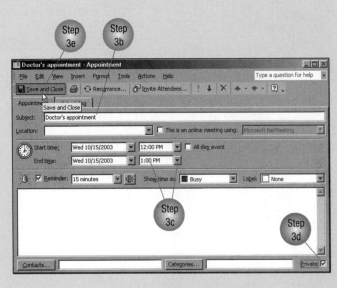

4. Click the Print button on the Standard toolbar. With *Daily Style* selected in the Print style section of the Print dialog box, click OK.

5. Click *Inbox* on the Outlook bar.

Sending and Receiving Newsgroup Messages

A newsgroup is a collection of related messages about a particular topic that have been posted by users to a news server. Newsgroups are generally focused on members sharing information with each other or offering comments for discussion on a topic such as a software program, or a hobby such as gardening or traveling. Newsgroups can be a valuable source of information; however, keep in mind that anyone can join a newsgroup and post messages regardless of their professional experience or training.

You access newsgroups through a news server that is maintained by your company or ISP. Companies can create private newsgroups accessible only by employees through an Intranet. Public newsgroups are available for every imaginable subject you can think of. To read and post messages to a newsgroup you need a newsreader application.

If you have not set up a specific newsreader program on the computer you are using, Outlook will automatically start the Outlook Newsreader. To start the default newsreader, make sure you are connected to the Internet, click View, point to Go To, and then click News. The Microsoft Outlook Newsreader will open as shown in figure 6.14.

FIGURE

6.14 *Microsoft Outlook Newsreader Window*

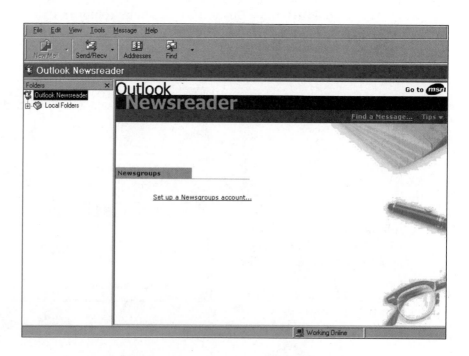

OUTLOOK

To subscribe to a newsgroup you need the name of the news server, and in some cases, an account name and password. As shown in figure 6.14, the Outlook Newsreader looks similar to the regular Outlook window with the Folder List pane open. To the right of the Folders pane is the Messages pane. Once you have subscribed to a newsgroup, messages will appear in the Messages pane with a Preview pane at the bottom which displays the first few lines of the selected message.

In a newsgroup a message is called a *post*. When someone posts a message on a particular subject and someone else responds to the message, the original message and the response message are grouped together by the subject. A plus symbol next to a message header, indicates there are more messages related to the subject that are not displayed. Click the plus symbol to expand the message subject and view the related messages. This group of related messages is called a *thread*. Think of a thread as a conversation between members in a newsgroup about a particular subject.

To read messages in a newsgroup, click the newsgroup name in the Folders pane. The messages in the selected newsgroup will download into the Messages pane. Click a message header to preview it in the Preview pane. Double-clicking a message opens it in a message window.

New messages appear in bold similar to e-mail messages in Outlook. As soon as you preview or open a message, it is no longer displayed in bold. Use the View, Current View menu to reduce the messages listed in the Messages pane by the following categories: *Show All Messages, Hide Read Messages, Show Downloaded Messages, Show Replies to my Messages, Hide Read or Ignored Messages.*

exercise 13

CREATING A NEWS ACCOUNT, SUBSCRIBING TO A NEWSGROUP, AND OPENING MESSAGES

(Note: This exercise and the next exercise work on the assumption that the computer you are using is already set up to access your news server and that the default newsreader program is Outlook Newsreader. Check with your instructor if necessary for alternate instructions.)

1. With Outlook open and the *Inbox* folder active, click <u>V</u>iew, point to <u>G</u>o To, and then click News to open the Outlook Newsreader program.
2. Set up a newsgroup account in order to post and reply to messages by completing the following steps:
   a. Click <u>T</u>ools and then click Accounts.
   b. Click the <u>A</u>dd button in the Internet Accounts dialog box and then click News. The Internet Connection Wizard starts.
   c. Key **Student Name** (where your name is substituted for *Student Name*) in the <u>D</u>isplay name text box and then click <u>N</u>ext. The name you key is the name that will appear in the From line on any messages that you post to the newsgroup.

Step 2b

Your list of Accounts will vary.

d. Key your e-mail address in the E-mail address text box and then click Next.

e. Key **news.microsoft.com** in the News (NNTP) server text box and then click Next. Microsoft Corporation maintains this news server for individuals to find information related to Microsoft products.

f. Click Finish at the last Internet Connection Wizard dialog box. You are returned to the Internet Accounts dialog box and the news server *news.microsoft.com* is added to the Folders pane.

g. Click the News tab in the Internet Accounts dialog box to view the news account just added.

h. Click Close.

i. Click Yes at the message box asking if you want to download newsgroups from the news account you added. When the download is complete, the Newsgroup Subscriptions dialog box appears. *(Note: Downloading newsgroups may take a few moments to complete depending on the amount of newsgroups maintained on the news server and the speed of your Internet connection.)*

3. Subscribe to a newsgroup on the Microsoft news server by completing the following steps:

a. With the Newsgroup Subscriptions dialog box open and the All tab selected, scroll down the first few screens of newsgroup names in the Newsgroup list box to see the various newsgroups available for Microsoft products.

b. Key **office xp** in the Display newsgroups which contain text box.

c. Scroll down the Newsgroup list box and then click *microsoft.public.jp.officexp.outlook*.

d. Click Subscribe. An icon of a message in a folder with a red push pin appears next to the newsgroup name.

e. Click the Subscribed tab at the bottom of the Newsgroup list box. The newsgroup *microsoft.public.jp.officexp.outlook* appears in the Newsgroup list box and the Unsubscribe button becomes active.

f. Click OK to close the Newsgroup Subscriptions dialog box. The subscribed newsgroup name appears in the Folders pane below the news server name.

4. Download messages from the news server, browse, and then open a message by completing the following steps:

a. If necessary, drag the right border of the Folders pane to the right to increase the width and view the entire newsgroup name.

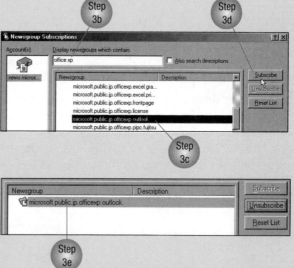

b. Click *microsoft.public.jp.officexp.outlook* in the Folders pane. The first 300 message headers are downloaded. The number of additional messages on the news server that have not been downloaded appears on the Status bar.

c. Scroll down the Messages pane and view the entries in the *Subject* column. Messages that appear to have garbled characters in the *Subject* column indicate that the message was posted in a language other than English.

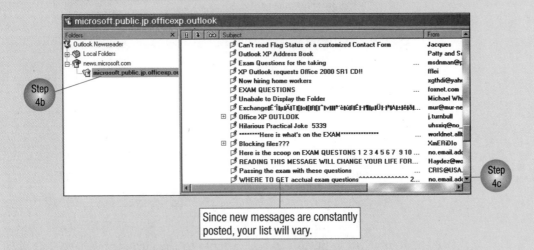

Since new messages are constantly posted, your list will vary.

d. Click a message header in the Message pane to view the first few lines of the message in the Preview pane.

e. Double-click a message header to open the message in a message window. Read and then close the message.

f. Look for a threaded message with a plus symbol next to it. Click the plus symbol to expand the thread. Double-click the first message to read the question or comment that was posted to the newsgroup and then close the message window. Double-click the indented message below it to read the threaded reply from another user and then close the message window.

To unsubscribe to a newsgroup, click <u>T</u>ools and then click Ne<u>w</u>sgroups, or click the Newsgroups button on the toolbar to open the Newsgroup Subscriptions dialog box. Click the Subscribed tab, click the newsgroup name in the Newsgroup list box, and then click <u>U</u>nsubscribe.

Posting Messages in a Newsgroup

The Standard toolbar in the Microsoft Outlook Newsreader contains two buttons that can be used to post a message in a newsgroup: *New Post*, and *Reply Group*. Use the New Post button to post a new message to the newsgroup. A message window opens with the name of the newsgroup automatically entered for you as shown in figure 6.15. Key a subject and message, and then click the Send button.

6.15 *New Post Message Window*

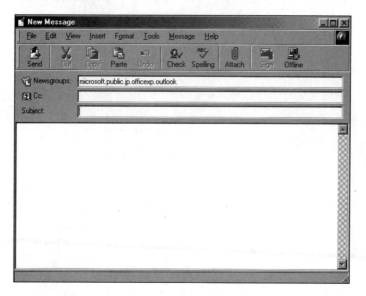

Use the Reply Group button to post a reply to the current message that you are reading in the Messages pane. This results in a thread being posted to the original message. The newsgroup name, original subject, and original text are automatically inserted in the message window. Key your response in a similar manner that you would reply to an e-mail message, and then click Send.

Do not post a message in a newsgroup until you have read quite a few of the existing messages and are comfortable with the style and content that is consistent with the existing messages in the newsgroup. You will also get a feeling for the subjects that have been exhausted by reading through threads to avoid bringing up a matter that has been thoroughly discussed. When you decide to contribute to a newsgroup by posting a message, keep the message short and to the point.

There are test areas set up in newsgroups where new members can post a test message to practice the steps before using a "live" newsgroup. In the next exercise you will post a message to one of these test areas.

exercise 14

POSTING A MESSAGE TO A NEWSGROUP

1. With Microsoft Outlook Newsreader open, click Tools and then click Newsgroups, or click the Newsgroups button on the toolbar to display the Newsgroup Subscriptions dialog box.
2. Subscribe to a test newsgroup and post a message by completing the following steps:
   a. Key **test** in the Display newsgroups which contain text box.
   b. Click *microsoft.test* in the Newsgroup list box and then click Subscribe.
   c. Click OK to close the Newsgroup Subscriptions dialog box.
   d. Click *microsoft.test* in the Folders pane.

OUTLOOK

e. Post your own test message to the newsgroup by completing the following steps:
1) Click the New Post button on the Standard toolbar.
2) With the insertion point positioned in the Subject text box, key **Testing a new message**.
3) Click in the message editing window and then key **This is a test of posting a message to a newsgroup**.
4) Click Send.
5) Click OK if a dialog box appears

telling you the message has been sent to the news server and that it may not appear immediately. You may need to check back at a later time to see your message posted.

3. Click File and then Exit to close Microsoft Outlook Newsreader and return to Outlook.

Sending and Receiving Instant Messages

Communicating in real time (immediately) is fast becoming a popular alternative to e-mail. Instant messaging (IM) is similar to an online chat with the exception that there are usually only two participants. IM runs in the background all of the time that you are working on your computer. When a message for you arrives or one of your contacts goes online, a pop-up screen informs you of the activity on the messenger service.

To use instant messaging you must install Instant Messaging client software for the messenger service that you want to use and obtain an IM address. Outlook includes support for MSN Messenger Service and Microsoft Exchange Instant Messaging Service.

MSN Messenger

To send and receive instant messages in Outlook, you need to add the instant message address for each contact with whom you want to communicate in the IM address field in the contact window. Likewise, the other individual needs to add your address to their instant messaging program so that messages sent from you are accepted at their end.

(Note: Check with your instructor before completing this exercise in case the computer you are using already has IM client software installed and accounts have already been created for your class on the IM service. If you are using the Windows XP operating system, it automatically includes the Instant Messaging client software.)

1. With Outlook open and the *Inbox* folder active, click File and then Exit to close Outlook.

2. Download the instant messaging client software and obtain an IM address by completing the following steps:

   a. Start Internet Explorer.

   b. Key **http://messenger.msn.com** in the Address text box. *(Note: Web sites and procedures are often updated—if the screen that you see does not match with the instructions in this exercise, check with your instructor, or substitute appropriate alternate instructions.)*

   c. Click Download Now on the MSN® Messenger for Windows®.

   d. Click Download Now at the Get MSN® Messenger Software page.

   e. Click Run this program from its current location in the File Download dialog box and then click OK. *(Note: Depending on the speed of your Internet connection, the software may take a few moments to load.)*

   f. Click Yes at the Security Warning dialog box asking if you want to install and run the Messenger software.

   g. Read the license agreement presented in the Messenger dialog box and then click Yes to accept the terms of the license agreement. The software will begin installing on the computer you are using. When the installation is complete, the MSN Messenger dialog box displays.

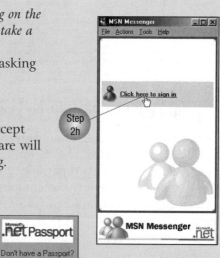

   h. Click in the MSN Messenger window over the link *Click here to sign in*.

   i. If you have an existing hotmail account, close all windows and proceed to exercise 16. If you do not have a hotmail account, click the *Get one here* link below *Don't have a Passport?* in the Sign in to .NET Messenger Service - MSN Messenger dialog box.

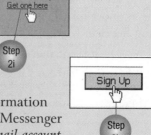

   j. Key the required field entries in the Profile Information and Account Information sections of the .NET Messenger Service Get a free Passport page. *(Note: The hotmail account address and password that you create will be your sign-in name and password for the Messenger Service.)*

   k. Click the Sign Up button at the bottom of the page.

l. Key the required field entries in the Profile Information and Account Information sections of the Microsoft .NET Passport Member Services Registration page, scroll to the bottom of the page, read the Agreement between you and Microsoft section, and then click I Agree.

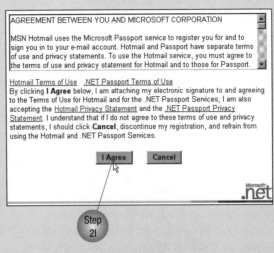

m. Click Continue in the Registration is Complete Corporation section on the MSN Hotmail page.

n. Scroll to the bottom of the WebCourier Free Subscriptions page and then click Continue.

o. Scroll to the bottom of the Special Offer Newsletters page and then click Continue to E-mail.

p. Close the Hotmail Home Page window.

q. Close all other open windows.

exercise **16**

ADDING A CONTACT TO MSN MESSENGER

(Note: Check with your instructor before completing this exercise to find out which student in the class you will be partnered with for this exercise and the next exercise. In this exercise you will add the student to your contacts in MSN Messenger and in the next exercise you will load Outlook and use IM within Outlook. If the computer you are using has a different IM software application, the steps you complete to add a contact and the screens you will see will vary from those shown below.)

1. Click *Start*, point to *Programs*, and then click *MSN Messenger* to start MSN Messenger.

2. Log in to the MSN Messenger Instant Messaging service by completing the following steps:

   a. Click in the MSN Messenger window over the link *Click here to sign in*.

   b. Key the hotmail address you created in exercise 15 in the Sign-in name text box in the Sign in to .NET Messenger Service - MSN Messenger dialog box.

   c. Click in the Password text box and then key the password you created in exercise 15.

   d. Click OK. The Instant Messaging service verifies your identity and then presents the MSN Messenger window. *(Note: If the student that you are partnered with for this exercise and the next has already completed this exercise, you will see the message shown in figure 6.16. Click OK. MSN Messenger will automatically add him or her to your contact list and you can proceed to exercise 17)*

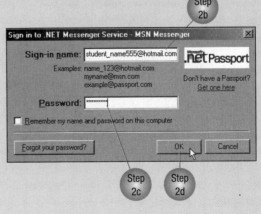

e. Click *Add a Contact* in the I want to section of the MSN Messenger window.

f. With By e-mail address or sign-in name selected in the How do you want to add a contact? section of the Add a Contact dialog box, click Next.

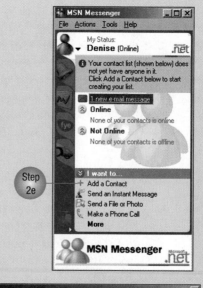

Step 2e

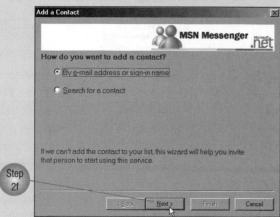

Step 2f

g. Key the e-mail address of the student to whom you will be sending an instant message in the Please type your contact's complete e-mail address text box, and then click Next.

Step 2g

h. Click Finish at the Add a Contact dialog box that says the student was added to your list.

i. Click the Close button on the MSN Messenger window Title bar. Click OK if a dialog box appears telling you the program will continue to run in the Taskbar. The *MSN Messenger* icon is added to the Taskbar next to the current time.

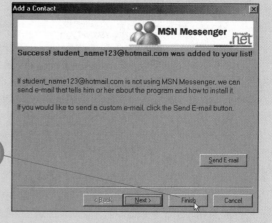

Step 2h

OUTLOOK

Clicking the *MSN Messenger - Signed In* icon on the Taskbar will cause a pop-up menu to appear with options for launching the MSN home page, checking your hotmail account, sending an instant message, changing your online status, signing out, or exiting. Double-click the icon to open the MSN Messenger window.

If a person adds your IM account to his or her contact list, the dialog box shown in figure 6.16 appears. Clicking OK will automatically allow the person to see when you are online and add their account to your contact list.

FIGURE

6.16 *MSN Messenger Dialog Box*

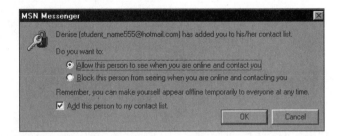

exercise 17

SENDING AN INSTANT MESSAGE FROM OUTLOOK

(Note: The screens shown in this exercise were created using MSN Messenger. If the IM client you are using is a different application, your screens will vary from those shown below.)

1. Start Outlook.
2. Click the *Contacts* icon on the Outlook bar.
3. Add a contact record for the student to whom you will be sending an instant message by completing the following steps:
   a. Click the New Contact button on the Standard toolbar.
   b. With the insertion point positioned in the Full <u>N</u>ame text box, key the student's first and last name.
   c. Click in the IM address text box and then key the student's complete hotmail account address.

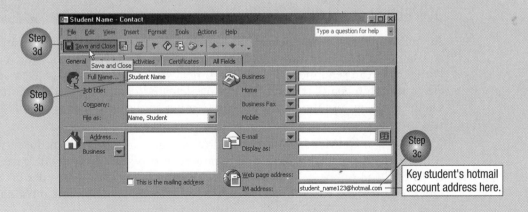

d. Click _S_ave and Close.
4. Send an instant message to the student by completing the following steps:
   a. Double-click the contact record for the student you added to your Contacts list in step 3. A yellow information box displays below the tabs in the Contact window informing you the contact is online.
   b. Click over the text _Click here to send an instant message_ in the Contact window. A Conversation window for the student will open.
   c. Key **Instant Messaging is fun**! in the message text box at the bottom of the window and then click Send.

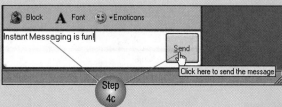

d. Send a few more messages back and forth to each other.
   e. When you are finished using MSN Messenger, click the Close button on the Conversation window Title bar.
   f. Click the Close button on the Contact window Title bar.
5. Click _Inbox_ on the Outlook bar.
6. Sign out of MSN Messenger by completing the following steps:
   a. Click the _MSN Messenger - Signed In_ icon on the Taskbar next to the current time.
   b. Click Si_g_n Out at the pop-up menu.

Scheduling an Online Meeting

An online meeting can be scheduled in _Calendar_ where the participants can collaborate to work on the same document and view changes as they are made. Participants can send messages to each other, write notes or draw objects on an electronic whiteboard, transfer files, or participate in audio and video conferences. Online meetings use the Microsoft NetMeeting application that is included with Internet Explorer.

Hosting a NetMeeting requires additional software installed on the server that will be used for the workgroup collaboration. In this section, you will learn how to schedule an online meeting using NetMeeting in the _Calendar_ folder of Outlook; however, you will not be participating in an actual online meeting.

Complete the following steps to schedule an online meeting:

1. With the *Calendar* folder active, navigate to the day that the online meeting is to be held, click next to the desired time in the Appointment area, and then click File, point to New, and then click Meeting Request.
2. In the Untitled - Meeting window, click the This is an online meeting using checkbox. If necessary, click the down-pointing triangle next to This is an online meeting using, and then click *Microsoft NetMeeting* in the drop-down list. The Meeting window expands below the Location text box to include additional options as shown in figure 6.17 once the online meeting option has been selected.
3. Click the To button, and then select the names of the people who will be participating in the meeting from the Select Attendees and Resources dialog box.
4. Key a description of the meeting in the Subject text box. The entry in the subject text box is used as the NetMeeting conference name.
5. Enter the meeting end time in the End time time text box.
6. To have NetMeeting start automatically at the appointed day and time with a reminder, click the Automatically start NetMeeting with reminder check box.
7. Key the server address in the Directory Server dialog box. This is the server that the participants will be connected to during the meeting to allow workgroup collaboration. The system administrator for your network would provide you with this entry.
8. Key the e-mail address of the individual who is organizing the NetMeeting in the Organizer's e-mail text box.
9. If a document will be collaborated on during the meeting, key the path and file name for the document on the server in the Office document text box.
10. Click Send.

FIGURE

6.17 **Meeting Window with NetMeeting Selected**

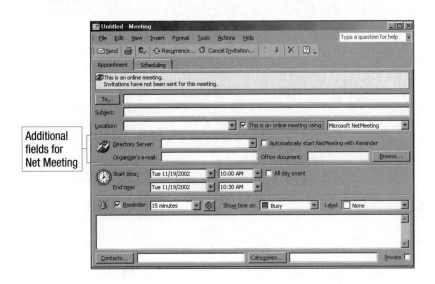

Additional fields for Net Meeting

A meeting request message is sent to each of the attendees. When the attendee receives the meeting request message, he or she clicks Accept, Tentative, or Decline to respond to the meeting invitation.

exercise 18

SCHEDULING AN ONLINE MEETING USING NETMEETING

1. With Outlook open and the *Inbox* folder active, click the *Calendar* icon on the Outlook bar.
2. Display the date *Wednesday, October 15, 2003* in the Appointment area.
3. Click next to 4:00 PM in the Appointment area.
4. Schedule a one-hour online meeting using Microsoft NetMeeting by completing the following steps:
   a. Click File, point to New, and then click Meeting Request.
   b. Click the check box next to This is an online meeting using. If necessary, click the down-pointing triangle next to This is an online meeting using, and click *Microsoft NetMeeting* in the drop-down list.
   c. Click the To button. Change to the Personal Address Book, add the name of the student you added to the PAB in chapter 1 to the Required list box, and then click OK to close the Select Attendees and Resources dialog box.
   d. Click in the Subject text box and then key **Online Meeting Demonstration**.
   e. Change the End time to *5:00 PM (1 hour)*.
   f. Click the Automatically start NetMeeting with Reminder check box.
   g. Click in the Directory Server text box and then key **http://servername**. *(Note: This is a fictitious server name for learning purposes only.)*
   h. Click in the Organizer's e-mail text box and then key your e-mail address.
   i. Click Send. The online meeting appears in the Appointment area as shown.

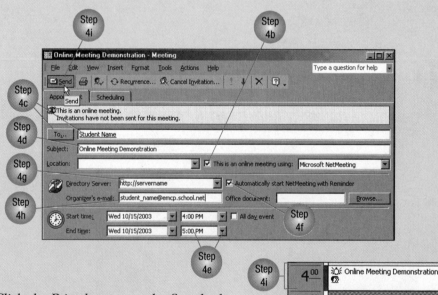

5. Click the Print button on the Standard toolbar. With *Daily Style* selected in the Print style section of the Print dialog box, click OK.
6. Click *Inbox* on the Outlook bar.

CHAPTER summary

➤ One of the methods that can be used to locate and/or manage messages is to associate a message with a keyword in the category list and then group messages by the category in the Advanced Find dialog box.

➤ *Tasks* and *Notes* can be integrated with *Contacts* by assigning a task to a person in the Contacts folder, or associating a task or note with the contact for which you are completing the work.

➤ Open a Contact window and then click the Activities tab to view all of the Outlook items associated with the contact in one place.

➤ A Word document, an Excel worksheet, or a PowerPoint presentation can be started from within any of the folders in Outlook by clicking File, pointing to New, and then clicking Office Document.

➤ Start the Import and Export Wizard to transfer data from other sources into Outlook, or to send data from Outlook to other applications. Click File and then click Import and Export.

➤ An archive is a file containing old messages that have been purged from the active mail folders.

➤ Outlook folders can be set to automatically archive old items based on the age of the item, or you can manually transfer old items to the archive file.

➤ The AutoArchive dialog box accessed from the Options dialog box is used to set the global archive options.

➤ Open the Properties dialog box for an individual folder to set different AutoArchive options that override the global options.

➤ Click File and then click Archive to perform a manual archive for a folder.

➤ The Mailbox Cleanup dialog box accessed from the Tools menu provides all of the folder management features in one location.

➤ Archived items can be restored by importing the archive.pst file back into Outlook, or by opening the archive file.

➤ A Web page can be assigned as the home page for any Outlook folder by keying the URL in the Address text box on the Home Page tab of the Properties dialog box for the desired folder.

➤ A folder can be shared with someone else by assigning the individual permission rights to access the folder on the Permissions tab in the Properties dialog, or by granting the individual delegate privileges in the Delegates tab of the Options dialog box.

➤ Click File, point to Open, and then click Other User's Folder to open a folder for which you have been granted permission rights.

➤ The Microsoft Office Internet Free/Busy Service is an application hosted by Microsoft Corporation in which you can publish free/busy blocks of your time to a secure shared Web-based location. This allows you to share your calendar information with other users not on the same network.

➤ Click the Private check box in the Appointment window to hide appointment details from other users of your calendar.

➤ A newsgroup is a collection of related messages about a particular topic that have been posted by users to a news server.

➤ Access to a news server is provided by your company or ISP.

➤ Click View, point to Go To, and then click News to start Microsoft Outlook Newsreader.

➤ In a newsgroup a message is called a post and a group of related messages is called a thread.

➤ Display the Newsgroup Subscriptions dialog box to subscribe and unsubscribe to newsgroups.

➤ Once a newsgroup has been subscribed to the newsgroup name appears in the Folders pane. Click the newsgroup name to download the messages.

➤ Reading, replying to, and posting new messages in Outlook Newsreader is similar to using e-mail.

➤ Do not post a message in a newsgroup until you have become accustomed to the style and content that is consistent with the newsgroup.

➤ Newsgroups sometimes provide test areas for new users to post a test message to practice the steps before using the live newsgroup.

➤ Instant messaging (IM) is similar to online chat with the exception that generally there are only two participants.

➤ Prior to using IM in Outlook, you need to have an IM client software application installed, have an IM account registered, and have added the IM contacts that you want to communicate with in the IM software.

➤ Key a participant's IM address in the *IM address* field in the Contact window of Outlook.

➤ Opening a Contact window for someone with whom you have set up instant messaging will cause a message to appear letting you know whether the individual is online or not.

➤ Online meetings using Microsoft NetMeeting can be scheduled in *Calendar* by opening a Meeting window and clicking the This is an online meeting using check box.

COMMANDS review

Command	Mouse/Keyboard
Advanced Find	Click Tools, Advanced Find
Archive	Click File, Archive
Assign category to a message	Click Edit, Categories
Create an Office document	Click File, New, Office Document
Open another user's folder	Click File, Open, Other User's Folder
Set Free/Busy options	Click Tools, Options, Calendar Options, Free/Busy Options
Set global AutoArchive options	Click Tools, Options, Other, AutoArchive
Start the Import and Export wizard	Click File, Import and Export
Start Newsreader	Click View, Go To, News

CONCEPTS check

Completion: On a blank sheet of paper, indicate the correct term, symbol, or command for each item.

1. Group messages by a category using this dialog box.
2. Click this tab in the Contact window to view all of the Outlook items that have been associated with the active contact.
3. Open this dialog box to start a Microsoft Excel worksheet from Outlook.
4. Use this wizard to transfer data to or from other applications and Outlook.
5. This is the term given to a virtual business card that is used to exchange contact information with other users.
6. This Outlook feature globally transfers items from the current Outlook folders to a separate file used to store old items.
7. Open this dialog box for an individual folder to change the time period for which items should be purged from the current folder.
8. Click this tab in the folder Properties dialog box to specify a Web page as the starting page for the folder.
9. This permission level allows the user to create, read, edit, and delete all items and create subfolders.
10. These two permission levels allow the user to edit and delete only the items that he or she has created.
11. Members of this service can share calendar information by publishing their free/busy blocks of time to a secure shared Web-based location.

12. Click this check box in the Appointment window to prevent the appointment details from being displayed to other users who have access to your calendar.
13. A message in a newsgroup is referred to by this term.
14. This is the term used in newsgroups to refer to a group of related messages.
15. This is the default newsreader that starts if no other newsreader is specified.
16. Subscribe or unsubscribe to newsgroups in this dialog box.
17. These are the steps that must be performed prior to using instant messaging in Outlook.
18. Open this window to send an instant message to one of your contacts in Outlook.
19. Online meetings in Outlook use this application that is included with Internet Explorer.
20. Scheduling an online meeting in Outlook generates this message to the attendees.

SKILLS check

Assessment 1

1. With Outlook open and the *Inbox* folder active, create and send a new message to yourself and assign it to a category as follows:
   a. Key your e-mail address in the To... text box.
   b. Key **Outlook Tips** in the Subject text box
   c. Key the following text in the message editing window:
      Assigning a category to a message is a way of grouping related messages together that can later be moved or copied to a new folder.
   d. Assign the *Ideas* category to the message.
2. Use the Advanced Find dialog box to view a list of messages assigned to the *Ideas* category.
3. Print an image of the search results displayed in the Advanced Find dialog box. *(Note: Refer to chapter 5, Assessment 2, step 2 if you need help with printing a screen image.)*
4. Close the Advanced Find dialog box.

Assessment 2

1. With Outlook open and the *Inbox* folder active, send a task request to a contact as follows:
   a. Display the *Tasks* folder and create a Task Request to Kenneth McTague.
   b. Key **Pennsylvania Trade Show Organization** in the Subject text box.
   c. Change the priority to *High*.
2. Display the *Notes* folder and create a new note as follows:
   a. Key the following text in the Note window:
      Send six cases of product brochures to Kenneth McTague in Pennsylvania for the trade show next month.
   b. Assign the note to the Kenneth McTague contact record.
   c. Close the Note window.
3. Display the *Contacts* folder and then open the contact window for Kenneth McTague.

4. Display all of the Outlook items that have been associated with Kenneth McTague in the Contact window.
5. Print an image of the contact record.
6. Close the contact record.
7. Display the *Inbox*.

Assessment 3

1. With Outlook open and the *Inbox* folder active, export the *Contacts* folder to a new personal folders file as follows:
   a. Make sure the student data disk is in the drive.
   b. Start the Import and Export wizard.
   c. Choose Export to a file at the first Import and Export Wizard dialog box.
   d. Choose Personal Folder File (.pst) at the second Import and Export Wizard dialog box.
   e. Select the *Contacts* folder in the Export Personal Folders dialog box.
   f. Key **A:\Contacts Ch 06 SA 03** as the file name to save the exported file as.
   g. Assign a password to the exported file in the Create Microsoft Personal Folders dialog box.
2. Use the File, Open, Outlook Data File command to open the exported pst file created in step 1.
3. Display the Folder List pane and then expand the Personal Folders list.
4. Click *Contacts* in the Folder List below Personal Folders.
5. Print an image of the Outlook screen.
6. Close the Personal Folders file.
7. Close the Folder List pane.

Assessment 4

1. With Outlook open and the *Inbox* folder active, complete a manual archive of the *Tasks* folder as follows:
   a. Make sure the student data disk is in the drive.
   b. Display the Archive dialog box.
   c. Select the *Tasks* folder to archive.
   d. Choose to archive any items that are older than the current date.
   e. Key **A:\Tasks Archive Ch 06 SA 04** as the archive file name.
2. Use the File, Open, Outlook Data File command to open the archived tasks file created in step 1.
3. Display the Folder List pane and then expand the Archive Folders list.
4. Click *Tasks* in the Folder List below Archive Folders.
5. Print an image of the Outlook screen.
6. Close the Archive Folders file.
7. Close the Folder List pane.

Assessment 5

1. With Outlook open and the *Inbox* folder active, create a new folder as follows:
   a. Key **Ch 06 SA 05** as the folder name.
   b. Click *Mailbox* or *Personal Folders* next to the *Outlook Today* icon in the Select where to place the folder list box.
2. Display the Properties dialog box for the *Ch 06 SA 05* folder and then assign the Web site www.usatoday.com as the default folder home page on the *Ch 06 SA 05* folder.

3. With the usatoday.com home page displayed in the Information Viewer, close the Folder List.
4. Print an image of the Outlook screen.
5. Display the *Inbox*.

Assessment 6

1. With Outlook open and the *Inbox* folder active, display the *Calendar* folder.
2. Display the appointments that are scheduled for Wednesday, October 15, 2003.
3. Mark the meeting scheduled at 10:00 am with Jona Thorne as private.
4. Print an image of the Outlook screen.
5. Display the *Inbox*.

Assessment 7

1. With Outlook open and the *Inbox* folder active, open the newsreader application.
2. Open the Newsgroup Subscriptions dialog box.
3. Display newsgroups that contain the word *certification* in the name.
4. Subscribe to the newsgroup microsoft.public.certification.
5. Download the messages from the microsoft.public.certification newsgroup.
6. Browse the message headers in the Messages pane and then open a message that interests you.
7. Print and then close the message.
8. Close the newsreader application.

Assessment 8

1. With Outlook open and the *Inbox* folder active, display the *Calendar* folder.
2. Display the appointments for Tuesday, October 14, 2003, and then click in the Appointment area next to 2:00 pm.
3. Schedule an online meeting using Microsoft NetMeeting as follows:
   a. Add the student that you added to the PAB as a Required attendee.
   b. Key **Sales videoconference** in the Subject text box.
   c. The online meeting will last one hour.
   d. The directory server name is http://meeting.servername.
   e. Key your e-mail address as the meeting organizer.
   f. Have NetMeeting automatically start with a reminder.
   g. Print an image of the Outlook screen with the Meeting Request window open.
4. Display the *Inbox*.

Assessment 9

1. With Outlook open and the *Inbox* folder active, display the Folder List pane.
2. Right-click *Web View Folder* in the Folder List and then click <u>D</u>elete "Web View Folder" at the shortcut menu.
3. Click <u>Y</u>es when prompted to confirm the deletion.
4. Delete the folder named *Ch 06 SA 05*.
5. Right-click *Deleted Items* in the Folder List and then click Empt<u>y</u> "Deleted Items" Folder at the shortcut menu.
6. Close the Folder List pane.
7. Exit Outlook.

OUTLOOK

OUTLOOK

OUTLOOK

configuring and customizing, 169-224

configuring security options in, 197-198

creating dial-up connection in, 201-206

creating forms in, 184-189

creating offline folders file in, 207-208

creating personal folders file in, 214-216

customizing commands review in, 219-220

customizing menus and toolbars in, 175-180

customizing Outlook bar in, 173-175

customizing view in, 181-183

downloading messages for remote use in, 211-213

exporting information from, 235-236

folders in, 5

information imported into, 233-235

instant messages sent from, 261-262

mail security and encryption options settings in, 196-201

Office document created from, 231

setting advanced e-mail options in, 189-192

specifying folders for offline use in, 209-211

specifying Startup folder in, 172-173

and using/customizing Outlook Today, 170-172

using for e-mail, 3-51

Word used as mail editor and viewer in, 195-196

working offline with, 208

Outlook bar

customizing, 173-174

hiding, redisplaying, and customizing, 174-175

icons on, 5, 217

shortcut menu, 174

Outlook components

integration/management, 225-270

archiving folders, 239-244

assigning Web page as folder home page, 244

categories assigned to messages, 226-228

commands review, 267

creating private appointment, 251-252

exporting information from Outlook, 235-238

importing information into Outlook, 233-235

Office document created from Outlook, 231-233

permissions assigned to someone else to share folder, 245-251

scheduling online meetings, 262-264

sending/receiving instant messages, 257-262

sending/receiving newsgroup messages, 252-257

tasks and notes assigned to contacts, 228-229

tracking activities for contact, 229-231

Outlook Folders, 188, 218

Outlook.pst, 214

Outlook Send/Receive Groups dialog box, 210

Outlook Send/Receive Progress dialog box, 209

Outlook Shortcuts, 173, 174, 217

Outlook Template format, 46

Outlook Today

page, 170

using and customizing, 170-172

Outlook Today icon, on Outlook bar, 170

Outlook window, starting/exploring, 4-6

Overdue Tasks list, 146

Owner, of task, 137, 163

Owner permission level, 245

P

PAB (personal address books) files, 16

Passwords, 7

for dial-up connection, 201

for newsgroups, 253

Permissions

assignment of, with other user for sharing folder, 245

delegate, 246

and sharing folders, 265

Personal Address Book, 46

adding entry to, and sending message, 18-19

creating, 16-17

Personal folders file, 233, 236

creating, 214-216

messages exported to, 238

Personal Forms Library, 188, 218

Personal Information Manager, 3

Personal information store, 214

Personal information store (pst) files, 169

Personal option, for appointments, 55

Phone Call option, for appointments, 55

PIM. *See also* Personal Information Manager

Plain Text format, messages sent in, 40

Plan a Meeting dialog box, 73, 74, 83

Plan a Meeting feature, 53

Planning meetings, 73-74

Plus symbol, for newsgroup messages, 253

Posting, messages to newsgroups, 253, 266

PowerPoint

automatic recording of documents in, 157

documents automatically logged in journal with, 159, 164

PowerPoint presentations, starting from folders in Outlook, 231, 265

Printing messages, 9, 11-12, 45

Privacy, with secured messages, 196

Private appointments, creating, 251-252, 266

Private key, 197

Private store, 214

Properties dialog box, 206, 218, 240, 244

Pst files, compacting, 216

Public key, 197

Publishing author permission level, 245

Publishing editor permission level, 245

Q

Quick Launch toolbar, Launch Microsoft Outlook button on, 4

R

Reading messages, 9

Read receipts, 46, 197

attaching to message, 20, 21, 22

requests, 41

Read Report Message, 22

Real-time communication, 257

Records

in Contacts folder, 90

locating, 108. *See also* Contacts; Forms; Notes

Recurrence button, 136

on Appointment window toolbar, 57

Recurring tasks, 136-137, 163

Red flags, 26

Reminder check box, for appointments, 55

Remote mail, 169, 207, 211

Reply button, on Standard toolbar, 10

Reply feature, 72

Reply Group button, in Standard toolbar for Microsoft Outlook Newsreader, 255-256

Replying to messages, 9, 10, 11-12, 45

Reply to All button, on Standard toolbar, 10

Reset Toolbar option, 179

Resource Schedule dialog box, 79

Resource scheduling, 68-71, 79, 83

Restricted sites security zone setting, 199

Reviewer permission level, 245

Rich Text Format, 46

messages sent in, 40

option, 36

Rules, 66

S

Save As dialog box, 36

Saving, file attachments to disk, 14-15

Schedule+, 234

Scheduling

appointments, 54-58

appointments from contacts, 116-117

automatic resource, 79

Calendar component for, 53-87

commands review, 84

events, 59

meetings and resources, 68-71, 78-79, 83

online meetings, 262-264, 266

recurring appointments, 57-58

Search In list box, 25

Second-rank options, 6

Secure receipts, 197

Security, 218

digital IDs, 197

global mail setting checks, 199

mail, 196

options in Outlook, 197-198

zones, 199-201, 218

Security dialog box, 200, 218

Security Properties dialog box, 198

Security Settings button, 19

Select Attendees and Resources dialog box, 83

with Resource selected, 78

Select Folders dialog box, 25